"Born from Coblentz's own expe_____ _____ _____ _____ _____ _____ ____
theological accompaniment of al.   ... with chronic depression. As
a systematic theologian, she expresses this love by offering new insight
into the classic theological discussion of suffering and by arguing that
those with depression deserve better than silencing or moralizing. Any
Christian theologian reflecting on what it means to be human should
read this book, as should anybody who lives with depression or ministers
to people with depression."

> —Elizabeth Antus, Assistant Professor of the Practice,
> Boston College

"This is the book I have been waiting for. With insight and sensitivity,
Jessica Coblentz offers a theological field guide for ministers and
communities hoping to faithfully accompany those stumbling through
the 'unhomelike' landscapes of depression. In *Dust in the Blood*, scripture,
systematic theology, and lived experience flow together into a wellspring
of resources for those of us with intimate knowledge of the depressive
wilderness."

> —Rev. David Finnegan-Hosey, author of *Christ on the Psych Ward*
> and *Grace is a Pre-Existing Condition: Faith, Systems, and Mental
> Healthcare*

"This is a remarkable work that integrates psychology in deliberate
theological reflection to disclose and probe some of the wrenching
spiritual pain and suffering of depression. Jessica Coblentz is rigorous
and poignant, resolute and passionate, uncompromising and gracious.
This book makes an important contribution to systematic, practical,
pastoral, and foundational theologies."

> —M. Shawn Copeland, Professor Emerita, Boston College

"Honoring first-person experiences of depression—including her own—Jessica Coblentz proposes ways of speaking theologically about depression that make space for the meaninglessness that so many depression sufferers know well. She turns to biblical stories of wilderness and the unsettling story of Hagar to offer a theological account of living with depression that takes dislocation and isolation seriously. Even as most of the wilderness stories lack resolution, Coblentz points to ways in which God shows up in those desolate spaces. She also offers a vision for what it means to accompany those who live with depression, including advocating for more access to psychiatric resources and care. A compelling and powerful addition to theological conversations about those who suffer from depression and all of us who love them."

—Deanna A. Thompson, St. Olaf College

Dust in the Blood

A Theology of Life with Depression

Jessica Coblentz

LITURGICAL PRESS
ACADEMIC

Collegeville, Minnesota
www.litpress.org

Cover design by Monica Bokinskie.
Cover art: *Gesture of Grace*, © Jan Richardson. janrichardson.com

Scripture quotations are from New Revised Standard Version Bible: Catholic Edition © 1989, 1993 National Council of the Churches of Christ in the United States of America. Used by permission. All rights reserved worldwide.

© 2022 by Jessica Coblentz
Published by Liturgical Press, Collegeville, Minnesota. All rights reserved. No part of this book may be used or reproduced in any manner whatsoever, except brief quotations in reviews, without written permission of Liturgical Press, Saint John's Abbey, PO Box 7500, Collegeville, MN 56321-7500. Printed in the United States of America.

1	2	3	4	5	6	7	8	9

Library of Congress Cataloging-in-Publication Data

Names: Coblentz, Jessica, author.
Title: Dust in the blood : a theology of life with depression / Jessica
    Coblentz.
Description: Collegeville, Minnesota : Liturgical Press Academic, [2022]
    | Includes index. | Summary: "Through first-person narratives of
    depression, contemporary theologies of suffering, and ancient biblical
    tales of the wilderness, especially the story of Hagar, Coblentz argues
    for and contributes to an expansion of Christian ideas about what
    depression is, how God relates to it, and how Christians should
    understand and respond to depression in turn"— Provided by
    publisher.
Identifiers: LCCN 2021038969 (print) | LCCN 2021038970 (ebook) |
    ISBN 9780814685020 (paperback) | ISBN 9780814685273 (epub) |
    ISBN 9780814685273 (pdf)
Subjects: LCSH: Depression, Mental—Religious aspects—Christianity. |
    Depressed persons—Religious life.
Classification: LCC BV4910.34 .C63 2022 (print) | LCC BV4910.34
    (ebook) | DDC 248.8/625—dc23
LC record available at https://lccn.loc.gov/2021038969
LC ebook record available at https://lccn.loc.gov/2021038970

To the God Who Sees,
I offer this long-labored prayer.

Contents

Part I

Surveying the Landscape

Introduction

Dust in the Blood

I was a twenty-six-year-old, fiercely independent young woman when depression took over my life with inestimable force. It was not my first experience with depression, but it had never been quite like this. I was paralyzed by everything. Not by anything in particular, but *everything*: relationships, grad school, part-time employment. Since eighteen, I had lived far from family, won scholarships and juggled multiple jobs to pay for school, maintained friendships and a busy social calendar. I had managed this through a master's degree and the first year of doctoral studies when suddenly the prospect of engaging in any one of these aspects of life seemed impossible.

Concerned by this shift, I sought the aid of a counselor, and at first our weekly appointments helped. There, I attended to my feelings as I had not in a long time, if ever, and I learned to extend this awareness to my everyday life. But as time went on, the self-examination only fueled my despair. I ruminated about my increasing inability to keep up with my coursework, not to mention the peer-reviewed publications, conference presentations, and other professional pursuits of my academic peers. So overwhelming was my fear of failure that I could barely write a single sentence. And the more I struggled, the more I hated myself. Guilt filled every cavity of my body, weighing me down to the point where even simple tasks were extraordinarily difficult. I could hardly get myself to complete an assignment or wash the dishes or show up to a social gathering.

Within a few months, my counseling regimen increased to multiple appointments a week: two, then three, sometimes five. Sometimes a day's work could only consist of going to my counseling appointment before retreating to the isolation of my apartment. I could do that, and I could cry. I cried every morning in therapy. I cried again every night for hours as I tried to sleep. Thoughts of all the ways I had failed everyone around me that day kept me awake despite my exhaustion. I cried at school. I cried in the parking lot, in empty classrooms, and sometimes quietly at my cubicle desk in the middle of the office when I could not conjure the energy for discretion.

Despite loyal friends and a family on the other side of the country that strained to be present, I experienced myself as utterly alone. I could not find the words to convey the depths of my depression. Communication is predicated on connection—on something shared, a common referent—and I could not relate to anyone. The words we shared could not capture what I felt. What "sadness" denotes did not apply. "Despair" and "guilt" were likewise unsuitable. Detached from the world and the people beyond me, I could not conjure an alternative tongue. Meanwhile, I was unable to hear a word of comfort. For some time, I could not read. My eyes jumped between words on the page and nothing of substance emerged, robbing me of the books that had been both my solace and my livelihood. I was trapped inside myself.

After more than a year and a half of therapy and struggle, I began to experience a recurring dream. Night after night, I dreamed I was in the backseat of a parked car that had made its way into the middle of a forest. Surrounding me were the woodlands of the Pacific Northwest where I had often wandered growing up. No one else was there, and not knowing how or why I was, I reclined on the cool leather of the backseat, letting my eyelids droop as I stared out the window at the tree canopy above. "It is only a matter of time," I thought to myself each night in this dream. I knew I would die there.

I started to wonder why this dream had come. I wondered if it remained in my memory each morning because it was something special, like dreams in the biblical tales that I delighted in when I began reading the Bible as a teenager. Those ancient dreams were nocturnal messages from God, divine warnings or commissions to the dreamer. Perhaps I, too, remembered my dreams because God insisted. But what was God telling me?

The dream reoccurred over the course of weeks before one day I remembered another similar scene: the girl from high school who had propelled her car from a winding road down hundreds of feet into a densely wooded ravine. At first, no one knew where she went. Eight days passed before a local woman received a vision right in the middle of her suburban living room: She saw the car and its young driver alive in the forest. She thought she recognized the place, so she got into her minivan and went looking. When the woman found the wrecked car and its driver still alive, the people around me called it a miracle: the vision, the discovery, the fact that this girl survived the car's descent and remained alive so many days later. Some also began to whisper that the wreck was not an accident. This beloved teenager—beautiful, popular, athletic—had been trying to kill herself. But God had saved her, they said.

Remembering the girl, I wondered if my dreams were sleeping prayers for divine rescue—for a miraculous intervention like the one she had received. Maybe God would send someone another vision and she would come looking for me.

I also wondered if the woods that filled my sleeping hours were an ethereal version of my therapist's office, where I spent so many waking hours. After all, it had green walls and a stillness similar to the forest. It was dark there, too, when I arrived nearly every morning for her first appointment of the day. Lying atop the carpeted green chaise, I stared out the window past the curtains embroidered with leaves. Perhaps the dream was a divine foreshadowing of the fate to which I might have to resign myself: Would I be a perpetual patient, stuck in depression and helpless to move forward for the rest of my life? Would I live forever lost in this depression?

I wondered, too, if the dream was a sacred commissioning to another place I knew. My apartment was a few miles from Harvard's McLean Psychiatric Hospital, and when the depression continued to worsen, I found myself driving by, looking through the wall of trees along its perimeter. I wondered if I would be better off on the other side of the hospital's verdant boundary. Maybe these were the woods that surrounded me in my dreams. Was it on the stiff bench of the hospital where I would finally lie down and find rest?

This book would not exist had my life with depression not improved in the months and years following that severe episode in my twenties. But it would also not exist had the depression and those dreams never come. When I resumed my graduate studies, passing my comprehensive exams and deliberating prospective dissertation topics again, my condition and those dreams had become part of me, like "dust in the blood," a descriptor the poet Robert Lowell once used to characterize his own depressive states.[1] I had planned to pursue a research project in feminist theology or one of the other political or liberation theologies that had long grounded my studies. But as I waded through all that literature's compelling insights about suffering and God's responses to it, I found myself always ultimately wondering where depression fit in. What was this suffering I lived with, I pondered, and how was God working in its midst? How should I have related to it as a Christian, and how should I relate to it if it ever consumes me again?

Were depression *my* suffering alone, it would not have warranted the dissertation I would go on to write, nor the book before you now. But in fact depression is a relatively common condition in the United States, my native country, with one measure estimating that 17.3 million Americans experienced a major depressive episode in 2017 alone.[2] Other studies suggest that rates of depression are increasing globally as well,[3] with one study estimating that 264 million people across the world suffered depression in 2017.[4]

---

1. Jeffrey Meyers, ed., *Robert Lowell: Interviews and Memoirs* (Ann Arbor, MI: University of Michigan, 1988), 169.

2. Jonaki Bose et al., "Key Substance Use and Mental Health Indictors in the United States: Results from the 2017 National Survey on Drug Use and Health," *Substance Abuse and Mental Health Services Administration*, September 2018, https://www.samhsa.gov/data/sites/default/files/cbhsq-reports/NSDUHFFR2017/NSDUHFFR2017.pdf.

3. Ethan Watters offers a critical account of this phenomenon in *Crazy Like Us: The Globalization of the American Psyche* (New York: Free Press, 2011).

4. Global Burden of Disease Collaborative Network, "Global Burden of Disease Study 2017," *Institute for Health Metrics and Evaluation*, 2018, https://ourworldindata.org/grapher/number-of-people-with-depression.

Research consistently shows that a number of socially marginalized groups experience depression at higher rates. Women suffer depression at higher rates than men.[5] Transgender youth are nearly four times more likely to experience depression than their non-transgender peers.[6] Meanwhile, cis lesbian, gay, bisexual, and queer teens experience significantly more depressive symptoms and higher rates of suicidality than their heterosexual peers.[7] The disproportionate rates of depression in the LGBTQ community evince the importance of investigations into the effects of oppression on mental health, which is a concern depression researchers also bring to their studies of race and class. Studies of racial and ethnic differences among depression sufferers find that while racial minorities are less likely to be diagnosed with acute episodes of major depression than white Americans, these minoritized populations are more likely to experience extended and severely debilitating symptoms when they do suffer depression.[8]

Upon learning of depression's prevalence and its disproportionate effects on marginalized groups, the scarcity of theological resources that address this condition alarmed and perplexed me. Theology ought to consider the implications of this widespread suffering for Christianity's teachings and practices. At the very least, theological reflection on depression could enrich Christian understandings of the human condition. What's more, if God resides in a special way among the poor and vulnerable, as Christianity's "option for the

5. For statistics on this gender disparity in the U.S., see Bose et al., "Key Substance Use and Mental Health Indictors"; for statistics on this gender disparity across the globe, see Global Burden of Disease Collaborative Network, "Global Burden of Disease Study 2017." For an overview on this topic, see Lori M. Hilt and Susan Nolen-Hoeksema, "Gender Differences in Depression," in *Handbook of Depression*, 3rd ed., ed. Ian H. Gotlib and Constance L. Hammen (New York: Guilford, 2014), 355–373.

6. Sari L. Reisner et al., "Mental Health of Transgender Youth in Care at an Adolescent Urban Community Health Center: A Matched Retrospective Cohort Study," *Journal of Adolescent Health* 56, no. 3 (2015): 274–279.

7. Michael P. Marshal et al., "Suicidality and Depression Disparities Between Sexual Minority and Heterosexual Youth: A Meta-Analytic Review," *Journal of Adolescent Health* 49, no. 2 (2011): 115–123.

8. Rahn Kennedy Bailey, Josephine Mokonogho, and Alok Kumar, "Racial and Ethnic Differences in Depression: Current Perspectives," *Neuropsychiatric Disease and Treatment* 15 (February 2019): 603–609.

poor" affirms, then studies of depressive suffering could also reveal important insights about who God is.

Faced with this lacuna, I was mindful that academic theologians like me must approach this topic with great care. Theologians during the last half century have learned that studying suffering is a delicate task because the discipline, both in its silence and in its speech, has often failed when confronted with the struggles of our world. On one hand, the silence of theologians concerning suffering has at times called into question the integrity and sheer relevance of the Christian tradition. This was the case during and after the Shoah, when too many Christian theologians said nothing to decry Nazi violence. This problem endures in the relative silence of my own community of Catholic theologians, who—overwhelmingly white—too rarely speak of the suffering engendered by anti-Black racism in the United States. On the other hand, the Shoah and other atrocities across the globe—from the brutality of nuclear warfare to the everyday, dehumanizing exploitation of factory workers—have also exposed inadequacies in how many theologians treat suffering when they *do* venture to speak of it. Utilizing rational proofs, theodical explanations, and intellectual apologies, many theologians speak of suffering only to justify its existence before God and, in doing so, explain away the grave horrors of history.

In the wake of these theological failures, theologians such as Johann Baptist Metz, Dorothee Sölle, and Edward Schillebeeckx have insisted that theologians *must* address suffering. Yet when they do, theologians must utilize specific modes of reflection in order to do so humanely.[9] These theologians argue for narrative theological approaches to suffering that uphold the particularities of suffering, including its contradictions and fragmentations, and, as Metz puts it, its "non-identity" with Christianity's tidy theories of God. Only by humbly bringing together complex and concrete narratives of suf-

---

9. See Johann Baptist Metz, *Faith in History and Society: Toward a Practical Fundamental Theology*, trans. J. Matthew Ashley (New York: Crossroads, 2007); Dorothee Sölle, *Suffering*, trans. Everett R. Kalin (Philadelphia: Fortress, 1975); Edward Schillebeeckx, *Jesus: An Experiment in Christology*, The Collected Works of Edward Schillebeeckx, vol. VI, trans. Hubert Hoskins and Marcelle Manley (New York: Bloomsbury, 2014).

fering and the revealing memories of the Jewish and Christian God will theology be possible in a world of such pain, he insists.

It is in view of Christian theology's failings and the subsequent turn of many theologians to concrete narratives of suffering that I have come to see my own experience as a potential asset in my development of a theology of life with depression. I know—again from decades of insights from liberation and political theologies—that there are epistemological gains born of experience. Ada María Isasi-Díaz, the late founder of *mujerista* theology, names the affordances of first-person experience for theology in her reflections on *lo cotidiano*, the everyday experience of Latina women. *Lo cotidiano*, she argues, is both a source of knowledge and a hermeneutic through which *mujerista* theologians see God and the world.[10] This insight from Isasi-Díaz, along with other analogous theological affirmations of the knowledge born of experience, has led me to attend to how my firsthand experiences of depression direct me to dimensions of this elusive experience that outsiders might not be so inclined to apprehend. There are some things one knows from living them, even suffering them, and the story of depression that I explore in this book is one that circulates in my veins. I know it by heart.

At the same time, I am well aware of the hazards that accompany my relationship to depression. My experience of depression might leave this research vulnerable to charges of "navel gazing" or of "bias." In response, I concede that my personal story of depression informs the representations of the condition and the theological claims I develop in this book. I, like all theologians, cannot wholly suspend these biases. Many inductive theologies emphasize the contextual reality of the theological enterprise to argue that all theologies arise from and reflect a particular historical location and its people, whether or not an author acknowledges this situatedness. That the concrete reality of my depression informs my views of God, Jesus Christ, the Holy Spirit, the human person, and the church is undeniable and unavoidable to some extent, and this would be the case even if I gave myself to a research topic seemingly disconnected

---

10. Ada María Isasi-Díaz, *Mujerista Theology: A Theology for the Twenty-First Century* (Maryknoll, NY: Orbis, 1996), 66–73.

from depression. Taking on depression as the *locus theologicus* of my work simply makes explicit that which will inevitably shape any topic I take on. A body that has known depression is the only body from which I can theologize.[11]

Still, it is not my own story that I forefront as the sole or even primary account of depression that grounds this project. Chapter 1 draws on many published, first-person narratives of English-speaking sufferers to offer a portrait of life with depression, particularly in its chronic and recurring forms. While each account of depression has unique features, just like every life story, I focus on patterns that emerge across these stories to convey what this depression is like for many sufferers. I then utilize the insights of phenomenologists of depression to sharpen and interpret the narrative contours of depressive experience, arguing ultimately that depression can be thought of as a particular experience of "unhomelikeness" (*Unheimlichkeit*). What results is a narrative-phenomenological account of depression that differs significantly from the condition's prevailing emotional profile. Over the course of the first chapter, I demonstrate why this far-less-common description of depression is preferrable to others. Thus, and henceforth, my own story of depression is but one among many others that belong to a cloud of witnesses. And while I am predisposed to narratives that are in accord with my own, I have tried to relativize my experience and offer a richer presentation of depression through engagement with these other narratives and expert interpreters.

Whereas chapter 1 explores what depression is through the stories of numerous depression sufferers and the perspectives of various secular scholars of depression, chapter 2 examines how Christians in the contemporary United States tend to understand this condition. There, I present two popular theologies of depression that circulate

---

11. Dorothee Sölle offers another response to concerns about personal bias: "I consider the separation of the personal from the professional, of one's own experience from reflections that then vault themselves as 'scientific' philosophical-theological thought, to be a fatal male invention, the overcoming of which is a task for any serious theology that intends to be a theology of both men and women." See Dorothee Sölle, *The Window of Vulnerability: A Political Spirituality*, trans. Linda M. Maloney (Minneapolis: Fortress, 1990), 35.

among U.S. Christians today. Gathered from Christian self-help books, pastoral writings, websites, and social-scientific research, these theologies represent the attempts of pastors and other Christians to bring their religion to bear on this harrowing condition. In addition to outlining these theologies with illustrative examples, I connect their underlying logic to the Enlightenment worldview that underpins some of the secular approaches to depression featured in chapter 1, as well as well-known theodical theories of God and suffering that are emblematic of the modern Western mindset. I suggest that the modern logic underlying these popular theologies of depression may contribute to their widespread appeal among Christians. However, this modern logic also limits them theologically. These popular theologies of depression reinforce a presumption that faithful Christian interpretations of suffering necessarily entail a coherent, logical justification of suffering before God, no matter how extraordinary the suffering in question may be.

Chapters 3 and 4 grapple with what to make of these prevailing popular theologies of depression. Do they offer a suitable Christian understanding of depression? And if so, how does one determine this? Other scholars of Christianity and mental illness cast doubt on the validity of these popular theologies, and their critiques could provide grounds to reject these theologies in favor of other prescriptions for how Christians ought to make sense of this condition. Wholly rejecting these popular theologies raises other problems, however. Drawing on the incisive work of theologian Karen Kilby, I argue that the tendency of scholars to dismiss these popular attempts at Christian meaning making transgresses theology's ethical boundaries. These rejections overdetermine how others make meaning of the mystery of suffering in relation to the Mystery of God. I then consider what it might look like for theologians and other Christians to contribute to theological reflection about depression without violating the boundaries of theological "restraint" that Kilby exhorts. These chapters thus amount to an extended methodological reflection that informs the chapters to come, where I propose additional resources for Christians trying to theologize depression.

When I set out on this research, I did not anticipate that my intellectual investigation would lead me back to the wilderness of my dreams. That lonely, recurring dream of the forest ceased as the severity of my depression lessened, and once it dissipated from my sleep, I thought of the dream only occasionally in the months and years that followed. When it did cross my mind, however, the dream captivated me, like a vivid flashback. No matter the time that had passed since the depressive episode that overtook my life, that dream of the wilderness endured as an arresting representation of what I had lived.

It was not until I revisited Delores Williams's classic, *Sisters in the Wilderness: The Challenge of Womanist God-Talk*, that I began to consider the dream as not only a memory of my depression but also a lens through which I might explore the theological questions that my struggle engendered.[12] As I explore at greater length later in this book, Williams identifies the suffering of African American women with the wilderness experience of Hagar, the woman of the Hebrew Scriptures who was enslaved by Sarah and her husband, the patriarch Abraham (Gen 16, 21). The similarities between the suffering of Hagar and of African American women lead Williams into the wilderness traditions of Judaism, Christianity, and the African American community. From the convergences of these traditions, all of which assign theological significance to desolate landscapes, Williams develops a groundbreaking account of suffering and salvation in the lives of African American women.

The theological truths born of the suffering of the African American women with and for whom Williams theologizes resonated profoundly with some of the reflections that arose from my early thinking about God and depression. They did so despite the fact that I—a white woman of European descent—encounter God and suffering from a decidedly different social location. Yet these resonances are not entirely surprising. Williams, like many of her Black and womanist contemporaries, was attuned to psychological suffering within the Black community. Consequently, her project presents important truths that pertain to many forms of psychological distress, including the experiences of depression that I share (at least to some degree)

12. Delores Williams, *Sisters in the Wilderness: The Challenge of Womanist God-Talk* (Maryknoll, NY: Orbis, 1993).

with many women in the Black community. Williams's work also reveals truths about God, the human person, and the Christian community that are relevant to Christians of all races and psychological conditions.[13]

The influence of Williams's text is apparent in chapter 5, which marks a constructive pivot in *Dust in the Blood*. In search of theological resources for ongoing Christian reflection on depression, I explore biblical images of the wilderness. Throughout Christian history, theologians have brought together the Scriptures' tales of harsh landscapes and applied them analogously to contemporary experiences, including instances of psychological and spiritual distress. I invite depression sufferers to continue this theological tradition by bringing the wilderness worlds of the biblical text to bear on contemporary depression, and I use the work of biblical theologian Walter Brueggemann to elucidate the possible theological affordances of doing so.

It is in chapter 6 where I demonstrate in greater depth how biblical wilderness narratives can afford theological alternatives to popular theologies of depression in particular. I do so by reading the Hagar story from the book of Genesis as a tragedy in the classical sense, a tale where suffering is undeserved, inexplicable, and serves no apparent purpose from the perspective of the audience or the sufferer herself. This reading shows Hagar's wilderness experience to be one that not only resonates experientially with what many depression sufferers describe but also one that affirms the possibilities of meaninglessness that many sufferers experience. At the same time, this interpretation of the biblical tale upholds that senseless suffering is not necessarily antithetical to an affirmation of divine presence. Hagar's story shows that some wilderness experiences are tremendously difficult, utterly baffling, and still coexist—inexplicably, even incoherently—with an affirmation of a personal and benevolent God.

---

13. On this point, I have in mind M. Shawn Copeland's charge that, against a history in which the white, male, bourgeois subject was taken for granted as the universal subject for all Christian theology, all Christians must consider the theological truths revealed by a "new anthropological subject," namely, the "poor, despised woman of color" who is also centered in Williams's project. See M. Shawn Copeland, *Enfleshing Freedom: Body, Race, Being* (Minneapolis: Fortress, 2010).

This, too, can be a Christian theological interpretation of depression. This proposal notably differs from existing popular theologies of depression and their resonant theodical counterparts in that it offers a Christian interpretation of depressive suffering without the rational justifications and requisite meaning making that accompany these and so many Christian views of suffering.

Chapters 7 and 8 draw out some of the implications of theologizing depression with this tragic interpretation of Hagar's wilderness experience. In chapter 7, I reflect on how it might inform claims about the doctrine of God and how God relates to depressive suffering. Next, and with the aid of Delores Williams, I consider how the story of Hagar can inform Christian notions of salvation amid the wilderness of depression, especially in its chronic and recurring forms. In chapter 8, I reflect on the implications of the Hagar story for Christian discipleship. In particular, I focus on how a recognition of depressive suffering as tragic suffering invites Christian disciples to adopt particular ethical and spiritual dispositions in relation to the suffering of others. Here, Rowan Williams's work on the tragic imagination affords a helpful framework for Christians who accompany depression sufferers as friends, family, ministers, and people of faith.

Across these chapters, I do not wade into Christian debates about the morality of suicide, a topic many might expect from a project on depression. They might expect this because, though most depression does not end in suicide, most people who die by suicide experience a mood disorder such as depression.[14] Suicidologists who study the factors that lead to suicide attempts and completion help us understand why this is the case: The forms of psychological pain that most often contribute to an individual's desire for death have much in common with features of depressive suffering, including perceived disconnection, ineffectiveness, and hopelessness.[15] Greater attention to these dimensions of depressive suffering, which are commonly downplayed and misunderstood in and beyond the Christian com-

14. Thomas Joiner, *Why People Die by Suicide* (Cambridge, MA: Harvard University, 2005), 152–153, 164, 191, 199, and 201; Kay Redfield Jamison, *Night Falls Fast: Understanding Suicide* (New York: Vintage Books, 1999), 100–105.

15. See Joiner, *Why People Die by Suicide*, 36–42, 164; Edwin S. Shneidman, *The Suicidal Mind* (New York: Oxford University, 1996).

munity, can thus contribute to a better understanding of some of the circumstances that lead to suicidality. Any debate about the morality of suicide must take into account these circumstances, as my own Catholic tradition's teachings on suicide increasingly acknowledge (despite the suicide stigma that still endures within this denominational community, to be sure).[16] So while this book does not engage in debates about the morality of suicide, it can contribute to the necessary groundwork for these discussions by replacing some operative misunderstandings about depression with a more accurate account of the circumstances that often occasion suicide.

Dust in the Blood is unequivocally a product of who I am. I am an academic theologian, and this is a work of academic theology, as is evident in my citational practices and my engagement with interlocutors from the theological academy. I am also someone who has suffered with depression, and this, too, is a book from and for depression sufferers—many of whom are in the academy, certainly, but also beyond it, of course. Additionally, I hope and anticipate that this book will serve those who accompany depression sufferers, which statistically speaking, includes every one of us. Ultimately, my great hope is that engagement with this book, whether critical or sympathetic, will spur more dialogue about depression in any number of Christian settings and mediums, from the theological classroom and our Sunday liturgies to religion news media and official church teachings. In defiance of the stigma that has long hidden this suffering—confining it to the privacy of counseling offices, confessionals, and sometimes only the silent prayers of our hearts—I hope for more discussion of what depression is, who we are, what we ought to be for one another, and who God is in the midst of this difficult condition.

---

16. For the history of Catholic perspectives on suicide, see Ranana Leigh Dine, "You Shall Bury Him: Burial, Suicide, and the Development of Catholic Law and Theology," *Medical Humanities* (July 2019): 1–12, esp. 6–7. Elizabeth Antus explains that greater theological attention to the mental suffering that usually occasions suicide would reflect a paradigm shift that has already taken place in suicidology more broadly. See Elizabeth L. Antus, "Covid-19 and Religious Ethics," *Journal of Religious Ethics* 48, no. 3 (September 2020): 380.

Chapter 1

Depression as Unhomelikeness

Of all people, Martha Manning is well-positioned to speak to experiences of depression, for she is both a sufferer and a psychologist who spends her days caring for patients with this and other mental-health conditions. In her memoir, *Undercurrents*, she weaves her personal experiences and psychological expertise to convey what depression is like. And yet seventy pages in, she confesses, "Sadness carries identification. You know where it's been and you know where it's headed. Depression carries no papers. It enters your country unannounced and uninvited. Its origins are unknown, but its destination always dead-ends in you."[1] Elsewhere, recounting a conversation with her therapist, she writes, "I struggle to articulate how awful and isolating this feels, but I can't find the words."[2] "I feel like English is my second language," she remembers, "I am almost mute."[3]

The elusiveness of Manning's depression is not unique. Across depression memoirs, authors regularly testify to its unspeakability.[4]

1. Martha Manning, *Undercurrents: A Life Beneath the Surface*, rev. ed. (San Francisco: HarperOne, 1995), 70.
2. Manning, *Undercurrents*, 85–86.
3. Manning, *Undercurrents*, 110.
4. I survey book- and essay-length narratives written in English by sufferers in the U.S. and Western Europe during the last forty years. I limit my study to this

17

From the pages of the Pulitzer Prize winner to the self-published pamphlet of a local writer, these texts name the inadequacy of ordinary language for conveying what depression is like. "Depression is awful beyond words or sounds or images," explains another psychologist, Kay Redfield Jamison, in her memoir of life with bipolar depression.[5] "It is mysterious even to those who suffer from it," confirms Matt Haig.[6] Acclaimed author William Styron similarly describes depression as "so mysteriously painful and elusive in the way it becomes known to the self—to the mediating intellect—as to verge close to being beyond description." He concludes, "It thus remains nearly incomprehensible to those who have not experienced it in its extreme mode."[7]

These testimonies present a challenge that scholars, including theologians, face when they embark on a study of depression: It is a mystifying condition. How, then, should we understand it—a condition that even sufferers struggle to grasp and convey? Difficult though this question may be, this is requisite for every Christian who desires to reflect theologically on this suffering, and it is the aim of this chapter to offer some description of and language for speaking about it. I look first at various scholarly accounts of depression, many of which may be familiar to readers. Then, departing from more widely known accounts of the condition, I argue in favor of some common first-person descriptions of depression, which I read with insights from phenomenology. What these first-person

---

geographical and historical context because of research on the cultural contingency of both conceptions and experiences of depression. See Aurthur Kleinman and Byron J. Good, eds., *Culture and Depression: Studies in Anthropology and Cross-Cultural Psychiatry of Affect and Disorder* (Berkeley, CA: University of California, 1986). Tracing the contours of depressive experience in another time and place might result in a different image of this condition. Though I elucidate consistencies across these first-person narratives, they are not indicative of all depressive experience, even within this historical context.

5. Kay Redfield Jamison, *An Unquiet Mind: A Memoir of Moods and Madness*, First Vintage Books Edition (New York: Vintage Books, 1995), 217.

6. Matt Haig, *Reasons to Stay Alive* (New York: Penguin, 2016), 14.

7. William Styron, *Darkness Visible: A Memoir of Madness*, First Vintage Books Edition (New York: Vintage Books, 1994), 7.

narratives and phenomenologies offer is an account of depression as "unhomelikeness," a description that grounds the theological reflection of subsequent chapters.

Depression according to Its Origin

Though scholars respond differently to the question of what depression is, many share a methodological commitment to investigating depression's origins. Such an approach assumes that pinpointing the cause of depression will afford insight into its essential composition. This is a well-tried, even ancient line of reasoning (I think here of Aristotle's taxonomy of causes). Still, among scholars who approach depression this way, of which I will highlight three examples, consensus about depression's nature remains elusive.

Many scholars in the sciences, for example, approach depression as a disease. To say that depression is a disease is to make an etiological claim—that is, a causal claim—for a "disease" presumes a "distinct sustaining cause" that when removed, results in the corresponding removal of its effects, which are often expressed as symptoms.[8] Scientists presume that the causal composition of a disease can be reliably demonstrated for empirical observation.[9] But, despite the ubiquity of this view of depression among medical professionals and scientists as well as the general public, researchers have yet to demonstrate the definitive cause of depression that they presume. There

---

8. See "Concept of a Distinct Sustaining Cause" from Bernard Gert and Charles M. Culver, "Defining Mental Disorder," in *The Philosophy of Psychiatry*, ed. Jennifer Radden (New York: Oxford University, 2004), 419–420. This is an admittedly broad and morally neutral definition of disease. Some have argued that the label "disease" is inherently tied to moral norms, and therefore it ought always to be defined in a manner that names its normativity. Disease, in this view, is a demarcation that pathologizes and stigmatizes. I opt for a morally neutral conception of disease here in order to explore how even neutral understandings of depression as a disease entail significant shortcomings. For a brief overview of current debates on the relationship of disease and social norms, see "Criticisms of the DSM Definition of Mental Disorder" from Gert and Culver, "Defining Mental Disorder," 418–419.

9. James Aho and Kevin Aho, *Body Matters: A Phenomenology of Sickness, Disease, and Illness* (Lanham, MD: Lexington, 2008), 3.

are researchers who believe that depression probably results from a particular gene,[10] or hormonal composition,[11] or unique constellation of gut bacteria,[12] or chemicals in the brain[13]—or a yet-isolated combination of some or all of these. But these remain contested positions within the scientific community because, at present, these causal theories lack the necessary evidence to discount other theories. This is one reason why it is so difficult to treat depression: Doctors and scientists do not know what causes it on a biological level.

Psychoanalytic interpretations of depression offer another, very different causal account of what depression is. Sigmund Freud, the founder of psychoanalysis, argued that his patients' illnesses were not the result of biological triggers but rather an unconscious reaction to interpersonal loss, repression, and introjection. Depression, according to his famous 1917 essay, "Mourning and Melancholy," is a sufferer's unconscious response to the loss of a beloved "object," most often the sufferer's mother. Stanley Jackson summarizes this position: "This lost 'loved object,' or aspects of that person, had been 'taken into' the melancholic by a process of introjection, and an identification with that person had occurred, that is, aspects of the lost object had become internalized aspects of the person who has now become the melancholic sufferer."[14] Melancholy, then, is essentially the experience of mourning a lost object. Rather than typical

10. Jennifer Y. F. Lau et al., "The Genetics of Mood Disorders," in *Handbook on Depression*, 3rd ed., ed. Ian H. Gotlib and Constance L. Hammen (New York: Guilford, 2014), 165–181.

11. Russell T. Joffe, "Hormone Treatment of Depression," *Dialogues in Clinical Neuroscience* 13, no. 1 (March 2011): 127–138; and Russell T. Joffe and Anthony J. Levitt, "The Thyroid and Depression," in *The Thyroid Axis and Psychiatric Illness*, ed. Joffe and Levitt (Washington, DC: American Psychiatric Press, 1993), 195–254.

12. Giacomo De Palma et al., "Microbiota and Host Determinants of Behavioural Phenotype in Maternally Separated Mice," *Nature Communications* 6 (July 28, 2015), http://www.nature.com/ncomms/2015/150728/ncomms8735/full/ncomms8735.html.

13. Michael E. Thase, Chang-Gyu Hahn, and Olivier Berton, "Neurobiological Aspects of Depression," in *Handbook on Depression*, 3rd ed., ed. Ian H. Gotlib and Constance L. Hammen (New York: Guilford, 2014), 182–201; see also Francisco López-Muñoz and Cecilio Álamo, eds., *Neurobiology of Depression* (London: CRC, 2012).

14. Stanley W. Jackson, *Melancholia and Depression: From Hippocratic Times to Modern Times* (New Haven, CT: Yale University, 1990), 224–225.

mourning in which grief eventually facilitates a letting go of loss and a movement toward a new relationship to the object, the melancholic person clings to lost objects and atypical mourning persists.

As a result of this theory, Freud believed that treating depression is not a matter of biological makeup and medicinal remedies. It necessitates a form of intensive talk therapy in which the analyst (the therapist) guides the analysand (the patient) in free association that unearths the loss that manifests itself unconsciously in the form of melancholy. The task of the analyst is to move the patient from melancholia to healthy mourning, which will have a lasting effect on the analysand's depression. Many of Freud's immediate disciples established their own branches of psychoanalysis, and the field has continued in flux since then. The central insight that melancholy (now called depression) results from personal loss still prevails, however.[15] Psychoanalysis remains prevalent in parts of Western Europe, but it has fallen out of favor in American mental healthcare for a variety of reasons, including the absence of what many deem to be sufficient scientific backing for its etiological theories and therapeutic techniques.[16]

Whereas most scholars of depression, regardless of their disciplinary affiliation, concede that cultural forces magnify the symptoms of depression, social constructionists take a more radical stance, offering yet another account of this condition. "Construction implies the emergence of some new structure, in which various items or various features, previously separate, are brought together to form a new whole," explains philosopher Jennifer Church. "In the case of a socially constructed mental disorder, an assortment of behaviors and experiences are brought together and ordered in some new way

---

15. See, for example, Melanie Klein, *The Writings of Melanie Klein*, vols. 1–3, ed. Roger Money-Kyrle (New York: The Free Press, 1975); Melanie Klein, "Mourning and Its Relation to Manic-Depressives States," in *Essential Papers on Object Loss*, ed. Rita V. Frankiel (New York: New York University, 1994), 95–122. See also the work of Julia Kristeva, especially *Black Sun: Depression and Melancholy*, trans. Leon S. Roudiez (New York: Columbia University, 1989).

16. See Michael Lacewing, "The Science of Psychoanalysis," *Philosophy, Psychiatry, and Psychology* 25, no. 2 (June 2018): 95–111.

that plays a role in the life of that society."[17] In contrast to biological and psychoanalytic accounts of depression that explore the causes that trigger or bring about the experience of depression and that assume the possibility for depression is somehow naturally latent in the constitution of the human person, social-constructionist accounts assert that social forces invented depression. That is to say, either a particular set of social forces engender the experience of depression or cultural conditions have facilitated the invention of the concept of depression by grouping experiences and symptoms together and assigning them their own ontology as a means of social stratification.[18] Yet like other causal accounts of depression, social constructivists face criticism for the tenuous assumptions that operate in their views of depression.[19]

These efforts to nail down depression as a disease, as neurotic grief, or as a social construction are pragmatic. Not only would a clear origin of depression aid in illuminating the nature of this condition, but it would also afford a way to curtail its difficulties. A clear and re-

17. Jennifer Church, "Social Constructionist Models," in *The Philosophy of Psychiatry: A Companion*, ed. Jennifer Radden (New York: Oxford University, 2004), 395.

18. Some notable examples of social-constructionist accounts of depression include Matthew Bell, *Melancholia: The Western Malady* (Cambridge, UK: Cambridge University, 2014); Ann Anelin Cheng, *The Melancholy of Race: Psychoanalysis, Assimilation, and Hidden Grief* (New York: Oxford University, 2001); Jonathan Cobb and Richard Sennett, *The Hidden Injuries of Class*, repr. ed. (New York: W.W. Norton, 1993); Ann Cvetkovich, *Depression: A Public Feeling* (Durham, NC: Duke University, 2012); Alain Ehrenberg, *The Weariness of the Self: Diagnosing the History of Depression in the Contemporary Age* (Quebec City, Canada: McGill-Queen's University, 2010); Michel Foucault, *Madness and Civilization: A History of Insanity in the Age of Reason*, Vintage Books 1988 ed., trans. Richard Howard (New York: Vintage Books, 1988); Michel Foucault, *History of Madness*, ed. Jean Khalfa, trans. J. Murphy (New York: Routledge, 2006); Gary Greenburg, *Manufacturing Depression: The Secret History of a Modern Disease* (New York: Simon & Schuster, 2010); Thomas Szasz, *The Myth of Mental Illness: Foundations of a Theory of Personal Conduct* (New York: Harper Perennial, 1974); Thomas Szasz, *The Manufacture of Madness: A Comparative Study of the Inquisition and the Mental Health Movement* (New York: Harper, 1970).

19. For example, for criticisms of Thomas Szasz, a widely known advocate for a social-constructionist view of depression, see Jeffrey Schaler, ed., *Szasz Under Fire: A Psychiatric Abolitionist Faces His Critics* (Chicago: Open Court, 2004).

liable map of depression's causes would presumably enable researchers to identify a route for reversing and preventing this condition. As it stands, however, linking the identity of depression to its cause is of limited use because its cause or causes remain elusive. In such circumstances, these causal claims often disclose more about the worldview of a particular theorist—such as a scholar's disciplinary assumptions about human nature and how it ought to be explained and assessed—than they disclose about the identity of depression itself. For instance, the scientists who confidently assert that depression has an empirical and quantifiable cause may do so not because of conclusive evidence specific to depression but because they are trained to account for the world through empirical and quantifiable cause-and-effect relationships.

What's more, and importantly for the aim of this chapter, the discovery of a clear cause for depression might not afford a sufficient portrait of the experience of depression itself. Already, some theologians have cautioned against such tidy explanations of suffering because they can elide the condition's more complex phenomenological dimensions. "Limiting our speech to scientific language leads to an ever-increasing silence; 'whatever cannot be said clearly,' to use Wittgenstein's phrase, then remains untreated," warns Dorothee Sölle.[20] In response, she insists that theology has "the task of enlarging the border of our language. A theology that could wrest land away from the sea of speechless death would be a theology worthy of that name."[21] The fact that depression sufferers struggle to represent and explain their own suffering should give us pause as we consider the suitability of etiological accounts of depression, popular as they may be across depression studies. They may not capture the fullest portrait of what it is to live with this condition.[22]

---

20. Dorothee Sölle, *Suffering*, trans. Everett Kalin (Philadelphia: Fortress, 1975), 7.

21. Sölle, *Suffering*, 7.

22. For more on the limitations of common descriptions of depression, see John Swinton, *Finding Jesus in the Storm: The Spiritual Lives of Christians with Mental Health Challenges* (Grand Rapids, MI: Eerdmans, 2020); and Jessica Coblentz, "What Can Theology Offer Psychology? Some Considerations in the Context of Depression," *Journal of Moral Theology* 9, no. 1 (2020): 2–19.

Depression as an Emotional State

At present, these inconclusive investigations leave many scholars and mental healthcare professionals to operate with what Matthew Bell calls a "causal agnosticism."[23] "Psychiatrists can be agnostic about the nature of any underlying neurochemical or neurobiological processes. What matters is that a meaningful cluster of symptoms occur together and follow a distinct course."[24] In other words, while investigations into the cause or causes of depression remain inconclusive, many simply define it as a particular conglomeration of observable traits.

A well-known example of this view of depression is found in the American Psychiatric Association's *Diagnostic and Statistical Manual of Mental Disorders* (DSM), which includes the diagnostic criteria most commonly used by healthcare providers and insurers in the United States. Many of the leading mental-health advocacy organizations in the U.S. also rely on the *DSM's* description of depression.[25] As a result, even Americans who have not heard of the *DSM* often unknowingly associate depression with the manual's symptomatic profile. Beginning with the third edition of the *DSM* in 1980, where the manual shifted from etiological definitions of mental disorders to symptomatic criteria for diagnoses, the *DSM* defined depression as a particular constellation of symptoms. For instance, the *DSM*, now in its fifth edition, identifies major depressive disorder as the co-occurrence of five or more of the following symptoms for the minimum duration of two weeks: depressed mood, loss of interest, weight loss or gain, insomnia or hypersomnia, psychomotor agitation or retardation, fatigue, feeling worthless or excessive guilt, decreased concentration, and thoughts of death and/or suicide. One of the first two symptoms—depressed mood or loss of interest—must be present to constitute depression, and together the constellation of remaining symptoms must "cause clinically significant distress

23. Bell, *Melancholia*, 11.

24. Bell, *Melancholia*, 11.

25. American Psychiatric Association, *Diagnostic and Statistical Manual of Mental Disorders*, 5th ed. (Washington, DC: American Psychiatric Publishing, 2016), 160–161.

or impairment in social, occupational, or other important areas of functioning."[26]

While this particular constellation of symptoms was new to the *DSM-III*, a number of historians and philosophers argue that, in the West, there has long been a human condition demarcated by the co-occurring symptoms of sadness and despondency, two of the key symptoms featured in *DSM's* definition of depression. These scholars argue that though this condition has had many labels across history—such as melancholia, acedia, and of course, depression—these two defining symptoms link the *DSM's* current emotional profile of depression to conditions of the past.[27] In fact, Stanley Jackson identifies a "remarkable consistency" across the history of these conditions on through today, pointing to the co-occurrence of sadness and despondency as the thread.[28]

Across the history of the *DSM*, the manual has progressively disregarded issues of context and cause in its definitions of depression in favor of this symptomatic profile. Though the *DSM-III* included a "bereavement specifier," which excluded from the diagnosis of depression anyone who exhibits the symptoms of major depressive disorder but has lost a loved one within the last two months, Horwitz, Wakefield, and Lorenzo-Luaces note that the *DSM-III* did not "exclude people whose symptoms arose from other life events such as the dissolution of a romantic relationship, loss of a valued job, or failure to achieve a long-desired goal, thus suggesting that these responses are not 'expectable' or 'culturally sanctioned.' This reasoning was contrary to the centuries-long understanding that such people do not have individual dysfunctions but are responding naturally to undesirable losses in their lives."[29] This decision by the American Psychiatric Association (APA) suggests that, with the

---

26. American Psychiatric Association, *Diagnostic and Statistical Manual*, 161.

27. Allan V. Horwitz, Jerome C. Wakefield, and Lorenzo Lorenzo-Luaces, "History of Depression," in *The Oxford Handbook of Mood Disorders*, ed. Robert J. DeRubeis and Daniel R. Strunk (New York: Oxford University, 2017), 11; Bell, *Melancholia*; Jackson, *Melancholia and Madness*; Jennifer Radden, *On the Nature of Melancholy: From Aristotle to Kristeva* (New York: Oxford University, 2002).

28. Jackson, *Melancholia and Madness*, ix.

29. Horwitz, Wakefield, and Lorenzo-Luaces, "History of Depression," 20.

exception of bereavement, the potential contextual causes of one's symptoms are irrelevant for diagnosing the condition. For the most part, then, it is the constellation of symptoms themselves that define depression. The APA emphasized this further when, in the fifth edition of the *DSM*, published in 2013, the bereavement specifier was officially omitted. This not only emphasized the irrelevance of context and cause for defining depression, but it also "show[ed] significant regression in understanding the most basic of all distinctions—the difference between normal sadness and depressive disorder."[30]

This last observation from Horwitz, Wakefield, and Lorenzo-Luaces—that a symptom-based definition of depression blurs the boundaries of normal and pathological mood—reveals some concerns about the *DSM's* portrait of depression. First, Horwitz, Wakefield, and Lorenzo-Luaces imply that they believe depression importantly differs from "normal sadness." This is significant in light of the fact that depression is so often identified with the emotion of sadness in the *DSM* as well as in the general public's imagination. Second, they suggest that context, such as a situation of bereavement, should play a central role in differentiating "normal sadness" from depression. Sadness appears to correspond with a cause—such as a death, loss of relationship, a trauma or other crisis—that understandably warrants a shift in mood. Depression, they imply, is unlinked to a single cause in one's life—or, if there is significant cause for a mood shift, then that shift can only be viewed as depression when it appears disproportionate to its cause.[31] Although Horwitz, Wakefield, and Lorenzo-Luaces emphasize the importance of the distinction between "normal sadness" and depression, they also note that a bereavement specifier and other causal qualifiers would not entirely eliminate confusion between the normal and the pathological. Even with such specifiers, a depression diagnosis hangs on how a particular healthcare professional differentiates between "proportionate" and "disproportionate" sadness, a distinction that is both culturally contingent and individually subjective. As long as depression is defined as a

---

30. Horwitz, Wakefield, and Lorenzo-Luaces, "History of Depression," 21.

31. Horwitz, Wakefield, and Lorenzo-Luaces, "History of Depression," 12–16, 21–22.

form of sadness, scholars and healthcare practitioners will face this definitional conundrum. Thus, while today's *DSM* offers a practical symptomatic account of depression that seemingly obviates the gridlock of causal debates and definitions, it has settled on an emotional profile of depression that is difficult to distinguish from ordinary emotion. The ambiguity between ordinary and pathological emotion and between proportionate and disproportionate sadness continues to garner criticism from scholars and healthcare practitioners.[32]

Outside these professional and scholarly debates, observations of depression in everyday life also signal the shortcomings of the *DSM's* definition. Consider the voices that opened this chapter: If depression was simply a magnification and extension of commonplace emotions—the sadness, hopelessness, and guilt that all persons experience at some point in their lives—then depression would be easily communicable and highly relatable. Yet depression sufferers repeatedly distance their condition from ordinary emotional experiences. "Depression is not just sadness and sorrow," writes Kathryn Greene-McCreight. "Depression is not just negative thinking. Depression is not just being 'down.'"[33] Judith Belushi, too, writes, "Sadness is part of it, but you can be sad without being depressed. Depression is deeper and more encompassing."[34] Pressing this further, Meri Nana-Ama Danquah asserts, "Depression isn't the same as ordinary sadness."[35] The negations that fill the pages of depression memoirs—it is *not* sadness, or *not just* negative thinking—indicate the inadequacy of identifying depression with sadness. It is this inadequacy that leads philosopher and psychiatrist Matthew Ratcliffe to conclude that unlike ordinary emotions, experiences of

32. For a discussion of these critiques, see Paul Bebbington, "The Classifications and Epidemiology of Unipolar Depression," in *The Wiley-Blackwell Handbook of Mood Disorders*, 2nd ed., ed. Mick Power (Malden, MA: Wiley-Blackwell, 2013), 8–10.

33. Kathryn Greene-McCreight, *Darkness Is My Only Companion: A Christian Response to Mental Illness* (Grand Rapids, MI: Brazos, 2006), 21.

34. Kathy Cronkite, *On the Edge of Darkness: Conversations about Conquering Depression* (New York: Delta Trade Paperbacks, 1994), 27.

35. Meri Nana-Ama Danquah, *Willow Weep for Me: A Black Woman's Journey through Depression* (New York: W.W. Norton, 1998), 260.

depression "differ radically from many people's mundane, everyday experience."[36]

While Ratcliffe concludes that the *DSM* is misguided in portraying depression as an emotional state, he does not contest the APA's efforts to define depression by its experiential qualities. The *DSM* goes wrong not in its attempt to inventory the experience of depression but in the fact that it does not attend closely enough to the experience that it alleges to describe. Ratcliffe and other phenomenologists argue that a close look at first-person narratives of depression reveals that it is not fundamentally an experience of emotion. These first-person perspectives can present an alternative and more precise portrait of this condition.

Depression as a Place

Though I have noted the negations that reappear across depression narratives as sufferers struggle to articulate their conditions, sufferers do not resign to negations alone. Depression sufferers also frequently turn to the figurative language of analogy and metaphor. Anyone looking will notice the ubiquity of figurative imagery in depression narratives: Depression is death. It is falling. It is drowning. It is darkness. And so on. This imagery is not merely the stylistic flourish of people who write memoirs. Sociologist David Karp observes the same pattern in the interviews that composed his study of depression, *Speaking of Sadness*.[37] When interviewees lamented their inability to convey the pain of depression to those who have not experienced it themselves, they employed metaphors as an alternative medium of expression "as with literary prose writers whose art depends on translating ineffable emotions into written words."[38]

Theologians, too, have long employed figurative language to "translate the ineffable." Throughout the Christian tradition, fig-

---

36. Matthew Ratcliffe, *Experiences of Depression* (New York: Oxford University, 2015), 1.

37. David Karp, *Speaking of Sadness: Depression, Disconnection and the Meanings of Illness*, updated and expanded ed. (New York: Oxford University, 2017).

38. Karp, *Speaking of Sadness*, 93.

urative language for God has complemented apophatic negations concerning the divine. Elizabeth Johnson explains that while God is "incomprehensible, unfathomable, limitless, ineffable, [and] beyond description," human beings continue to strive to communicate about their experiences of God through analogical imagery.[39] The Scriptures talk of God as Mother and Father, Shepherd and Potter. Christian theologians including Johnson have extrapolated rich theories of analogy and metaphor to argue that, though ultimately inexhaustive, figurative language can nevertheless tell us something true about what God is like. And just as divine imagery is thought to reveal something true about qualities of the Divine Mystery, which by nature always exceeds our grasp, so too the recurring imagery of depression memoirs suggests something about the elusive human condition of depression.[40]

Time and time again, for example, sufferers represent depression using spatial imagery, conveying depression as a place. "I awoke into a different world," one recalls, "It was as though all had changed while I slept: that I awoke not into normal consciousness but into a nightmare."[41] Jeffery Smith writes that depression "remakes the world," transporting its sufferers from their native land to "another landscape."[42] "It begins, and the familiar world without is seen as if through isinglass: recognizable in its outlines but dimly. It loses substance: sight and sounds and scent alike are gone unaccountably bland. Your vision has gone within; you are enwrapped by inner experience, none of it pleasurable. You are resident now in some parallel universe, a place inclined to resist the concrete nouns, verbs, and adjectives we use to describe other landscapes."[43] "You've lost a

39. Elizabeth Johnson, *Quest for the Living God: Mapping Frontiers in the Theology of God* (New York: Bloomsbury, 2011), 12.

40. Karen Kilby carefully parses the similarities and differences between theological speech about the mystery of suffering and the Mystery of God in "Negative Theology and Meaningless Suffering," *Modern Theology* 36, no. 1 (January 2020): 92–104.

41. Dorothee Rowe, *The Experience of Depression* (Chichester, UK: John Wiley & Sons, 1978), 268–269.

42. Jeffery Smith, *Where the Roots Reach for Water: A Personal and Natural History of Melancholia* (New York: North Point, 1999), 21.

43. Smith, *Where the Roots Reach*, 61.

habitable earth," echoes James, a patient of psychologist Gail Hornstein. "You've lost the invitation to live that the universe extends to us at every moment. You've lost something that people don't even know is. That's why it's so hard to explain."[44] Likewise, Sally Brampton remembers her depression as "living in a parallel universe but a universe so devoid of familiar signs of life that we are adrift, lost."[45] For A. Alvarez, depression is a "closed, concentrated world, airless and without exits."[46]

In this brief litany, one sees that depression is not only likened to a place but to a particular kind of place—a place that is far more daunting than its typical associations with sadness and despondency suggest. To the point, first-person narratives frequently liken depression to a prison. Brampton remembers life with depression this way: "It is the glass wall that separates us from life, from ourselves, that is so truly frightening about depression. It is a terrible sense of our own overwhelming reality, a reality that we know has nothing to do with the reality that we once knew. And from which we think we will never escape."[47] Her image of confinement behind a glass wall mirrors Chase Twitchell's description of her early childhood memories of depression. "I knew I wasn't normal—at school there was clear glass between me and the playground, me and my young fellow humans." She describes herself as "the watcher."[48] Styron, too, describes depression as "the diabolical discomfort of being imprisoned in a fiercely over-heated room."[49] Danquah also recalls, "It seemed as if the world were closing in on me, squeezing me dry."[50]

44. Quoted by Gail Hornstein, *Agnes's Jacket: A Psychologist's Search for the Meanings of Madness* (New York: Rodale, 2009), 213.

45. Sally Brampton, *Shoot the Damn Dog: A Memoir of Depression* (New York: W.W. Norton, 2008), 65.

46. A. Alvarez, *The Savage God: A Study of Suicide* (New York: W.W. Norton, 1990), 293.

47. Brampton, *Shoot the Damn Dog*, 65.

48. Chase Twitchell, "Toys in the Attic: An *Ars Poetica* Under the Influence," in *Unholy Ghost: Writers on Depression*, ed. Nell Casey (New York: Harper Perennial, 2002), 23.

49. Styron, *Darkness Visible*, 49.

50. Danquah, *Willow Weep for Me*, 32.

Surveying images of imprisonment in depression narratives, Ratcliffe observes,

> According to some authors, the experience is somehow touch-like; one is 'immersed' or 'wrapped up' in something. Others emphasize an inability to act; there is an impenetrable barrier that prevents one from engaging with the world. And others couch the experience in visual terms; the world is dark, drained of colour. Many accounts appeal to a combination of vision and agency: one can *see out* but one cannot *get out*. . . . The enclosure is always oppressive, suffocating. . . . It is also solitary and inescapable; one is irrevocably alone, cut off from the rest of humanity. Another theme is that of stasis; the world of depression is bereft of even the *possibility* of change. . . . It involves feeling that things will not and cannot change. If nothing can change, then one cannot escape.[51]

Ratcliffe's observations capture how various dimensions of depressive experience combine to facilitate the feeling of entrapment and isolation within an entirely different world than what sufferers are accustomed to. This is a far more encompassing experience than ordinary emotional fluctuation. This isolation from others is also a feature of depression that renders its sufferers vulnerable to suicidal ideation. Suicidologist Thomas Joiner argues that those who desire to die by suicide almost always perceive a disconnection from or a lack of belonging among others.[52]

The phenomenological qualities that sufferers associate with imprisonment explain the prevalence of purgatory and hell imagery in depression narratives as well. Like the experience of being confined to prison, one imagines hell and purgatory to be alternative, all-encompassing places characterized by darkness, eternal stasis, and inescapable isolation. Nina, a woman interviewed by Karp, looks back on her depression and calls it a "purgatory." She worries that a recent layoff will trigger another depressive episode that will again confine

51. Ratcliffe, *Experiences of Depression*, 65.

52. Thomas Joiner, *Why People Die by Suicide* (Cambridge, MA: Harvard University, 2005), 117–136.

her to that place.[53] Tina Sonego, a sufferer interviewed by Andrew Solomon, characterizes depression as a "walk through hell."[54] This aligns with the words of Danquah who, when distancing depression from a typical emotional state, explains, "Depression isn't the same as ordinary sadness, it is hell."[55]

Thomas Fuchs offers a similar description from a depressed patient who recounted feeling as if he were already dead: "What looks like normal life is not. I found myself on the other side. And now I realized what the cause had been. . . . I had died, but God had removed this event from my consciousness. . . . A harsher punishment could hardly be imagined. Without being aware of having died, you are in a hell that resembles in all details the world you had lived in, and thus God lets you see and feel that you have made nothing of your life."[56]

The image of purgatory appears at the conclusion of William Styron's memoir when he quotes Dante: "In the middle of the journey of our life, I found myself in a dark wood, / For I had lost the right path."[57] Dante used this image of the "dark wood" to describe his journey through purgatory and hell. Styron appropriates Dante's journey as a poetic image that "summed up" his "fathomless" depression. "One can be sure that these words have been more than once employed to conjure the ravages of melancholia," Styron comments. "The return from the abyss [of depression] is not unlike the ascent of the poet [Dante], trudging upward and upward out of hell's black depths."[58] The spatial metaphors of the underworld and wilderness converge in the recurrent appropriation of Dante's *Inferno* across a number of depression memoirs. Therese Borchard alludes to Dante's famous opening, writing that she "felt [her] way,

---

53. Karp, *Speaking of Sadness*, 87.

54. Andrew Solomon, *The Noonday Demon: An Atlas of Depression*, new ed. (New York: Scribner, 2015), 442.

55. Danquah, *Willow Weep for Me*, 260.

56. Thomas Fuchs, "The Phenomenology of Shame, Guilt and the Body in Body Dysmorphic Disorder and Depression," in *Journal of Phenomenological Psychology* 33, no. 3 (2003): 238–239.

57. Styron, *Darkness Visible*, 84.

58. Styron, *Darkness Visible*, 84.

blindfolded, through the woods of depression and anxiety."[59] Dante's wilderness imagery also opens Parker Palmer's reflection on depression, where he recounts, "I found myself in the dark woods called clinical depression, a total eclipse of light and hope."[60]

Jeffery Smith's memoir of depression, *Where Roots Reach for Water*, is an extended exploration of associations between depression and place. It is there that he calls depression "another landscape," one that is "remote as the Yukon from the quotidian world."[61] There, too, he recounts the long history of the association between place and conditions like depression, such as melancholia. In 1688, Johannes Hofter believed that melancholia was a manifestation of "nostalgia"—that is, "grief for the lost charm of the Native Land, a continual melancholy, with incessant thinking of home."[62] In 1847, German physician Ernst von Feuchtersleben observed, "That turn of melancholia which seems caused by homesickness often leads to suicide."[63] Smith himself identifies resonances between depression and the experience of displacement or homesickness. During a visit to his family in the Allegheny Foothills after years away, Smith is suddenly taken by a feeling of at-home-ness that had been absent from his life in recent months as he struggled with depression. The feeling of being at home in the world—of "reveling, vibrant for the first time in many, many months," of familiarity with his surroundings, of feeling "restored" and connected to others—put into focus the contrasting qualities of the depressive state in which he had been living.[64] Depression is another "chambered and unearthly landscape, its origins obscure, its meridians unmapped," where no history exists and there are no connections across time.[65] It "is a state unto itself" where "just drawing breath after odious, laborious, stale breath

59. Therese Borchard, *Beyond Blue: Surviving Depression and Anxiety and Making the Most of Bad Genes* (New York: Center Street, 2009), xxvi.

60. Parker Palmer, *Let Your Life Speak: Listening for the Voice of Vocation* (San Francisco: Jossey-Bass, 2000), 57.

61. Smith, *Where the Roots Reach*, 21.

62. Smith, *Where the Roots Reach*, 132.

63. Smith, *Where the Roots Reach*, 133.

64. Smith, *Where the Roots Reach*, 130–131.

65. Smith, *Where the Roots Reach*, 21.

begins to seem pointless."[66] So taken is Smith by the similarities between his experiences of depression and of homesickness for Appalachia that he wonders if the old medical speculations of Hofter and Feuchtersleben are correct.

One need not affirm a causal relationship between homesickness and depression to appreciate the phenomenological similarities that Smith presents, especially in light of the other spatial descriptors that pervade depression narratives. What we learn from Smith and other sufferers is that depression often feels like displacement to a foreign landscape, like a forced exile from home. It is an unfamiliar and unruly place. It is a wilderness—not unlike the one I had dreamed of.

While the denials of depression memoirs distance the condition from its frequent identification with emotion, the recurring description of depression as a place—a world as unfamiliar as the afterlife, as constraining as a prison, and as inhospitable as the wilderness—presents a more textured and also more peculiar sketch of this condition: It is engrossing and yet elusive of description. It is strange relative to a sufferer's ordinary experience of the world.

Even though depression sufferers draw from a strikingly consistent inventory of figurative language to convey something of what it is like, their images remain partial. Like the images of God employed in theological reflection, these descriptors of depression are not literal. Sufferers describe their experience of depression as displacement to an unfamiliar landscape knowing they are located not in the forest but on the living room couch where they have been perched for months or under the covers of their beds, which for many become all-too-familiar refuges amid their struggles with depression. Inherent to these spatial representations of depression are implicit negations: Depression is a place and *not* a place. It is hell and *not* hell. It is prison and *not* prison. It is a wilderness yet *not* a literal, physical place. Especially because these recurring spatial images of depression are figurative and not literal, they require interpretation. For greater understanding, one must discern how depression is like and unlike the places that depression sufferers often associate with this condition.

66. Smith, *Where the Roots Reach*, 21.

Reading Depression Narratives with Phenomenology

These representations of depression show that, like the long tradition of theological reflection on God, this mysterious condition continues to escape the limits of even its most well-developed descriptions. To the theologian who credits the limits of God-talk to the nature of God, the limits of figurative speech about depression invite investigation. Why is it that depression eludes representation? What is it about depression itself that positions it beyond direct description?

Among the vast and important scholarship on depression, phenomenologists provide compelling responses to these questions. Phenomenology emerged in the nineteenth century as a distinct approach to examining human experience.[67] In contrast to scientists and other philosophers who brought an objectivist, etiological lens to the study of humankind, explaining phenomena in terms of cause and effect, Edmund Husserl and other phenomenologists in his lineage sought a more robust account of human life by attending to the subjective experience of oneself as a "lived-body" (*Leib*). This entails a "bracketing" (*epoché*) of the causal frameworks through which scientists view the body. For example, instead of defining the living body with reference to the biological factors that cause it to subsist (e.g., genetic makeup, brain function, proper nutrients, etc.), phenomenologists describe what it is like to *experience* oneself as living. Accordingly, they employ the term "lifeworld" (*Lebenswelt*) to denote the world as it presents itself to the subject. From the careful study of first-person accounts of life, phenomenologists theorize the structures of experience that shape how people find themselves in the world. These structures are often "pre-thematic"—that is, prior to one's immediate awareness. Over time, phenomenologists developed a catalogue of meticulous observations and technical terms to identify these structures of experience and their relationship to the more direct and immediate perceptions of human life.

By situating first-person accounts of depression into this larger and extraordinarily nuanced map of human experience, phenomenologists

---

67. For an introduction to the phenomenological approach to experience, see Dermot Moran's *Introduction to Phenomenology* (New York: Routledge, 2000).

elucidate the contours of depressive suffering, clarifying its particularities and distinguishing it from other dimensions of human
experience. In doing so, they provide rich portraits of depression,
an account of why sufferers so frequently describe depression
with spatial imagery, and an explanation for why it evades direct
description.

Depression as a Shift in Mood

A more in-depth look of the pre-thematic dimensions of human
experience is necessary for understanding how phenomenologists
make sense of depression and its unspeakability. A significant contribution of Martin Heidegger to phenomenology is his emphasis on
the multiple ways that people find themselves in the world, a variety
that is tied to these pre-thematic dimensions of experience. People
are "attuned" to the world in different "moods" (*Stimmung*), he observes. By "mood," Heidegger means something different than the
fluctuating psychological states suggested in our vernacular use of
the term. In its common usage, mood is synonymous with emotion,
and that is not what concerns Heidegger. Mood (*Stimmung*) grounds,
or pre-conditions, one's sense of belonging and possibility in the
world, whereas emotions are acts of consciousness that fluctuate
within the mood (*Stimmung*) in which one finds oneself.

Most of the time, explains Heidegger, people live in the taken-
for-granted mood of "everydayness" (*Alltäglichkeit*). This mood dis-
poses us to experience the world as meaningful and familiar. It is
characterized by a sense of "homelikeness" (*Heimlichkeit*) or of being
"at home" because we have a sense of belonging and connection to
what we experience. Ratcliffe illustrates this sense of belonging with
mundane examples: "Whenever I reflect upon my experience of a
chair, a table, a sound, an itch or a taste, and whenever I contrast my
experience with yours, I continue to presuppose a world in which we
are both situated, a shared realm in which it is possible to encounter
things like chairs and to experience things like itches." He continues, "This sense of being rooted in an interpersonal world does not
involve perceiving a (very big) object or believing that some object
exists. It's something that is already in place when we do that, and

therefore something that we seldom reflect upon."[68] As such, our interactions with the world are characterized by fluency and flow—by what phenomenologists call "attunement"—so much so that we unconsciously utilize tools and unthinkingly anticipate perceptions as we move from one thing to the next.[69]

Even amid this stable and pleasant backdrop of "everydayness," one can experience vast fluctuations of emotion: I might feel sad about the death of a pet or satisfied by a delicious meal. These emotions are tied to but distinct from the mood of at-home-ness that conditions my ordinary experience. Mood discloses the possibilities with which we experience the world, and these emotions are all possible when we find ourselves amid everydayness. Other moods may withhold this range of emotional possibilities, however. This is what leads philosopher Jennifer Radden to assert that moods have "ontological primacy over more cognitive states."[70] They condition the possibilities of our cognition, including our emotions. As such, they radically shape our experiences, even as "our moods are not as transparent to us as our more cognitive states."[71] "By their nature, then," Radden explains, "moods are important and ubiquitous, yet elusive and unbounded, blurring into other states."[72] For this reason, mood is frequently described as a "backdrop" of human experience.

The phenomenological distinction between mood (*Stimmung*) and emotion is key to understanding why the framework of emotion is inadequate for capturing what depression is like. When people identify depression with the emotions of sadness and despondency, they situate depression within one's ordinary experience of the world. This suggests that depression is but a long and severe version of the emotions that most people experience amid everydayness (*Alltäglichkeit*). And yet, were this in fact the case with depression, our vernacular

---

68. Matthew Ratcliffe, "The World of Depression" (unpublished paper, 2013), https://www.academia.edu/6054108/The_World_of_Depression.

69. Aho and Aho, *Body Matters*, 106.

70. Jennifer Radden, *Moody Minds Distempered: From Aristotle to Kristeva* (New York: Oxford University, 2009), 14–15.

71. Radden, *Moody Minds Distempered*, 14–15.

72. Radden, *Moody Minds Distempered*, 184.

repertoire for emotions would suffice when conveying what depression is like. One could simply say, "I am depressed: I have felt very sad for a long time. I am hopeless," and others could empathize based on their own experiences of these ordinary emotions. Instead, depression sufferers regularly reject emotional descriptions of their experiences.

Some phenomenologists of depression argue that depression is better understood as a shift in mood (*Stimmung*) than it is as an ordinary fluctuation of emotion. Locating depression in the backdrop of experience accounts for the preponderance of spatial imagery in depression memoirs: Depression is not primarily a change of something *within* one's ordinary experience of the world, such as emotion, but rather a more radical shift in the constitutive backdrop of one's experience *as a whole*. Because moods are the pre-thematic backdrop of human experience, they are all-encompassing of our experiences. Sufferers' images of a change of world or landscape reflect this radical and engrossing shift—one that, like a change in theatrical backdrop, relativizes everything else that is perceived in the forefront of one's experience.

This phenomenological sketch of *Stimmung* and the suggestion of some phenomenologists that depressive experience is fundamentally constituted by a shift in mood also affords insight into why depression consistently evades direct description. The language upon which we rely for everyday communication customarily refers to objects in our immediate consciousness, that is, in the forefront of experience. Meanwhile, it is more difficult to articulate shifts in mood because *Stimmung* "blurs" into other states and, as a pre-thematic dimension of experience, evades direct objectification. That is, it inherently evades the grasp of ordinary descriptions of consciousness. One of phenomenology's benefits for understanding depression is that it identifies and names these dimensions of human experience that we often otherwise miss.

Depression as Unhomelikeness

In addition to providing a technical explanation for why depression is frequently described with figurative spatial imagery, phenomenology also provides a sharper account of depressive experience through its inventory of various moods. I noted previously that depression is not merely depicted as a place but as a particular type of place. *Stimmung*, too, manifests particularly. Phenomenologists of depression have identified depression with a particular quality of mood, what is known as "unhomelikeness" (*Unheimlichkeit*). Those familiar with the technical phenomenological term *Unheimlichkeit* will know that the common English rendering of the term is "uncanniness."[73] Along with a number of phenomenologists of depression, I opt for "unhomelikeness," a translation closer to its literal etymology and one that retains the imagery common to first-person depression narratives, where sufferers often articulate their experience of depression with metaphors of displacement into harsh landscapes.

In Heidegger's studies of two manifestations of mood, anxiety (*Angst*)[74] and boredom (*Langeweile*),[75] he observes an experience of alienation or "unhomelikeness" that occurs with some shifts in *Stimmung*. This unhomelikeness, which individuals experience in contrast to the at-home-ness (*Heimlichkeit*) that constitutes most people's ordinary experience of everydayness, reflects the characteristics that regularly surface in figurative descriptions of depression.

Whereas the typical mood of "being-at-home" is experienced as "obvious" or ordinary and familiar, "everyday familiarity collapses"

---

73. According to philosopher Dermot Moran, Heidegger's use of "unheimlich," though commonly translated as "uncanny," nevertheless "carries the meaning of something being unfamiliar, un-homely." I simply highlight this meaning with my more literal translation of the term. See Dermot Moran, *Introduction to Phenomenology* (New York: Routledge, 2000), 241. Heidegger himself lends credence to this, as he explains in *Being and Time* that "here 'uncanniness' [*unheimlichkeit*] also means 'not-being-at-home' [*das Nicht-zuhause-sein*]." See *Being and Time*, trans. John Macquarrie and Edward Robinson (New York: HarperMillenial, 1962), §40. Commenting on this section, translators Macquarrie and Robinson note, "While '*unheimlich*' is here translated as 'uncanny,' it means more literally 'unhomelike,' as the author proceeds to point out" (233n1).

74. Heidegger, *Being and Time*, §40; Martin Heidegger, "What is Metaphysics?," in *Martin Heidegger: Basic Writings*, rev. and expanded ed., ed. and trans. D. F. Krell (New York: Routledge, 1993), 93–110.

75. Martin Heidegger, *The Fundamental Concepts of Metaphysics: World, Finitude, Solitude*, trans. William McNeill and Nicholas Walker (Bloomington, IN: Indiana University, 2001), §19–41.

in unhomelikeness.[76] The sense of connection and shared belonging in the world that constitutes everydayness falls away amid unhomelikeness, and other characteristics of everydayness dissolve as well. "The everyday world loses its felt richness and familiarity. Visual and audio cues are abstracted from a larger context and show up as simple sensations denuded of meaning. Otherwise compelling or tragic life events are experienced with emotional flatness and indifference."[77] Fuchs, drawing on the musical connotations of "attunement," characterizes unhomelikeness as a "'loss of bodily resonance' wherein one is rendered incapable of 'feeling themselves into the world.'"[78] In this description, we begin to see how a shift in the "backdrop" of mood affects the perceptions at the forefront of our experience. Whereas everydayness is the condition for the possibility of our experience of meaningfulness, presence, and connection with the world in which we find ourselves, *Unheimlichkeit* imposes a different set of conditions.

What is special about the moods associated with unhomelikeness, explains Fredrik Svenaeus, "is that they do not only open but also *block* our possibilities to be in the world together with others. . . . No particular thing in the world matters anymore and therefore it becomes possible to address the meaning of the being-in-the-world *as such*." Svenaeus continues, "They make the settling, the being at home in the world, hard since the world resists meaningfulness. The world becomes alien, making us long for another place to be in."[79] James and Kevin Aho illustrate this shift with some examples: "Expansive, unfettered connectedness to the world enables the gestures of colleagues, friends, and family to enter us as meaningful acts, not merely as mechanical operations. Upturned mouths become smiles; moisture on the cheek, tears; an empty palm held out to us, a sign

---

76. Heidegger, *Being and Time*, §40.

77. Aho and Aho, *Body Matters*, 118.

78. Aho and Aho, *Body Matters*, 119; Aho and Aho are quoting Thomas Fuchs, "Corporealized and Disembodied Minds: A Phenomenological View of the Body in Melancholia and Schizophrenia," *Philosophy, Psychiatry, and Psychology* 12 (2005): 100.

79. Fredrik Svenaeus, "Depression and the Self: Bodily Resonance and Attuned Being-in-the-World," *Journal of Consciousness Studies* 20, nos. 7–8 (2013): 22.

of peace. By the same token, the inability to feel into the world fore-closes any possibility of emotional connection to others. Instead, they present themselves as 'little robots.' "[80]

In this brief sketch of unhomelikeness, we see a number of similarities with depression. First, unhomelikeness is defined in contrast to the familiarity of everydayness that most people take for granted as they move through the world. The absence of familiarity, replaced by a sense of strangeness or not-at-home-ness, is mirrored in the recurring description of depression as a foreign place—an unfamiliar world. The strangeness that characterizes unhomelikeness sheds new light on the death imagery that fills depression memoirs as well. If homelikeness characterizes one's typical experience of the world, then the loss of that can quite reasonably be likened to death, an image that represents the antithesis of what we associate with ordinary life. To the point, phenomenologists use the term *Körper*, or "corpse," to denote a state of being-in-the-world that is contrary to the everydayness of the lived-body (*Leib*). To experience the world as unhomelike is to be in the world as "corpse."[81] It is unsurprising, then, that sufferers also describe depression as hell or purgatory, spaces antithetical to the familiar landscapes of the "living."

Second, understanding depression as a loss of homelikeness also accounts for the radical isolation sufferers often experience amid depression. Whereas the mood of everydayness is characterized by a sense of belonging, unhomelikeness is constituted by a loss of connection. The perception of some sufferers that they live with an invisible "wall" separating them from others and that they live as if confined in a prison cell can be read as attempts to describe this radically isolating state of unhomelikeness.

Third, the perception of isolation amid depression is magnified by the "resistance to meaningfulness" that characterizes unhomelikeness. The example from Aho and Aho of encountering "upturned mouths" and "empty palms held out to us" as meaningless gestures rather than smiles and signs of peace provides a glimpse of what it is like to find oneself in a world without meaning, a world that, as

80. Aho and Aho, *Body Matters*, 119.
81. Aho and Aho, *Body Matters*, 118.

a consequence, is incredibly isolating. Finding oneself in a world without possibilities of meaning would also compromise the pleasures and comforts of everyday life. This again accounts for sufferers' diminished ability to find enjoyment and purpose in the activities that once engaged them. Even when engaging the same people and activities they had previously, the shift in the backdrop of experience upon which meaningfulness and connection are predicated would obstruct the possibilities for pleasure that sufferers once took for granted. Again, this is not a mere shift in their emotional response to an activity or person. It is a radical shift in the available possibilities for emotional responses to the activity or person before them.

Fourth, understanding depression as unhomelikeness helps us make sense of the permanence and helpless entrapment that sufferers perceive. Unhomelikeness conditions people to experience the present as unending, like a prison from which one has no freedom to escape or a death that stretches into eternity. Ratcliffe describes moods as "worlds of possibility," and the unhomelikeness that constitutes depression is characterized by the perceived absence of possibilities for change. Ratcliffe points to Husserl's distinction between "instances" and "kinds" of possibility to illustrate how unhomelikeness affects a person's experience of possibility. "We can draw a distinction between *instances* of possibility, such as 'this cup can be touched' or 'this cup has the potential to be seen by others,' and *kinds* of possibility, such as 'being tangible' or 'being perceived by others.' In order to encounter anything as 'being tangible', or 'perceptually or practically accessible to others', 'relevant to a project', 'enticing' or 'fascinating', we must first have access to the relevant *kinds* of possibility."[82] Ratcliffe continues,

> Disturbances in existential feeling [that is, mood] are changes in the kinds of possibility we are open to, kinds that can be characterized in terms of the distinction I have drawn. At least some of these kinds of possibility are integral to the sense of reality and belonging. For instance, what would it be like to inhabit a world where nothing offered the possibility of *tangibility*? Of course, something can be ex-

---

82. Ratcliffe, *Experiences of Depression*, 51.

perienced as real, and more specifically, as "here, now" without its being experienced as tangible. Take the clouds, for example. However, there is a difference between a cloud's lacking tangibility and an absence of tangibility from experience as a whole. If everything ceased to offer the possibility of being touched or manipulated, if that *kind of possibility* were altogether gone, then experience would no longer include a contrast between the interchangeability of a cloud and the tangibility of a cup of coffee. Without the contrast, everything would look strangely distant, cut off, somehow not quite *there*, at least if one retained a *feeling* of loss (and one would, if kinds of possibility are integrated into complicated systems of anticipating, in relation to which their absence is noticeable).[83]

Ratcliffe observes that depression sufferers undergo a shift in the *kinds* of possibilities that their worlds entail. This is markedly different from the shifts in possibility one experiences within home-likeness, wherein one experiences shifts in *instances* of possibility. "Suppose two people both report that 'nothing matters anymore,'" as many depression sufferers often do. "It could turn out that one finds however many previously significant states of affairs inconsequential while the other inhabits a world from which the possibility

---

83. Ratcliffe, *Experiences of Depression*, 53. Also, "existential feeling" is more or less Ratcliffe's term for *Stimmung*. He prefers "existential feelings" to "mood" for several reasons relating to debates about emotion in contemporary philosophy. Though a thorough explanation of "existential feeling" exceeds the bounds of this chapter, the following passage conveys what's at stake for Ratcliffe in this term: "Although my 'existential feelings' have much in common with Heidegger's 'moods,' there are several reasons for adopting the former term. The English term 'mood' refers to a range of different phenomenon, not all of which play the phenomenological role described by Heidegger. . . . My departure from Heidegger is not just terminological though. His analysis also has shortcomings. For instance, he restricts himself to a fairly narrow range of emotional states. . . . However, the range of existential feelings is much wider than that. And we can, by drawing on Husserl's discussion of horizons, formulate a far more nuanced account of the kinds of possibility that experience incorporates. Furthermore, there is a need to accommodate the bodily dimension of existential feeling, something Heidegger explicitly declines to comment on in *Being and Time*. In this respect, Husserl is again more informative, in explicitly linking the background 'style' of experience to our bodily phenomenology." See *Experiences of Depression*, 58.

of anything mattering is gone."[84] The latter scenario is the case for many depression sufferers, and a similar shift in kind applies more generally to other experiences including despair, guilt, agency, and interpersonal connection, among others.[85] "The world of depression is bereft of even the possibility of change," Ratcliffe explains. "It involves a feeling that things will not and cannot change. If nothing can change, then one cannot escape. . . . One watches the dynamic lives of other people from inside a solitary, unchanging bubble."[86]

The loss of the possibility of change comes into focus when one considers the repeated assertions of depression sufferers that recovery from depression is impossible. "When you are depressed, the past and the future are absorbed entirely by the present moment, as in the world of a three-year-old. You cannot remember a time when you felt better, at least not clearly; and you certainly cannot imagine a future time when you will feel better," explains Solomon.[87] For Styron, "All sense of hope had vanished, along with the idea of futurity."[88] It is as if depression cuts one off from the world and its past, present, and future.

Ratcliffe links the fundamental shift in available possibilities to another aspect of depression that contributes to its perceived permanence—alterations in the overall structure of temporal experience. A shift in the temporal backdrop of one's experience is but one more reason why depression sufferers may characterize depression as such an unfamiliar experience. Ratcliffe writes, "Losses of hope involve the absence of certain kinds of possibility from the anticipated future and, in more extreme cases, from any imaginable future of remembered past. The conviction that one cannot recover is similarly bound up with what the future offers, as are experiences of diminished agency. And the most profound form of existential guilt involves a past that is frozen in place by the impossibility of redemptive change."[89]

84. Ratcliffe, *Experiences of Depression*, 44–45.
85. Ratcliffe, *Experiences of Depression*, 44–45.
86. Ratcliffe, *Experiences of Depression*, 65.
87. Solomon, *The Noonday Demon*, 55.
88. Styron, *Darkness Visible*, 58.
89. Ratcliffe, *Experiences of Depression*, 174.

Ratcliffe's observation about shifts in temporal experience arise from the testimony of depressed people. "I'd watch, incredulous, as putting cereal in a bowl took forever," remembers poet Gwyneth Lewis. "Sitting downstairs became a marathon of endurance because there was no escape from the dullness of each second, which had stretched so that it seemed like hours. . . . The ordinary afternoon light refused to change, it was going to stay like that all day and I'd never be able to move again and God why couldn't it do something instead of just continuing."[90] Rod Steiger recalls, "When you're depressed, there's no calendar. There are no dates, there's no day, there's no night, there's no seconds, there's no minutes, there's nothing. You're just existing in this cold, murky, ever-heavy atmosphere, like they put you inside a vial of mercury."[91] Solomon attests to this temporal shift as well: "You certainly cannot imagine a future time when you will feel better. Being upset, even profoundly upset, is a temporal experience, while depression is atemporal. Breakdowns leave you with no point of view."[92]

Whereas some phenomenologists characterize this shift in temporality as a change in the "flow" of time—that is, the velocity at which one experiences the shift between past, present, and future—others including Ratcliffe observe a heterogeneity of temporal experience that indicates an alteration in the more fundamental "structure" of temporality. Temporal structure refers to "how past, present, future, and the transition between them are experienced."[93] Both perspectives reflect a shift from the temporal perception of everydayness to a markedly different way of being in the world. According to Ratcliffe, a sufferer's inability to perceive the possibility of change

> could be construed as the depressed person's belief that *not p*, where *p* is the proposition "I will recover from depression." However, people do not state that they believed *not p* rather than *p*. What they almost always say is that they could not ever *conceive* of the possibility of *p*.

90. Gwyneth Lewis, *Sunbathing in the Rain: A Cheerful Book about Depression* (London: Harper Perennial, 2006), 14. Quoted in Ratcliffe, *Experiences of Depression*, 174–175.

91. Cronkite, *On the Edge of Darkness*, 46.

92. Solomon, *The Noonday Demon*, 55.

93. Ratcliffe, *Experiences of Depression*, 175.

By implication, they could not entertain the possibility of a choice between *p* and *not p*. *Not p* struck them as the only available option; it presented itself to them as absolutely certain. When we acknowledge that depression involves loss of any sense that things could change in a good way, it becomes clear why this is so.[94]

For many depression sufferers, the only possibility that presents itself is that things will stay the same or get worse. They live in a prison of the present—a hell-on-earth; an eternal, unfamiliar, and inhospitable landscape.

This experience of permanence is tied to suicide risk. Pioneering suicidologist Edwin Schneidman observes in suicidal patients a characteristic "narrowing or tunneling of the focus of attention" that he calls "constriction."[95] So constrained are the possibilities for living, for change, for meaning, for hope that a suicidal person can reach a state where death seems the *only* escape from one's psychological pain. "Everyone who commits suicide feels driven to it—indeed, feels that suicide is the *only* option left."[96] This informs Schneidman's view that, "[t]he single most dangerous word in all of suicidology is the four-letter word *only*."[97] And so while most depressive suffering does not end in suicide and depression itself is insufficient to complete suicide, the seemingly permanent collapse of possibility experienced by many depression sufferers affords insight into a suicidal state of mind.

Depression as a Particular Unhomelikeness

Identifying depression as unhomelikeness requires at least one important caveat. In his treatments of unhomelikeness, Heidegger presents it as a common feature of all human life. Though strange and uncomfortable by definition, it can be philosophically fruitful when one reflects on it in an authentic manner. In turn, one might

---

94. Ratcliffe, *Experiences of Depression*, 68.
95. Edwin Schneidman, *The Suicidal Mind* (New York: Oxford University, 1996), 59.
96. Schneidman, *Suicidal Mind*, 13.
97. Schneidman, *Suicidal Mind*, 59.

conclude that depression, seen as an experience of unhomelike-ness, is not so bad. Or one might surmise that, to the extent that depression is hard, its difficulties are always ultimately worthwhile because of some personal insight it can presumably produce, ac-cording to Heidegger's characterization. With this in mind, Fredrik Svenaeus disagrees with Heidegger, observing that the benefits of unhomelikeness for sufferers are tenuous. "The problem from the point of view of psychiatry . . . is that anxiety and boredom—two moods characterized by unhomelikeness—can become destructive, rather than productive, life experiences: they can be so overwhelm-ing that a return to homelikeness is impossible. Unhomelikeness is a necessary ingredient of life; it can be very rewarding insofar as it allows us to see things in novel, more nuanced ways. It must be balanced by homelikeness, however, lest we fall into a bottomless pit of darkness."[98] It is crucial to recognize that one cannot presume depression to be inherently fruitful and meaningful, for those suffer-ing with it often long to make meaning of their experience but cannot find or generate this meaning in their present state; some will never.

Many of the phenomenologists who have given themselves to the careful study of depression narratives associate the condition with this uncontrollable shift from at-home-ness to unhomelikeness that Svenaeus speaks of—this "fall into a bottomless pit of darkness." This seemingly irreversible displacement does not lend itself as read-ily to the happy or even meaningful endings that Heidegger seems to promise. This differentiates depression from other experiences of unhomelikeness that shape human life from time to time. Depres-sion, in this sense, is a relatively extraordinary experience, and an extraordinarily difficult one at that. This is important to keep in mind as the book turns to theological reflections on depression, which entail their own claims about if, when, and how suffering such as depression is meaningful.

As I proceed with this narrative-phenomenological portrait of depression, it is also important to mind the limitations of this ap-proach to human experience. While bracketing causal questions

98. Fredrik Svenaeus, "Do Antidepressants Affect the Self? A Phenomenological Approach," *Medicine, Health Care and Philosophy* 10, no. 2 (2007): 158.

about what and why depression is enables phenomenologists' rich description of experience, it suspends attention to factors that can contribute to the difficulties of this condition. The initial bracketing of phenomenology does not necessitate an enduring inattention to causal and magnifying factors, however, and at times it is important to attend to these, as we will see in some chapters ahead.

But first I turn in the next chapter to some views of depression that prevail in U.S. Christian communities. Though distinctly religious, these theological accounts of depression have much in common with the secular, etiological portraits of the condition that I have surveyed and criticized here in chapter 1.

Chapter 2

Popular Christian
Theologies of Depression

According to Christian psychologist Marcia Webb, mental illness, including depression, often "challenges our most basic ideas about ourselves."[1] We have already seen some evidence of this from depression narratives, which show how radically upending the dislocation of depression can be. Life in this unhomelike place entails the diminishment or loss of possibilities of meaningfulness, interconnectedness, agency, and futurity. From what many take for granted as essential to their experience of being-in-the-world, depression leaves sufferers unmoored.

Similar disorientations accompany other forms of suffering. Anthropologist Arthur Kleinman observes, "When we meet up with the resistance offered by profound life experience—the death of a child or parent or spouse, the loss of a job or home, serious illness, substantial disability—we are shocked out of our common-sensical perspective on the world."[2] Indeed, the "shock" of depression often rests not only in a radical shift in one's experience of the world but also in the concomitant challenge that this phenomenological

---

1. Marcia Webb, *Toward a Theology of Psychological Disorder* (Eugene, OR: Cascade, 2017), 92.

2. Arthur Kleinman, *The Illness Narratives: Suffering, Healing, and the Human Condition*, repr. ed. (New York: Basic Books, 1989), 27.

dislocation presents to the collectively held sources of meaning making that shape people's lives. Frequently, the "basic ideas about ourselves" threatened by suffering are religious ones.

Such challenges reveal what anthropologists like Kleinman teach
us about the cultural and religious realities that animate our everyday beliefs, values, and hopes. So entangled are our lives in these
cultural and religious systems that their influence often goes relatively unquestioned until a moment of crisis when we are desperate
for ways to make sense of our shifting experiences. The Gospel of
Luke offers one of my favorite examples of this when, in the wake
of Jesus's crucifixion, two disciples struggle with the divergences
between their Jewish worldview, with its foundational assumptions
about God and how God would save Israel, and the horrific death of
the Messiah that occurred just a few days prior (Luke 24:13–35). On
the road to Emmaus, they bemoan how their post-crucifixion reality
no longer maps onto the worldview of their Jewish faith. "We had
hoped that he was the one to redeem Israel," they lament (v. 21).

In times of needful searching, cultural and religious systems have
the potential to enrich our lives. For many, explains Kleinman, "local
cultural systems provide both the theoretical framework of myth
and the established script for ritual behavior that transform an individual's affliction into a sanctioned symbolic form for a group."[3]
In such instances, "shared moral and religious perspectives on the
experience of life crises anchor anxieties in established social institutions of control, binding threat in webs of ultimate meaning."[4]
This appears to have been the case for Luke's wandering disciples,
who eventually encounter a stranger who offers a reinterpretation
of their Jewish worldview for this post-crucifixion reality. In the
hermeneutical reconfiguration of their ancient tradition and these
recent events, the disciples perceive new possibilities for themselves
as persons of faith in this context. That helpful stranger they meet
is, of course, the risen Christ.

Yet for others in circumstances analogous to these disciples,
cultural and religious leaders and systems sometimes fail to offer

---

3. Kleinman, *Illness Narratives*, 26.
4. Kleinman, *Illness Narratives*, 27–28.

consolation and instead engender new crises.[5] When "we cannot situate this life with its suffering in any ongoing story carried by a community that can make this suffering person's life its own," then suffering can "drive us mad," observes Stanley Hauerwas.[6] Kleinman similarly notes that when people's experience of suffering fails to map onto prevailing religious myths and cultural scripts, sufferers are propelled into "a transitional situation in which [they] must adopt some other perspective on [their] experience."[7] When this occurs in the context of depression, sufferers live doubly displaced: displaced from phenomenological at-home-ness and from the communities of meaning making upon which they relied.[8]

Evidence of this double displacement resounds in the stories of depression sufferers. Reflecting on a recurrence of depression that Monica Coleman experienced during seminary, she writes,

> The faith that spent morning in quiet time with God was gone. The faith that believed that God would deliver dissipated overnight. I had gotten in the habit of turning to God. I pressed toward the wooden altar of the church to make things better. But all of a sudden, I couldn't. It's not that I didn't want to. I just couldn't. I didn't trust God to take care of me. I didn't trust God to hear me. And I didn't trust the church to understand.[9]

---

5. Gustavo Gutiérrez's *On Job: God-Talk and the Suffering of the Innocent* (Maryknoll, NY: Orbis, 2007) offers another biblical example of how religious systems—that of Job and of his friends—fail to sustain meaning and bring consolation amid Job's suffering.

6. Stanley Hauerwas, *God, Medicine, and Suffering* (Grand Rapids, MI: Eerdmans, 1990), 2.

7. Kleinman, *Illness Narratives*, 27.

8. The language of double displacement should not be taken too literally, as if one's religious belonging is entirely *separate* from one's way of being in the world in general or in the world of depression in particular. Because religious belonging (in the traditional sense) does not factor into all experiences of depression, I find it helpful to acknowledge it as a distinct (or, "additional") complicating factor for some who experience depression. The image of "double displacement" does this work for me.

9. Monica Coleman, *Bipolar Faith: A Black Woman's Journey with Depression and Faith* (Minneapolis: Fortress, 2016), 182.

Looking back on this period of her life, Coleman concludes, "My silence with God was my way of asking: where are you, God?"[10] Martha Manning recounts a similar spiritual displacement amid her depression. "It is hard to reconcile my old concept of a merciful God with my recent experience of a hateful, spiteful God, or a totally indifferent God who plays fifty-two-pickup with people's lives," she explains. "What did I do to deserve what I got? Will God keep me permanently on the shit list? Will I ever be forgiven?"[11] These doubts mirror what Manning elsewhere identifies as the "continual lament" of her depression: "Why me?"[12]

The respective questions of Coleman and Manning—"where are you, God?" and "why me?"—are the cries of many who struggle to make sense of depression within their Christian worldviews. Christianity professes a benevolent and relational God, one who creates the world and each one of its creatures. The world is beloved—called "good," "very good" even—and its humans are free but also finite and flawed (Gen 1–3). Because of God's love for the world, God actively works to transform it, bringing it into deeper communion with Godself through Jesus Christ and the Holy Spirit. Because the tradition presents a God who lovingly transforms the world for good, Christians anticipate evidence of divine intervention into history for the better. Suffering, particularity in its most harrowing and persistent forms, often seems to subvert this expectation. When resistance to suffering appears futile and one apprehends no means of amelioration, suffering can call into question the fundamental Christian affirmation of humanity's freedom and divinely intended flourishing. In such circumstances, suffering can leave a Christian disoriented, questioning the basic truths of the religious worldview that so deeply mediate her life.

Indeed, it can leave Christians such as Coleman and Manning doubting the basic truths of *every* aspect of the Christian worldview, for Richard Sparks observes that among Christians, making sense of

10. Coleman, *Bipolar Faith*, 203.

11. Martha Manning, *Undercurrents: A Life Beneath the Surface*, rev. ed. (San Francisco: HarperOne, 1995), 155.

12. Manning, *Undercurrents*, 107.

suffering always "involves one's concept of human nature (anthropology) as well as one's image of God (theology). For Christians, one also incorporates the message and person of Jesus (christology) and one's notion of redemption (soteriology)."[13] In short, suffering makes a claim on every dimension of the Christian worldview, sometimes generatively and other times perplexedly so.

Many struggle to make sense of depression in light of their Christian worldviews, piecing together conceptions of God and various truths of humankind from its sacred texts, ecclesial teachings, and ritual practices. They join other disciples who, from at least as early as that trek to Emmaus, have been disoriented by suffering in a variety of ways and have attempted to integrate new concrete realities into their religious worldviews. Along the way, it has been the task of the church to offer religious resources to sufferers in crisis in order to help them interpret their lives. Theologians play a particular role in this process, for they are tasked with articulating the beliefs and practices of Christianity across its variant and ever-changing contexts. They bring to this task intentionality, rigor, and a vast knowledge of the intricacies of the Christian worldview.

Because of this, theologians in recent decades have implored their peers to aid Christians whose lives and religious worldviews have been "undone" by suffering.[14] We encounter one such exhortation in Deanna Thompson's book, where, in reference to the incurable

13. Richard Sparks, "Suffering," in *The New Dictionary of Catholic Spirituality*, ed. Michael Downey (Collegeville, MN: Liturgical Press, 1993), 950.

14. The language of "undoing" comes from Deanna Thompson's book, *Glimpsing Resurrection: Cancer, Trauma, and Ministry* (Louisville, KY: Westminster John Knox, 2018). She is among theologians I have in mind here who are exploring these questions through the realities and theoretical frameworks of trauma. See Shelly Rambo, *Spirit and Trauma: A Theology of Remaining* (Louisville, KY: Westminster John Knox, 2010); Shelly Rambo, *Resurrecting Wounds: Living in the Afterlife of Trauma* (Waco, TX: Baylor University, 2017); Stephanie N. Arel and Shelly Rambo, eds., *Post-Traumatic Public Theology* (New York: Palgrave Macmillan, 2016); Serene Jones, *Trauma and Grace: Theology in a Ruptured World*, 2nd ed. (Louisville, KY: Westminster John Knox, 2019); Flora Keshgegian, *Redeeming Memories: A Theology of Healing and Transformation* (Nashville: Abingdon, 2000); Jennifer Erin Beste, *God and Victim: Traumatic Intrusions on Grace and Freedom* (New York: Oxford University, 2007); Deborah van Deusen Hunsinger, *Bearing the Unbearable: Trauma, Gospel, and Pastoral Care* (Grand Rapids, MI: Eerdmans, 2015).

cancer that she and many others live with today, she asks, "For those of us who claim the Christian story as *our* story, the most pressing question becomes 'How does the Christian story offer a framework of meaning to this cancer-filled life where meaning is constantly under threat?'"[15] Insofar as Marcia Webb is correct that depression "challenges our most basic ideas about ourselves," Thompson's question could also be asked in reference to depression-filled lives, wherein meaning is also constantly, and perhaps especially, under threat: How does the Christian story offer a framework of meaning for the world of depression?[16] And, I would add: How does the Christian story account for the persistent *meaninglessness* that many experience in the world of depression?

Scholars who study Christian perspectives on depression teach us that, in one sense, many Christians already offer accounts of how the Christian story affords meaning. In the writings, conversations, and church services of everyday Christians, people regularly draw on their religion to assign meaning to depression. What results are several theological "maps" of depression, so to speak. These maps position depression within the larger Christian worldview and in doing so offer sufferers prescriptions for navigating this strange terrain as faithful Christians. They posit interpretations of what depression is, why sufferers have come to dwell in it, and also how they can escape. They suggest, though often only implicitly, how Christianity's benevolent God relates to this condition as well. In the process of situating depression within the Christian worldview, these theologies assign meaning to it in various ways.

This chapter introduces two common "maps" or popular theological accounts of depression that circulate among U.S. Christian communities today. The first presents depression as a self-imposed moral evil, and the second casts depression as divine instruction. While these reflect how some sufferers make sense of their own condition, they frequently surface as messages that sufferers receive from their fellow Christians and which sufferers themselves may or may not appropriate. Though the two popular theologies that I will elucidate here diverge on a number of points, they share the

---

15. Thompson, *Glimpsing Resurrection*, 4.
16. Webb, *Toward a Theology of Psychological Disorder*, 92.

underlying assumption that, from a Christian perspective, depressive suffering possesses inherent meaning: It has a discernable cause, it serves a particular purpose within the Christian worldview, and its course unfolds according to a sensible sequence. With regard to these shared assumptions, these popular Christian perspectives on depression are not so different from the secular interpretations of this condition that I examined at the start of chapter 1.

"Will I Ever Be Forgiven?": Depression as a Self-Imposed Moral Evil

In her 2017 book, *Toward a Theology of Psychological Disorder,* Webb offers a taxonomy of popular Christian perspectives on depression that she, like other scholars of Christianity and mental illness, has drawn from Christian self-help books, social-scientific studies of Christian belief, depression memoirs, and from her own anecdotal encounters.[17] From these sources, she derives a set of "lay theologies"—what others might also term *ad hoc* or implicit or everyday theologies—that U.S. Christians commonly employ to make sense of mental illness within their religious framework.[18] Webb details a host of popular interpretations, yet in the eyes of a theologian, all those she examines appear as variations on the same underlying *theologic*. Namely, all the interpretations she charts present depression as a self-imposed moral evil.

17. Webb offers a brief overview of her data sources and their limitations in *Toward a Theology of Psychological Disorder*, 10.

18. Webb calls these perspectives "lay" theologies "because they do not appear to emerge from the discussions of trained professionals, such as theologians or mental health practitioners." *Toward a Theology of Psychological Disorder,* 9. Although I'm inclined to trust Webb's general assessment of her fellow mental healthcare practitioners, I provide many examples of professionally trained Christian mental healthcare workers who advance the very theologies that she designates as "lay." Though Webb might identify these as exceptions in the guild of Christian psychology, there is evidence that these individual examples mirror larger movements in professional Christian psychology. Also, for the sake of interdisciplinary clarity, I note that Webb does not apply the term "lay" in a theological sense (that is, she does not employ this to distinguish the ordained from the non-ordained). As my analysis in this chapter will demonstrate, there are many ordained members of the Christian community who espouse these "lay theologies" of mental illness.

The research of Webb and other social scientists shows that one of the most common theological interpretations of depression among contemporary U.S. Christians is the view that depression is an evil tied up with the sinfulness of the depression sufferer.[19] For Christians, evil is that which obstructs right relationship with God, "block[ing] or imped[ing] the possibility of loving God and sharing in God's eschatological hope for the world," explains John Swinton.[20] Moral evil is a manifestation of evil that results from human sin, where sin is any free action that compromises right relationship with God.[21] In associating depression with sin, Christians suggest that depressive suffering is, or is a result of, something that necessarily interferes with a sufferer's right relationship to God. Such a view moralizes depression as something unequivocally bad. Among Christians, this is not merely a phenomenological claim (e.g., depression *feels* bad), but an ontological one: Depression *is* bad because it is constitutive or symptomatic of one's disordered relationship with God. This negative moral assessment prompts preachers, spiritual advisors, counselors, and other Christians to prescribe repentance as the ultimate remedy for depression.

Already, the passing words of Martha Manning earlier in this chapter provided a glimpse of this theological view of depression. In her litany of questions, Manning blames herself for her condition: "What did I do to deserve what I got? Will God keep me permanently on the shit list? Will I ever be forgiven?" These self-indictments introduce one theological response to her own continual lament, a response that surfaces across so many popular Christian perspectives on depression. Manning asks, "Why me?" and with her own questions, she implies: "Because I've sinned."[22]

---

19. Both Anastasia Scrutton and Marcia Webb observe this. See Scrutton, "Is Depression a Sin? A Philosophical Consideration of Christian Voluntarism," *Philosophy, Psychiatry, and Psychology* 25 (2018): 261–274; and Webb, "Toward a Theology of Mental Illness," *Journal of Religion, Disability, & Health* 16, no. 1 (2012): 49–73.

20. John Swinton, *Raging with Compassion: Pastoral Responses to the Problem of Evil* (Grand Rapids, MI: Eerdmans, 2007), 56.

21. Swinton, *Raging with Compassion*, 56.

22. To be clear, Manning does not appear to endorse this interpretation. She is narrating the theological perspectives that she grappled with amid her depression.

Typically, the association of depression with sinfulness and needful repentance manifests in one of two ways.[23] The first identifies depression as a sin in and of itself. Webb explains the common reasoning that underwrites this view:

> [A]mong certain segments of the Christian population, particularly more conservative groups, psychological distress and disorder are not expected elements of Christian life. They are considered demonstrations of lack of faith and other sin, or the result of demonic influence. Similarly, when Christians do experience psychological distress or disorder, the emphasis may be on willpower and positive thinking to achieve psychological stability. The assumption is that believers can achieve instantaneous change through the appropriate dosage of faith and spiritual interventions such as prayers.[24]

We see in Webb's description some of the fundamental assumptions that make up this interpretation. One is that Christians have control over their experiences of the world. Referencing Saint Augustine's (in)famous pen pal, philosopher Anastasia Scrutton calls this a "Pelagian" conviction for its presumption of the individual's absolute freedom over and responsibility for her way of being in the world.[25] Also informing this interpretation of depression is the assumption that psychological distress is sinful. Among those who espouse this view, depression and other mental-health conditions are sinful because of the psychological distress they entail. "Depression is associated with sin because people experiencing depression are seen as lacking some of the spiritual fruits that are regarded as evidence of genuine Christian faith," observes Scrutton.[26] Christians

---

23. In Webb's *Toward a Theology of Psychological Disorder*, she organizes her "negative lay theologies" of psychological disorder differently than what I present here. I organize her "negative lay theologies" under the heading "self-imposed moral evil" because it utilizes the more technical theological terminology that is common to the theological guild that I address, and because doing so highlights the theological commitments that join these seemingly diverse perspectives.

24. Webb, "Toward a Theology of Mental Illness," 52.

25. Scrutton, "Is Depression a Sin?," 264.

26. Scrutton, "Is Depression a Sin?," 261–262.

with this view see depression or other mental health conditions as "a sign you don't have enough faith . . . a sin, because you don't have the joy in your life a Christian is supposed to have."[27] Some believe, with Steve Rudd, that "Jesus commanded us not to be anxious and to rejoice. Anxiety and depression are disobedient emotional choices in direct rebellion to Jesus Christ."[28] "All hopelessness is ultimately a denial of the resurrection," echoes Christian psychologist Edward Welch. "It falsely prophesies that the last words are death, despair, meaninglessness, ruin, and nothing."[29] The presumption is that good Christians harness their freedom to choose to be happy and thankful, while sinners choose to dwell in depression.[30]

An article about comedian Steve Harvey provides yet another example of this perspective on depression. In it, Harvey recounts a daily ritual of "gratitude prayer" in which he recites all the things he is grateful for. "It causes me to start my day in the right frame of mind. You cannot be depressed and grateful at the same time. . . . It's the two emotions that can't reside in the same space. So, I remove all depression and I start my whole day with gratitude," he explains.[31] Note that Harvey sees his affective experience of the

---

27. K. Camp, "Through a Glass Darkly: Churches Respond to Mental Illness," *Baptist News* (March 6, 2009), https://baptistnews.com/archives/item/3910-through -a-glass-darkly-churches-respond-to-mental-illness; cited by Scrutton, "Is Depression a Sin or Disease? A Critique of Moralizing and Medicalizing Models of Mental Illness," *Journal of Disability and Religion* 19 (2015): 288.

28. Steve Rudd, "Anxiety and Depression Are Sinful Behavior Choices Not Diseases," *The Interactive Bible*, http://www.bible.ca/psychiatry/psychiatry-junk-science -anxiety-depression-myth.htm.

29. Edward T. Welch, *Depression: Looking Up from the Stubborn Darkness* (Greensboro, NC: New Growth, 2011), 229.

30. When Sarah Coakley undertook a fieldwork investigation of prayer and the work of the Holy Spirit in among Anglican and post-Anglican charismatic Christians concerning the relationship between depression, low emotional states, and the work of the Spirit in prayer, her interviewees offered theological interpretations of depression and psychological distress that mirror those offered here. See Coakley, *God, Sexuality, and the Self: An Essay 'On the Trinity'* (New York: Cambridge University, 2013), 176–180.

31. Christine Thomasos, "Steve Harvey Reveals Morning Prayer Regimen to Stave Off Depression," *The Christian Post* (December 16, 2016), http://www.christianpost

world as entirely within his control. What's more, his bifurcation of depression and Christian gratitude assumes an unambiguous moral distinction: Depression is antithetical to Christian gratitude, and thus depression requires the free and active contrition of the sufferer. These assumptions frame depression as a sin.

The second iteration of the view that depression is a self-imposed moral evil posits that depression, though not necessarily a sin itself, is a consequence of or punishment for some other sin at work in a sufferer's life. Scrutton calls this a "moralizing account of mental illness" that includes "a family of ideas: that the person has not been saved, or is experiencing judgement for sin . . . or the result of demonic possession where the demonic possession is 'allowed' because of the person's sinfulness."[32] This list illustrates that, like reasoning that identifies depression as a sin, Christians who believe that it results from other sins share the assumption that individuals are morally culpable for their suffering. Sufferers have freely performed sinful actions that have left them vulnerable to this condition. They are therefore responsible for their depression.

Scrutton offers a number of concrete examples to illustrate how this theological interpretation operates in everyday Christian discourse about mental health.[33] She cites psychologist Kay Redfield Jamison, who, after the publication of her autobiography of bipolar disorder, received thousands of letters from readers, including ones who said "I deserved my illness because I was insufficiently Christian and that the devil had gotten hold of me."[34] On Christian websites, Scrutton finds other declarations that mental-health conditions are the result of "unbiblical and sinful choices" that lead to one's suffering.[35] Similarly, psychologist Matthew Stanford

---

.com/news/steve-harvey-reveals-morning-prayer-regimen-stave-off-depression -172168/. Welch offers another example of this: "The skill of thankfulness can hold the darkest depression at bay; it can even push back against depression and lighten it." See Welch, *Depression*, 239.

32. Scrutton, "Is Depression a Sin or Disease?," 288.

33. Scrutton borrows the concept of folk psychiatry from Nick Haslam, "Dimensions of Folk Psychiatry," *Review of General Psychology* 9, no. 1 (2005): 35–47.

34. Scrutton, "Is Depression a Sin or Disease?," 288.

35. Scrutton, "Is Depression a Sin or Disease?," 289.

conducted a social-scientific study of an online group of Christians with mental illnesses in which 31.4 percent responded affirmatively to the question, "Did the church make you feel like the mental illness was the result of personal sin?"[36] In a survey of best-selling Christian self-help books, Webb and co-authors Kathy Stetz and Kristine Hedden also found that Christians with mental-health conditions were "advised to 'confess any sins that may be causing emotional weakness or sickness.'"[37]

The nouthetic counseling movement, later called the biblical counseling movement, is one source of this view among Evangelical Christians. Founded by practical theologian Jay Adams in the 1970s, the nouthetic counseling movement posits that depression is the result of one's "unforgiven and unaltered sinful behavior."[38] David Murray summarizes the movement's interpretation of depression this way: "Following logically from Adams' belief that bad feelings are the result of bad actions is the usual nouthetic remedy: 'If you do right, you feel right.' If you get depressed because of sinful behavior, then, obviously, you get better by righteous behavior."[39]

The belief that depression results from sin also manifests in popular Christian claims about the relationship between mental illness and demon possession. Some Christian denominations hold that people are more vulnerable to demonic action when they are in a state of sin. This informs the assumption that depression sufferers must have sinned and thus made themselves vulnerable to the demonic activity that manifests as depression.[40] In turn, these

36. Matthew Stanford, "Demon or Disorder: A Survey of Attitudes Toward Mental Illness in the Christian Church," *Mental Health, Religion & Culture* 10, no. 5 (2007): 445–449.

37. Webb, "Toward a Theology of Mental Illness," 52; see also Marcia Webb, Kathy Stetz, and Kristine Hedden, "Representation of Mental Illness in Christian Self-Help Bestsellers," *Mental Health, Religion & Culture* 11, no. 7 (November 2008): 696–717.

38. Jay Adams, *Competent to Counsel* (Grand Rapids, MI: Zondervan, 1970), xvi.

39. David Murray, *Christians Get Depressed Too: Hope and Help for Depressed People* (Grand Rapids, MI: Reformation Heritage, 2010), 18; see also p. 23 for his treatment of the biblical counseling movement.

40. This reasoning is reflected widely in the literature, but it is worth quoting David Murray's summary of this interpretation of depression because it captures it concisely: "The idea is associated with some Pentecostal and charismatic churches

Christians prescribe repentance and call upon the power of Christ to exorcise depression. This logic appears in a story from Monica Coleman's depression memoir, where after she discloses her depression to a Christian pastor, the minister replies, "Depression is a tool of the enemy. Cast it out in the name of Jesus."[41]

Coleman is startled by this pastor's response. But Webb, Stetz, and Hedden report that demonic influence is the most frequently cited cause of depression in popular Christian self-help books.[42] Other social-scientific studies of Christian attitudes towards mental illness corroborate the prevalence of this view.[43] In Stanford's study of Christians with mental illnesses, 32.9 percent of participants attested to negative interactions with the church concerning their conditions, and 21 percent of these respondents were told that their mental disorder was the result of demonic activity. Another 19 percent said that their churches taught that their mental disorders were the result of a lack of faith and personal sin, which is often connected to claims about demonic activity.[44]

---

that place a large emphasis on spiritual warfare. The spiritual warfare movement takes the view that depression (just like alcoholism and immorality) is usually due to either demonic oppression or possession. The 'treatment,' therefore, is to effect 'deliverance' from or expulsion of these demons." See Murray, *Christians Get Depressed Too*, 15.

41. Coleman, *Bipolar Faith*, 181.

42. Webb, Stetz, and Hedden, "Representation of Mental Illness," 696–717.

43. See Norman Dain, "Madness and the Stigma of Sin in American Christianity," in *Stigma and Mental Illness*, ed. Paul Fink and Allan Tasman (Washington DC: American Psychiatric Press, 1992), 73–84; Kristine Hartog and Kathryn Gow, "Religious Attributions Pertaining to the Causes and Cures of Mental Illness," *Mental Health, Religion & Culture* 8 (2005): 263–276; Lois McLatchie and Juris Draguns, "Mental Health Concepts of Evangelical Protestants," *The Journal of Psychology* 118 (1984): 147–159; Webb, "Toward a Theology of Mental Illness," 59–62; Webb, Stetz, and Hedden, "Representation of Mental Illness," 698–699.

44. Stanford, "Demon or Disorder," 6. For two academic analyses of demonology and mental health, see Chris MacKenna, "Exorcism: Some Theological, Psychoanalytic and Cultural Reflections on the Practice of Deliverance Ministry in the Light of Clinical and Pastoral Experience," and Loren T. Stuckenbruck, "The Human Being and Demonic Invasion: Therapeutic Models in Ancient Jewish and Christian Texts," both in *Spirituality, Theology, and Mental Health: Multidisciplinary Perspectives*, ed. Christopher C. H. Cook (London: SMC, 2013), 75–93 and 94–123.

Together these perspectives reflect the underlying view that depression results from the sinfulness of the sufferer, either directly (e.g., depression is a sin) or indirectly (e.g., depression is a symptom of or punishment for other sin in a sufferer's life). In both iterations, the sufferer is the ultimate source of depression. And because charges of sinfulness always presume a degree of freedom on the part of the culprit, this view assumes that a sufferer is truly responsible for the depression she experiences.

Though viewing depression as a self-imposed moral evil is a decidedly religious perspective, it shares some notable similarities with prevailing secular accounts of this condition. I noted in the previous chapter that a number of professional and scholarly accounts of depression focus on cause. This is the case despite the fact that the precise etiology of depression remains elusive. Interpretations of depression as a self-imposed moral evil center on a causal narrative, too, though it is one that extends beyond the empirical world to include claims about God. And as we see in secular etiological accounts of depression, there is an affordance that accompanies this theological preoccupation with cause: Once we know the cause of depression, we can eliminate it. For some, attributing depression to sin affords a sense of empowerment by providing a clear path of escape from the condition: If one's free sins occasion displacement into the land of depression, then a way out logically rests in the free reversal of one's sin through repentance.[45]

The underlying similarities between this Christian view of depression and the etiological approaches of other secular disciplines will not surprise readers familiar with the influence of the Western Enlightenment on Christian theologies of suffering. Beginning in seventeenth- and eighteenth-century Western Europe during the

45. On this point, John Thiel draws attention to the keen observations of Bible scholar Elaine Pagels, who wonders why Catholics would adopt Augustine's view that "no one suffers innocently since all are born into sin for which they are guilty, even if not personally responsible. . . . People, she observes, 'often would rather feel guilty than helpless.'" Though here Pagels refers to the doctrine of original sin, the same could be said of depression sufferers who adopt the view that their condition results from their own sinful behavior: It may well be that some would rather feel guilty than helpless. See John Thiel, *God, Evil, and Innocent Suffering* (New York: Herder and Herder, 2002), 8; and Elaine Pagels, *Adam, Eve, and Serpent* (New York: Random House, 1988), 146.

historical era known as the Enlightenment, a particular set of truths about the world, humankind, and God's relationship to them began to shape Christian theology. "People assumed that the universe was rational, orderly, and essentially comprehensible, and that it could be controlled through reason by means of science and technology. Everything in the universe, including 'God,' was open to being broken down, analyzed, and explained," recounts John Swinton. "The mysteries of the universe and the complexities of God became acceptable loci for the ever-expanding gaze of science and human reason."[46] With the promise of understanding and explaining every facet of existence came the belief that realities such as suffering, which impede individual pleasure and happiness, need not be tolerated. It would only be a matter of time until human beings eliminate it, Enlightenment thinkers assumed, and to the extent that suffering persists, there must be some sensible reason why God—the Rational, Good, and All-Powerful Architect of the universe—permits it. That suffering was an unnecessary but enduring reality compelled philosophers and theologians to develop rational justifications for the existence of suffering, called "theodicies."

"Free-will theodicies" are among the most famous of these Enlightenment rationalizations of suffering. Free-will theodicies posit that suffering is an unfortunate consequence of the freedom that God benevolently bestows upon human beings. These theories trace "the origins of evil to human sin, manifested by destructive human choices that lead to negative consequences and subsequent suffering," explains Kristine Rankka. It is "[h]umans' disregard for God's intended and good purposes in creation [that] leads to evil and suffering."[47] This reasoning is precisely what we see in interpretations of depression as a self-imposed moral evil. Suffering is the fault of sufferers, directly or indirectly.

Commentators often critique the image of God forwarded by free-will theodicies. Accounts of depression as a self-imposed evil present an implicit image of God, too, one that is vulnerable to some of the same critiques as free-will theodicies. This image of God is easy to

46. Swinton, *Raging with Compassion*, 33.
47. Kristine N. Rankka, *Women and the Value of Suffering: An Aw(e)ful Rowing toward God* (Collegeville, MN: Liturgical Press, 1998), 38.

miss, however, as interpretations of depression as a self-imposed moral evil emphasize the sufferer's actions far more than God's. It is the sufferer whose free actions occasion depression, and it is the sufferer's repentance—or lack thereof—that depression's persistence hinges on. Insofar as God is involved in one's depression, it is as the distant, just judge who has arranged the universe such that individuals get what they deserve. According to this theological worldview, those who deserve depression will experience it, and those who repent from their sinful deeds are promised some corresponding relief from their condition. While these theologies rarely give an account of God's direct intervention, this economy of depression is presumed to be just because of God's benevolent oversight. Furthermore, this view preserves divine benevolence by redirecting blame for depression away from God and to the sufferer themselves.

"A Hell of a Mercy": Depression as Divine Instruction

If interpretations of depression as a self-imposed moral evil are unfamiliar to readers, it is likely due to the local denominational landscape. Research suggests that U.S. Christian perspectives on depression often vary along denominational lines. Webb reports on one study that found "Roman Catholics were less likely than Protestants to believe persons with mental illness could control their symptoms or were dangerous. They also reported fewer spiritually-oriented causes and treatments for psychological disorder than either Protestants or 'nondenominational' research participants."[48] When Catholic Christians do interpret depression in a religious frame, they frequently make sense of it in another way, espousing a different assessment of depression's cause and purpose, how it can be escaped, and God's relationship to it. This alternative theological perspective casts depression as a form of divine instruction. It posits that the condition, while trying, is ultimately gifted by God for the sake of advancing personal holiness. According to Scrutton, this Christian

---

48. Webb, *Toward a Theology of Psychological Disorder*, 13. Scrutton observes these denominational differences as well. See Anastasia Philippa Scrutton, "Two Christian Theologies of Depression: An Evaluation and Discussion of Clinical Implications," *Philosophy, Psychiatry, & Psychology* 22 (December 2015): 275–289.

perspective on depression posits that "a period of spiritual dryness and sense of abandonment by God is not a permanent devastation but part of the journey toward union with God."[49] Depression "happens for a reason," as the saying goes.

Commonly, notes Scrutton, this view surfaces in identifications of depression with the "Dark Night," a religious phenomenon described by Saint John of the Cross, a sixteenth-century spiritual master in the Carmelite tradition. In the Christian spiritual tradition, the Dark Night, though difficult, is an occurrence that deepens one's relationship with God. Composed of the dark night of the senses and the dark night of the spirit, it has been described as an "inability to practice discursive meditation combined with the absence of emotional satisfaction from the spiritual journey, while a deep commitment to Christ as a way to union [with God] is maintained."[50] As this description suggests, its context is an advanced life of prayer. Although the Dark Night is an affliction, it also ultimately serves as a spiritually fruitful "purification" of the soul at these advanced stages of spiritual development.

While some scholars with in-depth knowledge of Saint John's theology of the Dark Night have explored its relationship to contemporary depression, many Christians who identify depression as a Dark Night do not hold themselves to traditional or scholarly understandings of this spiritual phenomenon.[51] Frequently, what

49. Scrutton, "Two Christian Theologies," 277.

50. Phyllis Zagano and C. Kevin Gillespie, "Embracing Darkness: A Theological and Psychological Case Study of Mother Teresa," *Spiritus: A Journal of Christian Spirituality* 10, no. 1 (Spring 2010): 53.

51. For example, theologian Denys Turner argues that the "disintegration of an appropriate and healthy *sense of* self" that characterizes depression has much in common with the dislocation of the self that John of the Cross describes in the Dark Nights. See Denys Turner, "John of the Cross: The Dark Nights and Depression," in *The Darkness of God: Negativity in Christian Mysticism* (New York: Cambridge University, 1995), 227. Across these phenomena, the familiar and stabilizing experience of oneself in the world dissipates. Similarly, Kevin Culligan draws parallels between losses experienced in depression and in the Dark Night, which are often conveyed with the common metaphor of darkness: "John uses darkness as a metaphor to describe deprivations or losses that occur in the life of prayer. . . . For example, he speaks of our senses being in darkness when we deprive them of the gratification of their appetites in order to 'reach union with God.' . . . Or he describes persons who feel

Christians suggest in their appropriation of this concept is an understanding of depression as a divinely willed spiritual good that has some general phenomenological overlap with what is traditionally understood as the Dark Night. Thus, the Dark Night functions as a symbol for conveying certain phenomenological realities and theological beliefs—though not necessarily all the theological nuances traditionally associated with this spiritual condition. Rarely, if ever, do these popular interpretations of depression reference the rigorous and advanced life of prayer that traditional notions of the Dark Night presume, for example.

Nevertheless, Carmelite psychotherapist Kevin Culligan reports that the question he is most frequently asked in workshops on spiritual guidance is, "What is the difference between the dark night and clinical depression?," evincing the widespread association of these experiences.[52] In another example, Catholic Therese Borchard repeatedly refers to her depression as a Dark Night in her memoir.[53]

---

they are in darkness because they seem to have lost the possession of God. Similarly, persons today use the metaphor of darkness to describe clinical depression. . . . Here darkness is also used to describe losses, real or symbolic, that are experienced in clinical depression." See Kevin Culligan, "The Dark Night and Depression," in *Carmelite Prayer: A Tradition for the 21st Century*, ed. Keith Egan (New York: Paulist, 2003), 120. Note that Culligan also identifies a number of phenomenological discontinuities between depression and the Dark Night. In the Dark Night, "there is a loss of pleasure 'in the things of God' and in 'creatures,' but there is not the dysphoric mood, the psychomotor retardation, the loss of energy or the loss of interest or pleasure in hobbies and enjoyable activities, including sex, that one typically sees in clinical depression. And, while those in the dryness of the dark night of sense are unable to apply their minds and imagination to discursive meditation, they have little difficulty concentrating and making decisions in daily life. In the dark night of the spirit, there is a painful awareness of one's own incompleteness and imperfection in relation to God; however, one seldom utters morbid statements of abnormal guilt, self-loathing, worthlessness, and suicidal ideation." See p. 130.

52. See Culligan, "Dark Night and Depression," 119.

53. See Therese Borchard, *Beyond Blue: Surviving Depression and Anxiety and Making the Most of Bad Genes* (New York: Center Street, 2009), 3, 45, and 128. Perhaps because Borchard writes from a Catholic perspective, she takes this spiritual interpretation of depression for granted, never elucidating why she connects depression to the Dark Night. In later writings, she takes a more equivocal stance on this interpretation, due in part to the work of Kevin Culligan. To more recent identifications of depres-

Episcopal priest and theologian Kathryn Greene-McCreight does likewise and accordingly tells readers, "Mental illness is not an indication of the weakness of one's faith. It may be, however, a test and should be met like all other tests: with prayer that God will see us through it faithfully, that we will be seen faithful, and that we should be found at the last without reproach, that God will use it to our benefit and us to his glory."[54]

This interpretation of depression recently gained more attention when the letters and diaries of the contemporary saint, Mother Teresa, revealed her persistent struggles with sadness, despair, and the absence of God.[55] Many cite her writings as evidence of either depression *or* the Dark Night. Others question whether Saint Teresa of Calcutta experienced a combination of the two.[56] The fact of these debates is but another example of the symptomatic entanglement and confused relationship of these phenomena in contemporary Christianity.[57] My own experience as a Catholic theologian confirms the ubiquity of this perspective as well. The Catholics I speak with in both academic and parochial settings identify depression and the Dark Night with remarkable frequency.

Tim Farrington's memoir, *A Hell of a Mercy: A Meditation on Depression from the Dark Night of the Soul*, offers an extended interpretation of depression as a form of divine instruction.[58] Farrington presents

---

sion with the Dark Night, she has replied, "Um. Yes. And no." See Borchard, "The Dark Night and Clinical Depression," *Beyond Blue* (2009), https://www.beliefnet.com /columnists/beyondblue/2009/05/the-dark-night-and-clinical-de.html.

54. Kathryn Greene-McCreight, *Darkness Is My Only Companion: A Christian Response to Mental Illness* (Grand Rapids, MI: Brazos, 2006), 115–116.

55. Mother Teresa, *Come Be My Light: The Private Writings of the Saint of Calcutta*, ed. Brian Kolodiejchuk, MC (New York: Doubleday, 2007).

56. For an overview and one assessment of these debates in popular Catholic and secular media, see Zagano and Gillespie, "Embracing Darkness," 52–75.

57. Scrutton presents some of the public debates about Mother Teresa as an example of popular theologies of depression in "Two Christian Theologies," 278.

58. Tim Farrington, *A Hell of a Mercy: A Meditation on Depression from the Dark Night of the Soul* (New York: HarperOne, 2009). It is worth noting that some conflations of depression and the Dark Night do not reflect the theological view that depression is a testing from God in the sense that I explore here. A major reason for this is that some who connect depression and the Dark Night simply use the Dark Night as a

a vivid portrait of the first essential characteristic of this theological perspective, which posits that the source of depression is decidedly beyond the control of its sufferers. He sees God as the ultimate agent behind this pain:

> No one can know in advance how and where the night will come, and what form God's darkness will take. The soul is purged of its presumptions and illusions in the fire that it finds, wherever and whatever that fire may be. And no soul, once it feels the heat of that fire, wants to be there. The essence of the dark night is the arrival at the heart of human helplessness, the conscious realization of being immersed in a fire of misery so hot it burns away our every attempt at a remedy or escape. In our day of endless how-tos for the seeker of sacred competence, I don't think the involuntary nature of this plunge into the spiritual flame is sufficiently emphasized. The dark night is not something we do on purpose. Our purposes, indeed, are one of the main blocks to the work the dark night has to accomplish.[59]

By viewing depression as a Dark Night, Farrington suggests that it is not human aim or effort that facilitates depression but rather the will of God. And God wills depression in all its horror because it is a uniquely effective medium for divine instruction: "Our depressions, which we labor so to cure before they disrupt our self-enclosed routines, may be nefarious blessings, gestures by our stymied souls toward the conscious embrace of helplessness and suffering."[60]

Farrington clarifies his interpretation of depression with an appeal to the wisdom of Saint John of the Cross: "John adds, 'And in truth, there is no way out. Until God finishes purifying the soul in the way he desires to do it, no remedy can heal her nor is there relief from

---

much more general term for spiritual and psychological desolation. Consider, for example, psychiatrist Gerald May's *Dark Night of the Soul*, where he suggests that the Dark Night is not an experience exclusive to religious people. Such a claim departs so dramatically from what traditionally constitutes the Dark Night that it is quizzical why May opts to use the phrase "Dark Night" at all. See May, *Dark Night of the Soul: A Psychiatrist Explores the Connection Between Darkness and Spiritual Growth*, repr. ed. (New York: HarperOne, 2005).

59. Farrington, *Hell of a Mercy*, 41.
60. Farrington, *Hell of a Mercy*, 31.

her pain.' "[61] Farrington testifies that the helplessness of the sufferer amid the Dark Night gives way to a promising positive outcome; depression is thus a process of spiritual purification guided by God's noble purposes. Still more, an end to depression awaits the sufferer when "God finishes purifying the soul." It is not the sufferer who possesses the agency to halt depressive suffering, but rather God, the omnipotent caretaker who determines when an end to suffering best serves the sufferer. Therefore, the task of the depressed person is to embrace her fate and suffer as faithfully as possible, cooperating with the blessings God bestows through pain until she is ready for divine release from depression.

Like interpretations of depression as a self-imposed moral evil, Farrington's theology suggests that God ultimately desires to rid suffers of their depression, even as its existence has a necessary purpose within God's grand schema. Yet Farrington's theology differs from those who view depression as a self-imposed moral evil in his claim that God's will is the original source of depression. One benefit of this view is its representation of God's direct and intimate involvement in the life of the sufferer. This image of God differs from the more distant God of theologies that view depression as a self-imposed moral evil.

This account of depression's origin in God's will presents Christians with a conundrum, however: If God wills depression for the edification of the sufferer, then God—the divine teacher and caretaker—is at least somewhat responsible when sufferers do not find themselves better off for their suffering. Scrutton observes a semantic distinction that apologists for this position deploy to resolve this predicament: When depressive suffering is salutary, these Christians call it "spiritual depression."[62] Spiritual depression is constitutively positive in that God wills it; it promises to bear personal growth; and, when it does, one's suffering ends. Adherents of the view contrast spiritual depression from "pathological depression," or mental illness, which does not advance spiritual growth and is presumed, therefore, not to have its origin in God's will. This semantic distinction allows Christians

61. Farrington, *Hell of a Mercy*, 50.
62. Scrutton, "Two Christian Theologies," 277.

to renounce causal attributions to God whenever depressive suffering does not appear to serve some better, higher purpose in a sufferer's life. This logic maintains God's benevolence. However, it also leaves us wondering what to make of this other "pathological" (meaningless) depression from a Christian perspective.

Resonant with this view of depression is another well-established, modern-minded Christian theodicy, known as "soul-making theodicy." Articulated in John Hick's 1966 monograph, *Evil and the God of Love*, soul-making theodicies aver that suffering is a pedagogical necessity for humanity's spiritual advancement toward God.[63] Drawing on an Irenaean reading of humanity's "image" and "likeness" in Genesis 1:26, Hick argues that the world's benevolent and omnipotent God has structured the best possible universe to facilitate humanity's growth in union with God across history. The reality of suffering is central to this structure. In fact, Hick's soul-making theodicy contends "that pain and suffering are necessary for moral, spiritual, and intellectual growth," explains Mark Scott.[64] Scott, who advances his own version of soul-making theodicy based on Origen's work, explains that in this theodical worldview, evil "has constructive, productive, and positive value: it enables our development into divine likeness"—divine likeness being the *telos* of human spiritual growth.[65] "Without suffering, we would not realize our potential for divine likeness" at all.[66]

Surveying soul-making theodicies more generally, Rankka pinpoints the essential *theo*-logic that also animates views of depression as divine instruction. Soul-making theodicies conceptualize "suffering as a test imposed by God for the refinement or strengthening of an individual or humanity as a whole. In this model, that which seems harsh, difficult, or even unbearable is actually beneficial when seen in the proper light."

---

63. John Hick, *Evil and the God of Love*, 2007 ed. (New York: Palgrave Macmillan, 1966).

64. Mark S. M. Scott, *Pathways in Theodicy: An Introduction to the Problem of Evil* (Minneapolis: Fortress, 2015), 96.

65. Scott, *Pathways in Theodicy*, 96. For more on Scott's view of Origenian theodicy, see *Journey Back to God: Origen on the Problem of Evil* (New York: Oxford University, 2002).

66. Scott, *Pathways in Theodicy*, 106.

Here, suffering "acts as a stimulus to growth, offers the opportunity to learn humility, and reveals a greater depth of human experience and a richer understanding of the meaning of being human. Moreover, it can evoke in the sufferer a greater compassion and active concern for the suffering of others. . . . Such experiences, according to this perspective, are actually paths to wisdom, virtue, and greater strength and character, and suffering should be endured so that the benefits may be actualized."[67] This description calls to mind the previously cited comment from Greene-McCreight that mental illnesses such as depression may be "a test and should be met like all other tests" because "God will use it to our benefit and us to his glory."[68] Theological statements about depression such as this express a line of thinking about suffering that soul-making theodicies distilled and popularized. And because soul-making theodicies advance the Enlightenment mindset that already exists as a normative paradigm in the contemporary United States, this popular theology of depression may strike Christians as familiar and therefore more credible. It is no wonder this explanation of depression makes sense to so many Christians.

Popular Christian Theologies of Depression

So, what is depression? The popular theologies examined in this chapter represent two means by which many U.S. Christians currently attempt to answer this question. By extending to sufferers these accounts of how depression fits into a larger Christian worldview, faith communities may mitigate (or at least attempt to mitigate) the second component of that double displacement that many Christian depression sufferers experience. Though depression displaces its sufferers into an unfamiliar, unhomelike world, these popular theologies suggest that it is not a world beyond the bounds of the Christian faith and its God. The world of depression is one where divine benevolence persists, and some just and sensible logic still guides the happenings of life. Depression is a world where even the most harrowing suffering is explicable and serves some good

67. Rankka, *Women and the Value*, 41–42.
68. Greene-McCreight, *Darkness Is My Only Companion*, 115–116.

purpose in God's plan. It is a world where the promise of an end to suffering endures and can be actualized, if sufferers only cooperate with the good God behind it all.

These popular Christian theologies, for all their differences, share the underlying assumption that a Christian perspective on depressive suffering should illuminate some latent and inherent meaning. All suffering has a purpose, they commonly convey. As such, they are both constructive responses to one of this chapter's leading questions: How does the Christian story offer a framework of meaning for the world of depression?

Yet these popular accounts of depression may not sustain some Christians, including those who experience depressive suffering as a persistently meaningless condition. I pointed to this significant dimension of depressive experience with another important question at the outset of the chapter: How does the Christian story account for the persistent *meaninglessness* that many experience in the world of depression? Based on the prevailing Christian views of depression and the modern theodicies with which they have affinity, one gets the impression that there is no such thing as meaningless suffering from a Christian perspective. At the very least, these popular theologies leave us wondering whether this is the case. *Can* the Christian story account for the persistent meaninglessness that many experience in the world of depression? If we answer in the negative—that is, if Christianity is incompatible with what many experience as meaningless suffering, or if meaningless suffering must become meaningful suffering for one to sustain the Christian worldview—then the double displacement experienced by many Christian depression sufferers is all the more concerning. This would render the meaninglessness that often constitutes the primary displacement of depression irreconcilable with the Christian worldview. The only way to resolve the religious displacement many sufferers experience, then, would be to resolve—or erase, or ignore—the experienced meaninglessness that constitutes the original displacement of depression. So we mustn't lose sight of this question: *Can* the Christian story account for the persistent meaninglessness that many experience in the world of depression?

Chapter 3

Critiques of Popular Christian Theologies of Depression

Several factors coalesce to complicate speech about depression. Chapter 1 explored how the condition itself evades direct language, leaving its sufferers to approach it with the figurative language of analogy and metaphor. Additionally, mental-health stigma, the social process by which people are discredited and devalued because of their association with mental-health conditions, compels many sufferers and their loved ones to conceal depression from others. Despite these impediments, the last chapter showcased prevailing Christian efforts to speak about depression and to do so from a decidedly religious point of view. With their messages about what depression is, what it originates from, how God responds to it, and how sufferers should relate to it in turn, these popular theologies attend to the unmoored sufferer—the depressed person doubly displaced, first, from possibilities of at-home-ness in the world and, second, from one's typical experiences of religious meaning and belonging. Both popular Christian theologies, different as they are, attend to sufferers by asserting theodical justifications for suffering that assign depression some higher purpose within God's plan for individuals and for the world.

These efforts to address depression are not always welcomed, however, as I noted at the close of the last chapter. As readers might already anticipate, some depression sufferers and scholars of Christianity and mental illness disapprove of these popular theologies. Their concerns suggest that bringing a Christian voice to depression is not a good in itself; there are right and wrong ways to talk about depression. There are right and wrong views about what it is and what it is not in relation to the Christian theological worldview.

In this chapter and the next, I consider this matter of how Christians ought and ought not speak about depression. I do so not only because of existing charges against popular theologies of depression, which I engage at length in this chapter, but also because many Christians, especially Christian theologians who are inheritors of the Enlightenment, have often failed to respond to suffering as they should. As I mentioned in the book's introduction, theologians of the last century have frequently failed to address suffering with the care and concern it demands. Consequently, theologians continue to debate how best to talk about this vexing dimension of human experience.

I commence with a look at major critiques of the popular theologies from the previous chapter. I present these criticisms in three categories. First, according to critics, these theologies misrepresent common features of depression. Second, they forward inadequate portraits of the Christian God. And third, their ideas about God and suffering impinge upon the social liberation and overall flourishing of depression sufferers. To better understand these criticisms, I present each critique along with some supplementary insights from theologians who have critiqued other related theologies of suffering, ones that align with the popular theologies of depression examined here. I conclude the chapter with some observations about the assumptions that underpin these critiques, which are important for considering how Christians ought and ought not talk about depression.

Misrepresentations of Depressive Experience

Though popular theologies of depression claim to make sense of depressive suffering, some critics argue that they rely on misinformation about the lived realities of this condition. As such, they are not *really* talking about depression as much as they are talking about skewed conceptions of it and about the people who suffer from it. This is a driving concern in the work of Marcia Webb, who has contributed a great deal to mapping and critiquing popular theologies that present mental illness as a self-imposed moral evil. As we have seen, this interpretation of depression often alleges that sufferers have committed some unique type or quantity of sin that in turn triggers their depression.[1] Though this claim about the sinfulness of depression may resonate with the profound self-loathing and overwhelming experience of guilt that often accompanies this condition, it is ultimately unfounded, argues Webb.[2] "It will certainly

---

1. In addition to Webb's critiques that pertain to the misrepresentation of depressive experience, she identifies other reasons why interpretations of depression as a self-imposed evil are misguided. For example, these theologies are often predicated on the assumption that all psychological distress is sinful, which makes no sense in view of the numerous holy figures throughout the Bible who experience significant psychological distress. Jesus—a person free of sin—is but one example. See Marcia Webb, "Toward a Theology of Mental Illness," *Journal of Religion, Disability, & Health* 16, no. 1 (2012): 56–58. Matthew Stanford and David Murray offer similar critiques in their respective projects. Unlike Webb, however, they slip into anachronisms when they read today's mental-health conditions into the lives of biblical figures. Still, they legitimately challenge the belief that emotional distress is sinful when they point out holy figures who exhibit the symptoms that we often associate with depression today. See Stanford, *Grace for the Afflicted: A Clinical and Biblical Perspective on Mental Illness* (Downers Grove, IL: InterVarsity, 2008), 85; and Murray, *Christians Get Depressed Too: Hope and Help for Depressed People* (Grand Rapids, MI: Reformation Heritage, 2010), 2.

2. Webb explains that feelings of profound guilt are "so common in depression that the DSM lists 'excessive or inappropriate guilt' as a symptom of this disorder. . . . Prompted by a particular sort of superficially religious encouragement, these sensitive persons will readily conjure up any number of 'sins' for which they might imagine themselves now to be suffering with mental illnesses." See Webb, "Toward a Theology of Mental Illness," 59. Anastasia Scrutton confirms this, explaining, "Depression and sin accounts can have an intuitive plausibility to people that espouse them because depression often involves feelings of guilt . . . , so that people with depression are often able to think of a past (real or imagined) sins [*sic*], which are then posited as the cause of depression." See Scrutton, "Is Depression a Sin or Disease? A Critique of Moralizing and Medicalizing Models of Mental Illness," *Journal of Disability and Religion* 19 (2015): 292. Thus, despite the fact that there is nothing unique about the sin of those living with mental illnesses, the guilt commonly experienced by sufferers lends itself to this theological interpretation.

be the case that persons with mental disorders notice patterns of sin preceding the onset or exacerbation of symptoms. This is not evidence, however, that individual sins *cause* mental disorders. Instead, it suggests that mentally ill persons share the common fate of humanity; that is, they are sinners, too."[3] The claim that depressed people are uniquely sinful is therefore a misrepresentation of those who experience this condition.

Anastasia Scrutton takes on another key assumption about depressive experience that informs accounts of depression as a self-imposed moral evil. It is the view that "it is within a person's power to recover, such that remaining depressed is a choice."[4] She notes that this high estimation of human freedom contradicts depression narratives, where sufferers often report a significant diminishment of freedom when they are depressed. As a philosopher, Scrutton sees good reason to suppose "that people who experience diminished free will actually have diminished free will."[5] Her argument hinges on the fact that "one of the strongest arguments we have for free will is based on the phenomenology of free will (we believe we are free because we experience ourselves as free), and so if we believe that humans have free will at all, we ought to be consistent and regard a diminished experience of free will as indicative of an actual diminished ability to act freely in the world."[6] Scrutton thus concludes that "the voluntarist claim that depression is a choice (and the result of sin) can therefore not be maintained."[7]

Along these lines, I note that even if sufferers do conjure the will to "repent" according to the directives of the view that depression is a self-imposed moral evil, there is no indication that any amount of faithful repentance consistently curtails an episode of depression, which can stretch on for weeks and months and even years at a time. There is no evidence from the experiences of depression sufferers

---

3. Webb, "Toward a Theology of Mental Illness," 59.

4. Anastasia Scrutton, "Is Depression a Sin? A Philosophical Examination of Christian Voluntarism," *Philosophy, Psychiatry, & Psychology* 25, no. 5 (December 2018): 261.

5. Scrutton, "Is Depression a Sin?," 262.

6. Scrutton, "Is Depression a Sin?," 267.

7. Scrutton, "Is Depression a Sin?," 262.

that good Christian living will stave off a recurrence of another severe depressive episode, too. In manifold ways, then, the underlying logic of this theology does not hold up to the test of human experience.

Popular interpretations of depression as divine instruction also misalign with typical depressive experience in similar ways, according to critics. Whereas other theologies of depression assert that a sufferer's exceptional sinfulness is the cause of her depression, many theologies of depression as divine instruction claim the opposite: sufferers are gifted with depression because they are exceptionally holy, and this suffering is a necessary means to advance their sanctity more still.[8] Yet just as there exists no evidence that depression sufferers are on the whole more sinful than others without depression, so too there is no evidence from the testimony of depression sufferers to indicate that they are a quantifiably holier group.

Other versions of this interpretation of depression posit that sufferers do not necessarily begin as exceptionally holy persons, but they become holier through their suffering. While this may be the case for some individuals, it is a generalization that erases the experiences of all those who do not emerge from depression with any discernable spiritual advancement.[9] It erases the meaningless suffering that many endure, and furthermore, it does not account for the many sufferers who die by suicide, unable to endure this condition and no better for it. Both versions of depression as divine instruction critiqued here presume facets of depressive experience that are far from universal.

What we see in theologies of depression as divine instruction, then, is an overemphasis on depression's salutary possibilities and no acknowledgement of the many sufferers who do not experience depression as an edifying reality. This in turn elides the horrific and especially trying dimensions of suffering. This is akin to a problem some theologians have associated with soul-making theodicy, the modern theory of God and suffering that has commonalities with

---

8. Anastasia Scrutton, "Two Christian Theologies of Depression: An Evaluation and Discussion of Clinical Implications," *Philosophy, Psychiatry, & Psychology* 22, no. 4 (December 2015): 279.

9. Scrutton, "Two Christian Theologies," 279.

interpretations of depression as divine instruction. Speaking of soul-making theodicies, Kristine Rankka explains, "For many critics, the problem with this approach is that is raises all kinds of issues—e.g., suffering as a situation of test and trial can actually diminish and destroy rather than ennoble the person. Despite all the good will to endure or to grow from experiences of suffering, some are warped and damaged by the severity, diversity, and magnitude of suffering in their lives."[10]

John Thiel echoes Rankka's concerns in his analysis of soul-making theodicy, where he witnesses an "avoidance of the victim"—an inattention to the realities of those who suffer the most. Referring to John Hick, the original author of soul-making theodicy, Thiel observes,

> Hick offers a theodicy only for survivors. Although Hick concedes the existence of purposeless suffering, he never seems to consider its most horrible consequences. . . . [P]urposeless suffering quickly becomes purposeful suffering in Hick's account. And in order to become purposeful it must be meaningful for someone who still has a character capable of building. But what of the victim who cannot learn morally from suffering, the victim who is innocently victimized to death? What of innocent suffering that is wrenchingly scandalous precisely because the sufferer can no longer raise innocence to purpose? Hick's explanation would always turn discussion back to the living witnesses of such utter victimization, witnesses capable of transforming sheer innocence into a meaning that could posit God's goodness in suffering.[11]

Thiel is right to point out that the projection of positive meaning onto all suffering overlooks the diversity of experiences of suffering that exist, a critique that holds when we consider depressive suffering in particular. The claim that depression is good because it is a site of divine instruction rests on a universalization of the experi-

10. Kristine N. Rankka, *Women and the Value of Suffering: An Aw(e)ful Rowing toward God* (Collegeville, MN: Liturgical Press, 1998), 42.

11. John Thiel, *God, Evil, and Innocent Suffering: A Theological Reflection* (New York: Herder and Herder, 2002), 43–44.

ence of only those depression sufferers who survive the worst of it and subsequently find some way to make meaning of their suffering.

As with views of depression as a self-imposed moral evil, which wrongly promise relief from depression upon repentance, interpretations of depression as divine instruction also promise relief from suffering, if only sufferers patiently endure and cooperate with the spiritual growth allegedly born of suffering. Once some spiritual growth is actualized, depression will cease. Yet again, critics see no indication that depression necessarily ceases with the spiritual growth that some sufferers report, even as meaning making does appear to help sufferers endure persistent depression in some circumstances.

In both popular theologies of depression, the misrepresentations of depression named here are crucial for justifying the existence of this suffering before a loving God. The claim that depression is a self-imposed moral evil is predicated on the misunderstanding that sufferers are culpable for their suffering. The view that depression is divine instruction is predicated on the misunderstanding that sufferers are exceptionally holy and/or experience unique spiritual growth as a result of their depression. In both cases, these misrepresentations impute sufferers themselves: If depression is a self-imposed moral evil, then it is the fault of the free-but-sinful and unrepentant sufferer. If depression is divine instruction, then it is the fault of the sufferer if she cannot perceive the spiritual benefits inherent to her suffering. Because misrepresentations of depression and those who experience it are foundational to these theological explanations of depression, recognizing their wrongfulness is crucial for exposing their inadequacy, critics argue.

Misrepresentations of the Christian God

In addition to holding that a valid theological response to depression should be continuous with the truth of sufferers' lived realities, critics hold that the God of theologies of depression should align with Scripture and tradition, a common standard of orthodoxy in Christian discourse. By this measure, they argue that the examined popular theologies of depression should be rejected, for both perpetuate wrongful ideas about God.

In the case of theologies that cast depression as a self-imposed moral evil, Christians present the image of a God who has little or nothing to do with depression. The cause of depression rests entirely on human agency—on the sufferer's own sinfulness. Escape from depression is likewise contingent upon the free actions of the sufferer. As such, there is little to no affirmation of God's effort to join with the sufferer in overcoming this evil. As I noted in the previous chapter, God is at best a distant, just judge who created the world such that people "get what they deserve." If not a just judge, God appears as the absent, even neglectful, creator of the world.

In view of the resonances between popular theologies of depression and Enlightenment theodicies, this portrait of God is unsurprising. Critics have raised concerns about the impoverished conceptions of God that buttress modern theodicies.[12] Kenneth Surin notes that the God of these theodicies is the God of philosophical theism, which dominates the Enlightenment worldview that underpins theodical thinking. The God of Enlightenment theodicies is, in the words of Walter Kasper, "a unipersonal God who stands over against man as the perfect Thou or over man as imperial ruler and judge."[13] In this description we glimpse the central features of God in theologies of depression as self-improved moral evil too. God is "abstract" and "unipersonal." God is absolutely transcendent and disinterested in the perils of history. This transcendent God "stands over against" sufferers as "judge" of their sin, permitting depressive suffering accordingly. This view of depression so substantially reduces divine involvement in history that many are left wondering whether God has any relevance to everyday life whatsoever, not to mention any concern for or involvement in humanity's suffering. This is not the personal God of Scripture and tradition, critics note.

Whereas interpretations of depression as a self-imposed moral evil forward the image of an absent God who withholds interven-

---

12. For a sharp and concise critique of this portrait of God in Enlightenment theodicies, see Kenneth Surin, *Theology and the Problem of Evil* (Eugene, OR: Wipf & Stock, 1986), 3–7.

13. Surin, *Theology and the Problem*, 4. See Walter Kasper, *The God of Jesus Christ*, trans. Matthew O'Connell (London: SMC, 1984), 294.

tion into history, views of depression as divine instruction differ in their portrayal of God's involvement. Views of depression as divine instruction suggest God is closely involved in the lives of sufferers, for God gifts "spiritual depression" or this "Dark Night" to advance spiritual intimacy. In this sense, God is unquestionably concerned with the suffering of depressed persons. However, this account of God's involvement in depression has its own shortcomings. Attributing depressive suffering to the will of God could be said to be an instantiation of "theological sadism," a concept Dorothee Sölle uses to describe images of God as one who inflicts and rewards human suffering. In this view, suffering "is God's way of drawing near to us in order to win souls for himself."[14] In Sölle's critique of this image of God, she agrees with Ulrich Hedinger, who she deems "right to criticize radically every attempt to think of God as 'a God who justifies misery,' to reconcile God with misery."[15] For this God, "[b]rutality and salvation become brothers, suffering serves to teach obedience."[16] John Thiel captures the offensiveness of this view of God in his analysis of theologies that likewise attribute suffering to God's will: "The providential explanation imagines that God reaches into history, into an individual human life, and wills its suffering and death, which now are attributed to God's loving will."[17]

In Thiel's analysis of similar theologies of suffering, he observes, "Claiming that God's will is the agency of suffering and death may be consistent with a traditional affirmation of divine omnipotence. But this particular consistency can raise the specter of a divine wrath divorced from divine love. . . . This accommodation is unacceptable to many believers who find the prospect of God's purposeful willing of death to be utterly at odds with the expectations of faith in how God's providence is disposed toward the world."[18] In other words, the orthodox affirmation of God's power and involvement in suffering appears in tension with the central theological affirmation

---

14. Dorothee Sölle, *Suffering*, trans. Everett Kalin (Philadelphia: Fortress, 1975), 25.
15. Sölle, *Suffering*, 25.
16. Sölle, *Suffering*, 26.
17. Thiel, *God, Evil, and Innocent Suffering*, 72.
18. Thiel, *God, Evil, and Innocent Suffering*, 72–73.

of divine love. Though the prospect of a good God who willfully afflicts depression in service of some higher spiritual purpose leads
some to conclude that depression is ultimately good, it is easy to
see how critics might reach a very different conclusion—namely,
that a God who afflicts horrible suffering upon innocent humans is
a malicious God.

Therefore, when analyzing popular theologies that cast depression
as a self-imposed moral evil or as divine instruction, critics charge
that their images of God are incongruent with the witness of Scripture and traditional Christian views of God. This, in the minds of
critics, renders these theologies of depression unsatisfactory.

Impediments to the Liberation and Well-Being of Sufferers

In critiques of popular theologies of depression, a third concern
surfaces that once again identifies a problem with the content of
these theories. Some critics reject popular theologies of depression
because they impede the liberation and flourishing of sufferers by
reinforcing the mental-health stigma that already alienates sufferers
and magnifies their struggles.

Generally, these concerns about the social effects of theological
truth claims reflect an awareness that all language operates within
networks of power. Theological truth claims either advance or disrupt
the arrangements of social power in which they function. Liberation
and political theologians demonstrate this in manifold ways, naming and interrogating how theological ideas have reinforced racist,
sexist, heteronormative, and classist ideologies. In recognition of
this and from a perspective informed by their Christian faith, these
theologians argue that valid theological truth claims should promote
the liberation of sufferers from social injustice and advance the well-
being of a community's most vulnerable members. This is a norm
(orthopraxy) for determining the validity of a theological idea.

Critics measure popular theologies of depression against this
norm, rejecting them on the grounds that interpretations of depression as a self-imposed moral evil and as divine instruction perpetuate
ideas that stigmatize depression sufferers. As I noted earlier in the
chapter, stigma denotes a social process by which people are discred-

ited and devalued because of their association with a characteristic that their community deems unacceptable or undesirable.[19] In the case of mental-health stigma, individuals with symptoms or impairments associated with mental-health conditions, including depression, are subjugated and marginalized because of them.[20] Such stigma manifests in antagonistic stereotypes and interpersonal biases as well as structural discriminations imbedded in policies and institutions that deprive persons who experience mental illness of the same social, economic, and civic opportunities as "normal" (non-mentally ill) peers.[21] There is also growing attention to the effects of self-stigma, wherein sufferers internalize stereotypes and discriminate against themselves by opting out of opportunities because they believe their conditions render them incapable or unworthy.[22]

Scholars of mental-health stigma frequently claim that its effects are equally if not more harmful to sufferers than mental illnesses themselves. And while today the harmful effects of mental-health stigma are well-documented across disciplines and by many activist groups, studies indicate that mental-health stigma in the United States and in other places throughout the globe has increased in recent decades.[23] To make matters worse, research findings indicate that "[b]eing a member of a minority group and simultaneously

19. This definition is adapted from Alexandra Brewis and Amber Wutich, *Lazy, Crazy, and Disgusting: Stigma and the Undoing of Global Health* (Baltimore: Johns Hopkins University, 2019), 207.

20. There are some instances when people who do not experiences mental-health conditions nevertheless experience mental-health stigma because they exhibit symptoms or occupy social locations commonly associated with mental illness. See Patrick Corrigan, *The Stigma Effect: Unintended Consequences of Mental Health Campaigns* (New York: Columbia University, 2018), 54–55.

21. Corrigan, *Stigma Effect*, 49–53.

22. Corrigan, *Stigma Effect*, 52–53.

23. See Jo C. Phelan et al., "Public Conceptions of Mental Illness in 1950 and 1996: What Is Mental Illness and Is It to Be Feared?," *Journal of Health and Social Behavior* 41, no. 2 (2000): 188–207; Bernice A. Pescosolido et al., "A Disease Like Any Others? A Decade of Change in Public Reactions to Schizophrenia, Depression, and Alcohol Dependence," *American Journal of Psychiatry* 167, no. 11 (2010): 1321–1330; Philip T. Yanos, *Written Off: Mental Health Stigma and the Loss of Human Potential* (New York: Cambridge University, 2018), 28–29; Corrigan, *Stigma Effect*, 51.

having a mental illness constitutes a kind of double stigma," explains Stephen Hinshaw. Substantiating this, he cites the U.S. Surgeon General's report on race, ethnicity, and culture in connection with mental health, which finds that stigma is compounded "for individuals of color, particularly when poverty is involved."[24] This is but a glimpse of a growing body of scholarship that traces how encompassing and intersecting cultural systems of sexism, racism, homophobia, and capitalism devalue characteristics associated with depression, thus contributing to its widespread stigma.

In a context such as this, critics decry popular theologies of depression for their perpetuation of harmful portrayals of this condition. They note that the view of depression as a self-imposed moral evil is an apodictically negative moralization of depression.[25] Interpretations of depression as divine instruction can likewise perpetuate stigma, albeit more subtly. The assertion that depression necessarily exists for some good reason, for some benefit to the sufferer, provides warrant for onlookers to instruct sufferers to "look on the bright side" or "make the best" of their situation. Psychologist Philip Yanos calls dismissive and condescending statements like these "patronizing microaggressions," which his research with Lauren Gonzalez finds to be the most common type of mental-health microaggression in the United States.[26] These messages shame those who cannot "see the good" in their condition and can suggest that sufferers are deficient for their inability to do so. By contributing to mental-health stigma, these theologies risk compounding the difficulty of depression rather than supporting and consoling sufferers.

Further impeding the social liberation and well-being of depression sufferers are the justifications for depression at the heart of both popular theologies of depression. Like other theological justifications for suffering, they can breed apathy. When someone understands

24. Stephen Hinshaw, *The Mark of Shame: Stigma of Mental Illness and an Agenda for Change* (New York: Oxford University, 2007), 175.

25. See Marcia Webb, *Toward a Theology of Psychological Disorder* (Eugene, OR: Cascade, 2017), 91–92 passim; David Finnegan-Hosey, *Christ on the Psych Ward* (New York: Church Publishing, 2018), 44–48.

26. Yanos, *Written Off*, 42–44.

depression to be the warranted consequence of sufferers' sinfulness, or when one sees it has an ideal medium for spiritual growth, then one is not inclined to do anything to alleviate the difficulties of living with depression. According to the logic of these theologies, it is better to let depression run its divinely ordained course—to fulfill its God-sanctioned purpose. Recognizing that apathy is not a valid Christian disposition toward suffering, antitheodicists—the vocal critics of Christianity's theodical explanations of evil—have decried theologies that engender inaction rather than compassionate accompaniment or justice-inspired resistance.[27] It is no wonder, then, that critics of these popular theologies reject them for their obstruction of right Christian practice in response to depressive suffering. Rather than resisting mental-health stigma or inspiring compassion toward one's own depression and toward others who suffer, these popular theologies lend themselves to immoral tolerance and resignation, critics aver.

Searching for the Right Ideas about Depression

Though these critiques of popular theologies of depression and other like-minded Christian perspectives on suffering vary, they commonly reflect a conviction that the problem with the popular theologies of depression lies in their inaccurate claims about God and suffering. They share the assumption that the validity of a theology of depression hinges on right content. Namely, Christians ought to make sense of depression with claims that align with the lived realities of depression, or with a representation of God that is continuous with Scripture and tradition, or with assertions that promote the liberation and flourishing of depression sufferers in their social context.

The shared view that right content—determined according to these universal standards—makes for a proper Christian response to depression resonates with how many theologians think about the validity of Christian theological statements more broadly. As Thiel notes, "One of theology's responsibilities is to take a critical

27. See, for example, Surin, *Theology and the Problem*; John Swinton, *Raging with Compassion: Pastoral Responses to the Problem of Evil* (Grand Rapids, MI: Eerdmans, 2007); Terrance W. Tilley, *The Evils of Theodicy* (Eugene, OR: Wipf & Stock, 2000).

perspective on the doctrinal tradition by pointing out ways in which the conceptualization and practice of basic Christian beliefs may have negative consequences for the life of faith, for the church, and even for history." Furthermore, "Theological criticism can also have the unenviable responsibility of explaining to those consoled by a certain belief that its untroubled character *should* be troubling when placed in the larger context of the truthful witness of scripture, tradition, and experience."[28]

If, in accordance with these critics, we prioritize right content as the constitutive characteristic of a proper theological response to depression, then we have good reason to reject these popular Christian accounts of depression outright. In their place, Christians should develop alternative theologies of depression that are better aligned with typical depressive experience, that are in continuity with Christian Scripture and tradition, and that inspire Christian orthopraxis in response to depression and in service of sufferers' liberation and well-being. This is precisely the course that critics such as Webb have taken.[29] Presumably, once theologians and other Christians pinpoint the correct theological ideas about what depression is, why it occurs, how sufferers should respond to it, and how God relates to all this, then people of faith everywhere will know exactly how to talk—and how not to talk—about depression, be it their own depression or anyone else's. The question these content critics leave us with is, "If not the existing popular theologies, then what are these right theological ideas that all Christians should adopt for speaking about depression?"

---

28. Thiel, *God, Evil, and Innocent Suffering*, 71.
29. See Webb, *Toward a Theology of Psychological Disorder*, 95–150.

Chapter 4

How (Not) to Talk about Depression

How should Christians talk about depression, this condition that beckons but also evades speech in multifaceted ways? The previous chapter explored a number of criticisms concerning how U.S. Christians often talk about depression. These criticisms suggest that there are discernably correct and incorrect ideas about God and suffering, and proper God-talk about depression is contingent upon adjudicating the difference. This perspective on how rightly to speak of depression spurs Christians to diagnose the content errors latent in existing theological interpretations of depression, carve out those wrongful ideas, and then replace them with correct accounts of God and depression. If I agreed with these parameters for talk about depression, then I would forge ahead to replace existing Christian interpretations of depression with new and improved theological explanations and mandates.

Yet theologian Karen Kilby has given me reason to pause. Kilby's recent reflections on how Christians should and should not talk about suffering suggest that there are right and wrong positions from which to make meaning of suffering. She argues that it is positionality, not right content, that should be the primary factor for evaluating the legitimacy of Christian talk about suffering. Therefore, right and wrong theological engagements with depression primarily hinge not on content but on one's relationship to the suffering at hand.

This chapter considers Kilby's perspective on how Christians should and should not speak about suffering and endorses its insights for discerning and advancing a Christian theology of life with depression. I commence with an account of Kilby's argument about how Christians should and should not talk about suffering. I then weigh the implications, affordances, and questions that arise when we bring this perspective to bear on prevailing Christian interpretations of depression. Beginning with an account of how it exposes the shortsightedness of critics who prioritize content when judging the validity of Christian accounts of depression, I point to the strengths of Kilby's approach for Christian engagements with depression. I also show that Kilby's distinctive guidelines for proper God-talk about depression meet many of the concerns that motivate content critics—concerns for accurate representations of depressive suffering, orthodox views of God, and the well-being of sufferers. Kilby's parameters for how Christians, especially theologians, should talk about suffering inform my theological reflection on life with depression in the remainder of *Dust in the Blood*, so I conclude this chapter by considering their practical implications for this project.

Kilby on How (Not) to Talk about Suffering

As I have noted, Kilby's recent work argues that the validity of a theology of suffering principally hinges not on the content of that theology *per se* (e.g., whether it is in continuity with human experience, Scripture, and tradition) but rather on who, exactly, is interpreting the suffering at hand.[1] Kilby's reading of antitheodists grounds her methodological interest in who theologizes suffering in at least two ways.

First, antitheodicists have variously demonstrated the failure of theological and philosophical attempts to rationally justify the coex-

---

1. Kilby's prioritization of positionality is most clearly articulated in "Eschatology, Suffering and the Limits of Theology," in *Game Over? Reconsidering Eschatology*, ed. Christophe Chalame et al. (Berlin: De Gruyter, 2017), 279–292. Her proposal here reflects a concern for how theodicy wrongly reconciles people to suffering and for the utter incoherence of suffering, which Kilby also articulates elsewhere, including her monograph, *God, Evil and the Limits of Theology* (New York: T&T Clark, 2020), which includes a number of the previously published essays that I cite here.

istence of a benevolent and omnipotent God, on the one hand, and the reality of suffering and evil, on the other. Despite the intellectual energy invested in resolving this conundrum, resolution escapes us. What we humans are left with, then, is a "sense of bafflement before suffering, of being silenced by it, brought to the end of what can be explained."[2] Thus, how the Mystery of God relates to the mystery of evil and suffering remains unresolved in the human mind. And, according to antitheodists, those who continue to embrace theodicies misjudge the capacity of reason to universally account for the existence of evil and suffering in view of God. Kilby agrees with this.

Second, antitheodicists have demonstrated that ongoing attempts to resolve the conundrum of God and suffering via theodicy's abstract, rational, and universalizing theories not only betray the limits of human knowledge of God but also perpetuate evil. That is, theodicies are not just intellectually inadequate accounts of God and suffering but also, as Terrence Tilley argues, evil ones.[3] These rational justifications for suffering are evil because they promote reconciliation to suffering instead of spurring onlookers to action in support of those who suffer. "If one takes the long enough view, if one really gets the right perspective, the theodicists seem to say, everything is not so bad," Kilby notes.[4] This mentality is pacifying, hindering active ethical responses to suffering, which makes theodicies immoral. Instead of justifying the suffering of others, Christians ought to do what they can to prevent suffering when they can and accompany sufferers where suffering cannot be stopped or mitigated.

Underlying these two major antitheodical critiques is an indictment of how philosophers and theologians commonly *relate* to the mystery of God and suffering, Kilby suggests.[5] As universal theories, theodicies appeal to God to impose meaning onto all suffering, justifying its existence by assigning to suffering a (seemingly) sensible

---

2. Karen Kilby, "Negative Theology and Meaningless Suffering," *Modern Theology* 36, no. 1 (January 2020): 95.

3. Terrance W. Tilley, *The Evils of Theodicy* (Eugene, OR: Wipf & Stock, 2000).

4. Karen Kilby, "Evil and the Limits of Theology," *New Blackfriars* 84, no. 983 (January 2003): 15.

5. See Kilby, "Evil and the Limits," 14–16, and "Eschatology, Suffering and the Limits," 287–288.

cause and higher purpose. Theodicists' efforts to preserve the coherence of the Christian worldview by alleging to resolve the tension between the evil of suffering and the benevolence and omnipotence of God are precisely what spurs resignation to suffering: When suffering has a clear purpose within the Christian worldview, then one ought to let it run its course and not intervene. Criticizing this, Kilby argues that theodicy "puts oneself in the wrong *relationship* to evil: our response to evil should be found in various practices, including practices of resistance, not in a movement towards intellectual resolution."[6] Kilby crystalizes this antitheodical critique: "The issue is not just that the theodicy-maker is wasting time thinking when they should be acting: it is rather that the *kind* of thinking they are engaged in, which is all about being reconciled to the suffering that befalls other people, is a fundamentally unacceptable kind."[7] Kilby's critique suggests, for example, that free-will theodicies are not merely wrong because of their content—that is, because they proffer a misrepresentation of God and wrongly blame sufferers for their own pain—but also, and perhaps more importantly, because they use these ideas to impose a universal justification for suffering that reconciles everyone to it.

This does not lead Kilby to disavow all attempts to situate suffering in relation to God and the broader Christian story, however. Instead, she offers a set of practical, grammatical distinctions to delineate what kinds of talk about suffering immorally reconcile people to suffering and which do not. This delineation hinges upon *who* is thinking—that is, who is making meaning of the suffering at hand. In short, Kilby writes, "When one reflects on suffering, and when one considers anything in the realm of the *meaning* of suffering, it seems to make all the difference whether one is speaking in the first person, or the second, or the third." She elaborates:

> In relation to my own suffering, I may well be able to say "it was absolutely terrible, but I can see that there was actually some value in it," or "I now see it as quite meaningful." "I've a crumbling spine and I've been in significant pain for thirty years," someone can say to me, "but

---

6. Kilby, "Eschatology, Suffering and the Limits," 287.

7. Kilby, "Eschatology, Suffering and the Limits," 288.

I can see that many good things have opened up as a result of that."
So meaning and suffering can be brought together in the first person.
In the second person, in relation to someone I am encountering, it is
immediately more problematic. . . . For me to speak to you of your
suffering and presume it has meaning is in some fundamental way
for me to overstep a boundary.[8]

These distinctions indicate that a sufferer can reconcile herself to
her own suffering, but others are wrong to project meaning onto her
suffering so as to suggest or push or demand that she or anyone else
be resigned to it. This imposition of meaning onto the suffering of
another exemplifies the immoral relationship to suffering that antitheodicists have decried in their analyses of Enlightenment thinking.

Kilby's reflection on positionality sheds new light on Christian
talk about depression. For example, to posit in the second person that
"*your* depression is a justified consequence of *your* sinfulness and is
therefore an occasion for repentance" is a rational justification that
presumes this suffering is perfectly acceptable, even good, regardless
of how you experience it. Likewise, to posit that "*your* depression
exists to make you a holier person" justifies the existence of this suffering and prescribes resignation as everyone's rightful relationship
to your depression. These impositions of meaning onto the suffering
of others, which function to resign everyone to the suffering at hand,
are precisely what antitheodicists have decried as unethical in their
critiques of Enlightenment theodicies. Kilby therefore concludes, "we
cannot aim, even provisionally, to fill out, to sketch in, the content
of eschatological hope"—that is, the ultimate meaning, purpose, or
resolution of another's suffering. "We can hope that it will be all
woven into something meaningful and redemptive, but we cannot
even begin to imagine what that might be, to conceive of what could
make it meaningful, or understandable, or acceptable, the terrors
that befall other people. To try to do so is to try to occupy a position
we do not have, and almost inevitably, to wish to domesticate and
diminish the world's ills."[9]

8. Kilby, "Eschatology, Suffering and the Limits," 288.
9. Kilby, "Eschatology, Suffering and the Limits," 291.

A Challenge to Critics of Popular Theologies

The examples above show that Kilby would contest the universal application of popular theologies of depression. However, she would do so for different reasons than the content critics featured in chapter 3, who reject these theologies for their inaccurate claims about God and suffering. For Kilby, *who* espouses one of these popular theologies of depression at any given time would be the crucial factor for assessing these claims about the meaning of depression.

This is notable because, though depression narratives confirm that some individuals understand their own suffering according to these popular theologies of depression, these theologies frequently circulate via self-help books, church teachings, and pastoral counseling sessions as second- and third-person theologies. That is, they tell *others* how they ought to interpret their own suffering. When prescribed in the second or third person, these theologies constitute an ethical overreach and therefore a morally unacceptable relationship to the depression of others, regardless of whether or not the content of these interpretations is theologically sound by other measures.

That said, Kilby's argument indicates that those who espouse these popular theologies to make sense of their own suffering are in a rightful position to do so—something content critics would contest. Tim Farrington has a right to interpret *his* depression as a salutary "Dark Night," just as Steve Harvey can attribute *his* happiness as well as his depression to his free, moral actions. For, as Kilby writes, "meaning and suffering can be brought together in the first person."[10] She does not qualify this affirmation with concerns about the content of the first-person meaning making.[11] In fact, her examples of rightful first-person meaning making include a number of theological claims that many critics of popular theologies of depression would likely object to.

With Kilby's distinctions in mind, it is important to note that first-person meaning making can easily shift into the kinds of second- and third-person reflection that she condemns. As some memoirs of

---

10. Kilby, "Eschatology, Suffering and the Limits," 288.
11. Kilby, "Eschatology, Suffering and the Limits," 288.

depression show, sufferers who espouse these theologies in the first person often extend their theological interpretations to all depression everywhere, if not explicitly then implicitly. For Kilby, Tim Farrington has a right to interpret his depression as a salutary "Dark Night," but he transgresses the rightful boundaries of meaning making when he generalizes that all depressive suffering should be understood this way. Likewise, Steve Harvey can see his own depression as a result of his free, wrongful actions, but his suggestion that the depression of others also results from this is unacceptable. Such universal projections of meaning onto suffering are immoral, even when they begin as first-person reflections, for they reconcile people to suffering in ways that undermine the Christian imperative to resist and alleviate suffering.

Kilby's argument not only implicates those who impose popular theologies of depression onto others. It raises concerns about those who critique these popular theologies as well. If a depression sufferer embraces one of these popular theologies as her own, am I in any position to explain to her all the reasons why her interpretation of depression is unorthodox, as would critics of these popular theologies? Kilby's analysis suggests that such criticisms are only relevant in circumstances where a depression sufferer solicits input from me, and even in that situation, I ought not impose my perspective. Too, our conversation about her suffering should concern her suffering alone—not all suffering everywhere, or even some other suffering elsewhere.[12] Featured in the last chapter, the existing critiques of popular theologies of depression do not qualify their criticisms with concerns for *who* is interpreting depression. They reject interpretations of depression as a self-imposed moral evil or as divine instruction based on content and regardless of who espouses these views. In situations where these critiques inadvertently indict first-person theologizing about depression, they violate the right of depressed individuals to make meaning of their suffering as they see fit.

---

12. Kilby notes: "There is perhaps a degree of ambiguity around the second person relation to suffering, since, as I have suggested, one might find a kind of collaboration between the sufferer and the one who accompanies them in arriving at a sense of meaning" See Kilby, "Eschatology, Suffering and the Limits," 289.

In response to Kilby's ethical parameters for who can and cannot make meaning of depression, one might object with an appeal to the Mystery of God, the other theological point that surfaces in antitheodical critiques and which holds a place of prominence in Kilby's work on suffering. How can Christians permit first-person theologies that claim to know with certainty God's reasons for permitting suffering, God's intentions for suffering, or God's will for the sufferer? Though first-person claims about the meaning of depression sidestep the unethical, imposing overreach that concerns Kilby and other antitheodicists, don't they constitute an overreach of a different sort—an overreach of human intellect? Isn't it objectionable that these first-person theologies misrepresent what we can actually claim to know about God's relationship to suffering?

As I see it, Kilby's commitment to honesty about the mystery of God's relationship to suffering is precisely what informs her position on the unqualified permissibility of such first-person theologies of suffering. To critique a first-person interpretation of suffering presumes that the critic knows better than the suffer about how God does or does not relate to the suffering at hand. For those who take seriously the Mystery of God in relation to suffering, they cannot presume to know better than the sufferer about what God is doing and what this suffering means before God. Therefore, they are in no position to critique this first-person theologizing based on a disagreement about content alone. As such, Kilby's argument calls into question the utility and morality of universalized popular theologies of depression as well as the content critiques hedged against them.

Some Strengths of Kilby's Argument for Reflection on Depression

The strengths and perceptiveness of Kilby's proposal stand out when we consider its implications for Christian talk about depressive suffering in particular. I highlight three strengths here, and, in the process, I illustrate how Kilby's proposal satisfies content critics' concerns regarding the lived realities of suffering, the promotion of sufferers' well-being and flourishing, and orthodox claims about God even as her account of right talk about suffering differs from theirs.

First, Kilby assigns sufferers a place of incomparable privilege in theological reflection about suffering that enables them to represent their own experiences of depression. The authority of sufferers to convey their own experiences is important in view of how popular theologies—along with kindred modern theodicies—universalize suffering in ways that elide various experiences of depression, including experiences of meaninglessness. Investing sufferers with the authority to guide theological reflection on suffering leaves open the possibility of meaningless suffering, just as it leaves open the possibility that what sufferers experience could be meaningful. Either way, first-person theologizing empowers sufferers to navigate the Christian worldview in view of the particularities of their own depressive experience.

In the process of first-person reflection on depression, sufferers are also positioned with the authority to correct the misrepresentations of depression that concern critics of existing theologies of depression. At the same time, it equips sufferers to check the views of content critics as well. Content critics reject the generalizations about depressive experience that guide existing popular theologies, but their desire to replace these with "more accurate" representations of depression does not necessarily prevent a recurrence of the same issue in their own corrective proposals. Kilby's restrictions particularize theologies of suffering so as to curtail any further misrepresentations of depressive experience.

Second, Kilby's call to theological restraint can open outsiders to life-giving practices of first-person meaning making that are otherwise dismissed or overlooked when outsiders presume to know what is right or best for depression sufferers. This becomes clear when we cease interrogating content claims—e.g., "How can we possibly tolerate a first-person claim about depression that casts God as a sadist?!"—and instead consider a slightly different question: When critics reject the popular theologies that some sufferers apply to their own depression, do critics miss something of significance?

Dorothee Sölle's theology of suffering provides some answers to this question and offers further credence for Kilby's high regard for first-person meaning making about suffering. In Sölle's famous book, *Suffering,* she undertakes a phenomenology of what she calls "mute

suffering," which she deems the most severe instantiation of affliction because it encompasses the physical, psychological, and social
experience of the sufferer.[13] She calls it "mute suffering" because it
"reduce[s] one to a silence in which no discourse is possible any
longer, in which a person ceases reacting as a human agent. . . . It is
senseless because people affected by it no longer have any possibility
of determining a course of action, of learning from their experience,
or of taking measures that would change anything."[14] As a result, this
suffering "leads to the abandonment of all hope for oneself, to apathy
in the clinical sense of the word. . . . Death becomes increasingly
attractive in such situations—and one is then no longer capable of
wishing for anything except one thing, that everything might come
to an end."[15] The phenomenological resonances between this description and depression narratives abound.

For Sölle, any effort on the part of the sufferer to affirm the possibility of change amid the seeming endless pain, meaninglessness,
and isolation of mute suffering can itself be a remarkable, life-saving
effort. In such circumstances, meaning making constitutes a refusal
of resignation to something that steals all possible hope and purpose
from the sufferer. Very often, Sölle observes, this resistance manifests in bringing words to one's suffering, in finding "a language that
leads out of the uncomprehended suffering that makes one mute,
a language of lament, of crying, of pain, a language that at last says
what the situation is."[16] Indeed, "If they are to move from purely passive endurance to suffering that can humanize them in a productive
way, then one of the things they need is language."[17] She explains:

> The sufferer himself [*sic*] must find a way to express and identify his
> suffering; it is not sufficient to have someone speak on his behalf.
> If people cannot speak about their affliction they will be destroyed
> by it, or swallowed up by apathy. *It is not important where they find the*

13. Dorothee Sölle, *Suffering*, trans. Everett Kalin (Philadelphia: Fortress, 1975),
13–16.
   14. Sölle, *Suffering*, 68.
   15. Sölle, *Suffering*, 68.
   16. Sölle, *Suffering*, 70.
   17. Sölle, *Suffering*, 75.

language or what form it takes. But people's lives actually depend on being able to put their situation into words, or rather, learning to express themselves, which includes the nonverbal possibilities of expression. Without the capacity to communicate with others there can be no change. To become speechless, to be totally without any relationship, that is death.[18]

With the act of bringing language to one's suffering—"no matter what the language or the form it takes"—a sufferer begins to move beyond mute suffering in a shift that Sölle characterizes as a transition from "Phase One" of severe suffering to "Phase Two." She reiterates in various ways that it is the effort to bring language to mute suffering and not the content of the expression itself that is vital to this shift. Though Sölle was not shy in waging her own content critiques against some theologies of suffering, as I noted with her treatment of "theological sadism" in the previous chapter, she makes it clear that at these particularly severe phases of suffering, what is key is not the content of sufferers' efforts to voice their pain before God but rather that sufferers "learn to formulate things for themselves."[19] Even if we contest the universality of Sölle's claims about suffering, which we have good reason to do, a key point still stands:[20] Attempts to bring voice to and even make meaning of suffering can for some be crucial for their survival.

When we take seriously how, for so many, the world of depression resists meaningfulness—that is, how depression sufferers in the midst of a severe episode describe the diminishment or loss of the very possibility of meaningfulness—it puts into perspective how sufferers' efforts to claim meaning and purpose could function as acts of resistance; even attempts to name the meaninglessness of one's suffering could be subversive and life-affirming alternatives to mute suffering. Such efforts to bring voice to or make meaning of one's suffering can represent an act of hope against hope. This basic

18. Sölle, *Suffering*, 76, italics mine.
19. Sölle, *Suffering*, 71.
20. Karen Kilby cites Sölle's three-phase account of suffering as an example of the kind of universalizing theory of suffering that she rejects. See Kilby, "Negative Theology," 99.

fact can be true even when someone makes claims that do not hold up to the scrutiny of the content critiques featured in the previous chapter. That a sufferer decides to interpret or even make meaning of her depression in the first person may be more significant for her survival than the content of that meaning making. In the face of despair about one's own life, the very attempt to interpret one's suffering can be, literally, vital.[21]

A benefit of Kilby's unqualified affirmation of first-person theologies is that it turns our attention to the potentially subversive efforts that Sölle speaks of, efforts to bring language—be it an incoherent lament or, conceivably, the insights of a tidy theodicy—to the seemingly endless, isolating, encompassing reality of severe suffering. Kilby's proposal pushes theologians to recognize the potential truth latent in such efforts, regardless of their content: Even a first-person claim to meaning that, with regard to content, warrants theological critique (e.g., "God gave me depression for my own good") can represent a very important truth in the life of the sufferer—namely, that God has something to do with this suffering; that, despite her engrossing and endless experience to the contrary, she refuses to accept that life is without possibilities of meaning. It is important for theologians and all Christians to recognize that affirming this truth in the midst of depressive despair can be a radical act of life-sustaining resistance. Conceivably, it is an affirmation of the possibility that one's suffering matters amid a state of being in the world that is constituted by the absence of such possibilities.[22]

21. I am indebted to my former students at St. Mary's College of California for this insight. Only after studying theologies of suffering with them and hearing about their own experiences of first-person meaning making did I recognize this oversight in content-focused critiques of theodicy and other theologies of suffering.

22. Speaking specifically to experiences of depression and other mental illness, theologian William Lynch makes a related point: "An unpleasant fact is better than no fact at all, and anything is better than having *no* interior life and no self. This is why it is no help for the pious to say to the sick that they must have done something with negative feelings; this, at such a moment, might be ridiculous and a participation in the beginning of an act of self-annihilation. Some inward life that is existent is necessary, even if it is a dubious one. Do not, in the name of reason, remove it too quickly from the ill, because the hell of no feeling at all and no identity at all may be

The theological restraint of outsiders to suffering grants sufferers the room to interpret their own suffering by whatever means is
available and necessary for their survival and relative well-being at
the given moment. In this way, Kilby's parameters ensure that fellow
Christians do not impede the sometimes-lifesaving meaning making
that supports some sufferers' well-being. Insofar as this is the case,
I see Kilby's proposal meeting another concern of content critics
who call for theologies that support the well-being and flourishing
of sufferers.

Some content critics might object that first-person interpretations
of depression that serve an individual's survival may inadvertently
spread ideas that are harmful to others who are suffering. For instance, my belief in a sadist God may comfort me but play into
stigmatizing ideas about depression that widely and negatively affect
many other sufferers. If what is life-sustaining for me perpetuates
an idea that is oppressive to others, can my first-person meaning
making really be said to be good and true? I circle back to this issue
later in the chapter, but for the moment, I suggest that it is a good
thing that Kilby's proposal confronts us with this tension that sometimes emerges between the individual and the collective. Whereas
content critics might pass over this tension because they assume
the effects of theological ideas on sufferers as a collective ought to
be privileged over individual meaning making, Kilby's parameters
force us to at least reflect on the complexities of interpreting depression individually and collectively rather than presuming we already
know what is best.

A third and related strength of Kilby's proposal is its reverence for
the mysteries of God and suffering. This point builds on my previous

---

on the other side. Where we do not know what we are doing, we should let these
people be with their strange grasps on existence. We might better look to ourselves
with a question or two. It is not necessary to create a brief for negative thoughts or
negative identities to recognize that even these negative things, where there is nothing better or nothing promising to take their place, can come to represent existence
itself and can create horror at the thought of their disappearance. . . . Negative
identity represents a hold on reality. And a human being will hold on to any scrap
and the last scrap of reality." See Lynch, *Images of Hope: Imagination as Healer of the
Hopeless* (Notre Dame, IN: University of Notre Dame, 1965), 207–208.

discussion of Kilby's commitment to honesty about the Mystery of God in the face of evil and suffering. Her attention to the incoherence of God and suffering seems important for those engaging depression, in particular, as so many sufferers testify to its elusiveness, and scholars remain conflicted and uncertain about its origins. Experientially and empirically, then, it is elusive; theologically, it remains so, too, and Kilby's parameters acknowledge as much. For outsiders to depression, including many theologians, imposing a coherent explanation of depression would be a denial of how baffling this condition is from a Christian perspective. Imposing theological meaning onto the suffering of others erases the persistent mystery of evil. With this in mind, Kilby advises that "theologians may have to live with points of systematic incoherence that they cannot make go away, not even by dismissing the problem and changing the subject, and that we cannot resolve."[23] In light of this, it is "something like an apophatic moment" that theologians ought to bring to the mystery of suffering.[24]

Kilby's exhortation to this form of restraint seems to me an extension of her regard for the mysteries of God and suffering. To presume that I, as a theologian, know better than another depression sufferer when it comes to her suffering is to disregard the real, persistent mystery of evil in the Christian worldview. Instead of "correcting" this sufferer with my "right" ideas about God and suffering, which would at least indirectly impose parameters of meaning (and nonmeaning) onto the suffering of another, it would be better for me as an outsider to witness the complexities and even impossibilities of my own God-talk in the face of suffering's mystery.

This moral exhortation to theological restraint reflects a regard for orthodox representations of the Christian God, a third concern that underpins critiques of popular theologies of depression. As I noted earlier, when Christians abstain from imposing theological justifications for suffering, they also avoid the kinds of theological claims that often limit or misrepresent God at the behest of content critics. Abstaining from explanations of how God and suffering coexist, theologians honor the fact that they cannot grasp the Mystery of

---

23. Kilby, "Evil and the Limits," 24.
24. Kilby, "Negative Theology," 92.

God in this regard, and they honor this better than content critics who might be inclined to impose their own overextended claims about God after rejecting another.

In sum, Kilby's argument is amendable to reflection on depression for a number of reasons. Furthermore, her emphasis on right positionality meets the major concerns of content critics of popular theologies of depression and other theologies of suffering. She meets their concerns not by introducing alternative ideas about suffering but rather by exhorting theologians to refrain from imposing ideas altogether. If theologians and other Christians are going to position themselves in right relation to depression—and, in so doing, promote more accurate representations of the particularities of depressive experience, support the flourishing of sufferers, and honor the confounding Mystery of God in relation to the baffling mystery of others' suffering—then they need to heed Kilby's parameters for a right theological approach to depression.

How (Not) to Talk about Depression

Moving forward, I oblige myself to Kilby's directives for right talk about suffering. Still, with her, I admit "[t]his something-like-apophasis in the face of the suffering of others is difficult. We don't really want to know about suffering which we can neither eliminate nor absorb into a larger story with a satisfying shape. We are inclined to avert our attention, either by simply looking away, or by trying to nudge the suffering into a story whose shape gives comfort."[25]

This difficulty is especially challenging among theologians like me, who, through years of formal theological education, are habituated to teach others what to think about God and the difficult realities of our world. When people attribute their depression to a seemingly sadist God or place their hopes in the promise of a cure for depression that, surely, a benevolent God will deliver, I want to caution them against a God who is too small or a too-narrow, over-determined vision of hope. I have been trained to recognize such limited lines of theological reasoning. As a result, I am less practiced in the kind

25. Kilby, "Negative Theology," 98.

of theological restraint that Kilby exhorts, the kind that is born of humble bafflement before God and suffering.

Yet, intellectually convinced by Kilby's parameters, I have for some time now tried to rethink how to speak theologically about depression. I have even wondered: Does an embrace of these parameters necessitate that there be no more God-talk about suffering, save talk about one's own suffering and one's suffering alone? Is the only moral occasion for theologians to share their perspectives on suffering—suffering that does not belong to them—an explicit and direct invitation from the one who is suffering firsthand? "I want you to help me think this through"—that kind of direct invitation? And if so, should theologians cease writing theological tomes about suffering—including books on depression? Including this one? What does Kilby's moral theological restraint look like, in general, and with regard to this project, in particular?

As I look forward to more from Kilby on this topic, I have tried to sort out some answers of my own. These answers have resulted in two guiding convictions that shape my theological project: first, that theologians should not impose meaning onto the suffering of others, and second, that theologians have a responsibility to transform the present theological landscape wherein Christian interpretations of suffering typically amount to justifications for suffering and the imposition of meaning onto it.

Regarding this first conviction, what is unequivocally clear from Kilby's argument is that the imposition of meaning onto the suffering of others is immoral. What this book cannot be, then, is a prescriptive theory of the meaning of all depression, or even just some types of depression. At best, it seems that theologians like me can identify and develop resources for depression sufferers to draw from to interpret their own suffering in the first person, which can entail making meaning of it, if they so choose. It is the individual sufferer's place, not mine, to interpret her depression before God and with the Christian faith, and it is necessary to be clear on this, at the very least. What I can offer are resources for consideration, not prescriptions.

That being said, Kilby warns that it is easier for theologians to give lip service to this than it is to execute it successfully:

It is important not to see this difference between a first person and a second person relation to suffering as a mere matter of *tact*, of knowing when to speak and when to stay silent. The idea, in other words, is not that while I might see meaning in your suffering, I must be patient, keep my mouth closed and let you work it out for yourself, as I might for a student of mathematics who is a little slower than I am at doing a calculation. To ascribe meaning to your suffering, even silently, is something I have no right to do.[26]

How exactly a theologian can demonstrate the sincerity of her theological restraint remains unclear to me. I have tried to provide some context for my affirmation of multiple valid theologies of depression by extrapolating why Kilby's defense of first-person theologizing is compelling, especially with regard to depression. Hopefully, this substantiates my wish not to impose meaning but to expand the theological resources available to depression sufferers who wish to develop a Christian interpretation of depression for themselves. Acknowledging the real and continuous possibility of meaningless suffering is another way I have tried to demonstrate this too.

With regard to the second conviction, Kilby's argument clearly responds to a Christian context where one particular understanding of suffering reigns, and reflection on her arguments has convinced me that theologians must take responsibility for this. Kilby shows that theologians have tended to presume meaning of and impose meaning onto the suffering of others. They have often claimed some ultimate, discernable justification for all suffering, contributing to a context where suffering that appears to be *without* some theological justification or purpose can be perceived as un-Christian. This tendency to impose meaning onto suffering is epitomized by the free-will and soul-making theodicies that I engaged in the last two chapters. Contemporary theologians not only inherited these theodical approaches to suffering from previous generations but also adapted them and their underlying *theo*-logic for contexts of suffering today. It is no wonder, then, that the popular theologies of depression examined in chapter 2 propagate the tendency to presume

26. Kilby, "Eschatology, Suffering and the Limits," 288.

meaning of and impose meaning onto suffering: They emerge from a theological landscape where talking about suffering in a Christian fashion has overwhelmingly been a matter of assigning meaning to it.

Some theologians, upon recognizing their complicity in the creation of a theological landscape where meaning is presumed and imposed onto the suffering of others, might conclude that the best way to respond is to withdraw from discourse about suffering altogether. This would be a conservative, even extreme, manifestation of the theological restraint that Kilby exhorts. "No more talk of others' suffering. None at all!" some might conclude. "Leave sufferers alone to interpret depression for themselves, save the rare instance when they directly and explicitly invite a theologian to dialogue personally with them about it. Theologians have done enough damage."[27] According to this view, theologians' tendency to overstep and impose meaning onto the suffering of others should silence them entirely. The affordance of this response to the current context is that it does model another Christian response to suffering, if only indirectly. Rather than justifying suffering with the imposition of meaning, one remains baffled and literally silent before it. In contrast to the prevailing presumption that suffering ought to be explained and meaning ought to be made of it, this silence is potentially disruptive.

Although the most conservative manifestations of theological restraint seem morally preferable to continuing to impose meaning onto the suffering of others, I find myself discontent with this vision of restraint precisely because of the existing theological landscape that sufferers draw on to interpret their depression. Though silence can be disruptive, it can also preserve the theological status quo; risking the latter seems morally unacceptable for theologians too. Kilby's observations and critique of the prevailing tendency to justify

---

27. I should note that this absolutist interpretation of Kilby's imperative to theological restraint is not what Kilby herself exhorts, as I understand it. Her analogy to apophatic theology leads me to believe that what she calls theologians to is not an absolute silence but a disciplined form of speech: Just as apophatic theology is not absolute silence but is a mode of disciplined discourse before the Mystery of God, so too, it seems, theological restraint before the mystery of suffering could be not absolute silence but a particular form of restrained speech. See Kilby, "Negative Theology."

and impose meaning onto suffering convinces me that theologians should take some responsibility for transforming the theological landscape we have created, and absolute silence alone will not do this. Recognizing that theologians of the past and present have already overdetermined Christian interpretations of suffering, including depression, theologians have a responsibility to help change the theological landscape from which sufferers draw to interpret their depression in the first person. Theologians can meet this responsibility by ceasing to impose meaning onto others' suffering while also diversifying the widely available Christian resources for first-person theologies of depression. This requires us to keep talking about suffering, albeit with great discipline.

If theologians and other Christians have any chance of actualizing these dual parameters for rightly speaking about depression, we will have to continuously attend to how much easier it is to aspire to them than to realize them. Kilby makes it clear that any theological claim about the meaning of suffering must be considered with special care. Citing the example of theological reflections on depression, Kilby highlights the more subtle means by which theological justifications and meaning are often imposed onto suffering:

> [T]his weaving of suffering into larger patterns, especially patterns of value—seeing good in it, or good linked to it—is, to make a rather obvious observation, not always possible. True, many give accounts of the experience of grace amidst suffering, the occurrence of growth in and through suffering, the deepening of relationships to God and others through suffering—in some ecclesial contexts there is a strong tendency to turn any discussion of suffering in these directions. But however seriously we listen to such accounts, it is not possible to derive from them a law, whether of nature or of Christian experience. Suffering clearly often leads to more suffering, diminishing a person rather than ennobling them, destroying relationships rather than deepening them.[28]

I take Kilby's point here to be that theologians' focus on possibilities of meaning*fulness* amid depression can elide those experiences of

---

28. Kilby, "Negative Theology," 97.

suffering that have neither inherent meaning nor disclose any possibilities of meaning at all. This is a far more subtle way of imposing meaning than that of many Enlightenment theodicies, which explicitly assign meaning to all suffering everywhere. These theologies of depression impose meaning by way of presumption and diversion: Theologians *presume* that there is purpose to be found in suffering, and in pursuit of this, *divert* attention away from those instantiations of suffering that are meaningless. This focus on meaning elides any "apophatic moment" that theologians encounter in depressive suffering. Speaking to this point, Kilby continues:

> It is because there is *not* always a tale of the experience of grace or growth or greater intimacy in suffering that the possibility of an apophatic response to suffering on the part of the one who suffers is important. "This is terrible, and, in spite of what I believe about God working for the good in all things, I can't see any good attached to it whatsoever." Such an unresolved and in a sense uncomprehending attitude is not easy to sustain; there are social, cultural, and ecclesial pressures to know what it is all about and to have something positive to report in relation to suffering. And yet without the possibility of such an unresolved, uncomprehending attitude, the believer is forced into a range of distortions in their relationship to their faith and to the reality of their situation.[29]

If theologians do not actively attempt to counteract the prevailing pressures to assign meaning to suffering—"social, cultural, and ecclesial pressures to know what [suffering] is all about and to have something positive to report in relation to suffering"; pressures that erase the meaninglessness experienced by many depression sufferers—then theologians will remain complicit in constraining the interpretive resources available to Christian depression sufferers.

Particularly in light of the fact that theologians have long contributed to a context where resources for thinking about suffering in a Christian frame are so very limited, might theologians have a responsibility to identify additional Christian resources that could

---

29. Kilby, "Negative Theology," 97.

serve as an alternative to the existing ones that overwhelmingly posit theological justifications of depression as the only means of affirming that depression matters for the Christian and is significant before God? Might theologians today offer more resources to desiring members of the Christian community could draw from that affirm the reality of suffering without imposing coherence and justification for it? Resources that could demonstrate the possibility that meaningless suffering need not be understood as un-Christian? Theologians' radical withdrawal from discourse about suffering would constitute a resignation of responsibility for the theological landscape we have in part created and a neglect of the opportunity to actively and correctively expand the resources available to sufferers as they develop Christian interpretations of their suffering.

I see two ways that theologians can meet this responsibility. First, theologians can demonstrate that meaningless suffering is not necessarily antithetical to the Christian worldview. In so doing, theologians can offer sufferers resources that show that suffering coexists with God, even as it cannot be reconciled with the goodness and omnipotence of God in a coherent fashion. Such resources would uphold the "apophatic moment" of suffering within the Christian worldview for the consideration of those seeking to interpret their own suffering.

I should note that, in order to identify and develop Christian resources that affirm the reality of meaningless suffering, theologians have to attend to the content of theological resources. I do not see this as a contradiction to Kilby's argument, for though Kilby argues for the priority of positionality when it comes to theologizing suffering, she does not dismiss the significance of content altogether. Considered with an eye toward the priority of positionality, insights from critics of popular theologies of depression and other theologies of suffering can be helpful. If nothing else, their critiques clarify existing theologies and point to new, uncharted horizons for diversifying the available resources for theological thinking.

Complementing this affirmation of meaningless suffering is a second way Christian theologians can carry forth Kilby's proposal. In a context where the resources for Christian theologies of suffering, in general, and depression, in particular, are relatively homogenous in that they tether meaning to theological justifications for suffering, I see a place for theologians to offer additional and more diverse theological resources for generating meaning in the context of depression, especially resources that affirm meaning without presuming its necessity or prescribing it onto the suffering of others.

Offering *more* resources for theologizing suffering may seem a counterintuitive response to Kilby's persuasive call to restraint and her cautions against outsider claims about the meaning of suffering. Indeed, when identifying and developing possible resources for meaning making, theologians risk the more subtle imposition of meaning that Kilby already cautions against in relation to theologies of depression: By continuing to communicate to sufferers that Christian meaning making is possible in the context of depression, theologians like me could reinforce the presumption that goodness and hope can (and therefore, should) be found amid depression, which risks eliding or at least downplaying the very real experiences of meaninglessness that also occur within depressive experience. To avoid this, theologians must affirm the reality of meaningless suffering at the same time that they expand the resources available to sufferers for Christian meaning making—meaning making that names the possible goodness that can be made of a life with depressive suffering. That is, we should try to expand possible resources for first-person meaning making without requiring and imposing meaning. In a passing footnote, Kilby affirms something like this, noting the potential use of "a profusion of possibly contradictory, inconsistent images" such as "what we find in Scripture." These could "be understood precisely as the cataphatic counterpart to eschatological apophasis."[30]

Kilby's gesture toward this profusion of images calls to mind the work of William Lynch, whose theological reflection on the role of imagination in mental illness gives credence to the importance of theologians' ongoing efforts to change and expand the theological landscape available to depression sufferers. To support depression sufferers, Lynch exhorts a search for "those many forms of reality and of psychic life that know how to give . . . surcease, small or large, from neurosis or madness."[31] Identifying such resources is imperative for Lynch because he demonstrates, as I have in previ-

---

30. Kilby, "Negative Theology," 104n50.
31. Lynch, *Images of Hope*, 47.

ous chapters, that "hopelessness usually involves a constriction of the imagination," of one's perception and experience of the world.[32] "Hopelessness means to be ruled by a sense of the impossible," he explains, and in turn, "hope is, in its most general terms, a sense of *the possible*, that what we really need is possible, though difficult."[33] To survive this hopelessness, he argues, "it is necessary to imagine context and perspective and a way out, in other words to meet hopelessness with some enlargement of the imagination."[34] This is because the depressed person can be helpless and "operating within his [*sic*] own closed system of fantasy and feeling, unable, as a result, even to see or imagine what is on the outside. He needs another's imagination that will begin to work with his own, and then the two can do it together. He must put on another's imagination in order to rediscover his own."[35] Theologians—like therapists and others who accompany depression sufferers—could offer sufferers the resources of our own imaginations of what might be possible for them, which, for some, could support a vital expansion of their own imaginations beyond what they, themselves, can fathom amid depression. This could include possibilities for meaning making yet unforeseen by sufferers themselves; it could also include possibilities for affirming the meaninglessness of one's own suffering within a Christian worldview, within the purview of God's benevolent care and concern.

Lynch admits, "No one is going to come up with a cure-all for the dense and manifold ills of the mind," which is all the more reason for Christians and other theologians to refrain from imposing general theories of depression onto others. But we could support the expansion of the sense of the possible among Christian sufferers, notes Lynch. "We can add, however slightly, to the weight and number of ideas that are counter-agents to the forces for illness."[36]

Again, my interest in this arises from a concern about the immorality of *withholding* such theological resources from depression sufferers. While erasing the non-meaning of others' suffering is an

32. Lynch, *Images of Hope*, 143.
33. Lynch, *Images of Hope*, 32.
34. Lynch, *Images of Hope*, 143.
35. Lynch, *Images of Hope*, 77.
36. Lynch, *Images of Hope*, 47.

immoral overstep, the opposite extreme—intentionally withholding assistance from those who desire a way beyond meaninglessness, especially those who desire to make meaning of their suffering without claiming any inherent meaning—seems to constitute another kind of wrong relationship to the suffering of others. So while theologians ought not assume that all suffering should or can result in meaning making, theologians also ought not abandon sufferers to an experience of meaninglessness when so many convey that they want help escaping from at least that dimension of their suffering—which, as Kilby affirms, is their right as those reflecting on suffering in the first person. And many sufferers do yearn for some theological assistance in this way, especially if and when they deem prevailing popular theologies of depression inadequate (and many do, often for the reasons named by content critics). Identifying and developing diverse theological resources will require theologians such as myself to affirm the possibility of suffering's persistent meaninglessness—its purposelessness, its inexplicability before God—while also offering sufferers access to theological resources that expand possibilities for meaning making in the context of depression. And of course, we must do so while articulating a clear stance against the imposition of meaning.

What could potentially result are more resources that obviate the tension that can presently arise between the life-giving affirmations of first-person theologizing and the collective good of all those who suffer from depression. Recall the anticipated critique of Kilby's proposal that asks: If a theology that is life-sustaining for *me* perpetuates an idea that potentially stigmatizes *others*, then is this theology really morally permissible? Rather than condemning such first-person theologies and thus "blaming the victims"—here, sufferers who are often doing the best they can to interpret their suffering in a life-affirming fashion—theologians should concern themselves with the larger theological landscape that they have extended to these sufferers. Let's direct our attention to developing and humbly offering more life-affirming and non-stigmatizing resources for interpreting depression instead of correcting Christian depression sufferers who are struggling amid this unhomelikeness.

Adding such resources to the theological landscape from which depression sufferers draw to interpret their suffering in relation to the Christian worldview would correct the hegemony of the existing Christian resources that impose meaning onto all suffering. These additional resources would contribute to a theological landscape that equips sufferers with more resources to interpret depression in a way that reflects the particularities of their experience, that supports their survival and relative well-being, and that accounts for the possible incoherence of their suffering in relation to God.

Conclusion

I have offered these reflections on how to talk about depression to clarify what I do and do not intend to accomplish in subsequent chapters. What follows is not an attempt to argue that there is one right way to interpret depression from a Christian perspective. With Kilby, I view that as an unacceptable disposition to bring to the harrowing mystery of depressive suffering. Many sufferers make and will continue to make meaning of their suffering as best they can and in ways that I am in no position to invalidate. Sometimes these sufferers seek out the aid of theologians for this first-person work; other times they do not. Sufferers have a right to engage in either process when it comes to interpreting their own suffering before God.

What I do attempt in the forthcoming chapters is to offer more theological resources for interpreting depression—including those that represent the meaninglessness of suffering from a perspective of faith and those that make meaning of depression while maintaining possibilities of meaninglessness. I offer these theological resources with hopes that some sufferers, especially those who might find themselves frustrated with or only temporarily sustained by existing Christian interpretations of depression, may find the proposals generative for their own theological reflection. For others who are not acquainted with the desolate experience of depression firsthand, I hope that the proceeding chapters better equip them for occasions when others, undone and dislocated by depression, may solicit aid in navigating its difficult terrain.

Part II

Sketching New Maps

Chapter 5

Depression as a Wilderness Experience: Theological Foundations

"Where are you, God?" queries Monica Coleman. "Why me?" asks Martha Manning. The methodological reflection of the last chapter leaves onlookers with only one assured response to the theological questions that emerge from depression memoirs. That is, "I don't know."

Still, I have argued that, while upholding what we cannot know about God and depression, we can—and should—wonder about these questions with depression sufferers. We should wonder because, when our response to these questions is merely silent resignation, we leave sufferers to grapple with only the prevailing Christian theories of God and suffering—theories that, due in no small part to generations of theologians like me, are limited, imposing, and fairly homogenous. Nourishing as these available theories may be for some sufferers, there are others who remain mystified and doubly displaced, still plagued by their questions, "Where are you, God?" and "Why me?"

In this chapter, I begin the work of offering theological resources to depression sufferers who are still trying to navigate the difficult and desolate world of depression from within the Christian faith. Guiding my efforts are the parameters for theological reflection on depression that I advanced in the previous chapter. I heed Kilby's charge that only sufferers themselves are rightly positioned to interpret their suffering: what it is, theologically speaking; how Christians should relate to it; how God relates to it; and what God will make of it now and eschatologically. Christians like me must exercise restraint so as to not impose meaning onto them and elide the incoherence of Christian claims about God's goodness and the real mystery of suffering in our world. At the same time, my task as a theologian and fellow sufferer is to expand the available theological resources for potential engagement among those navigating their own depression. It is for sufferers to engage, reject, or embrace the proposed theological resources on their own terms.

In view of the fact that the popular theological resources in the U.S. context mirror well-established, Christian patterns of meaning making about suffering, I focus my efforts on identifying alternative resources for interpreting depression in a Christian frame. I seek resources that affirm divine goodness and the innocence of depressive suffering while also refusing attempts to justify why one suffers from depression and claims about its inevitable resolution. I seek means for theologizing meaningless suffering and for theologizing meaningful suffering without presuming that its meaning is necessary and inherent. I start developing these resources in this chapter, where I explore biblical tales of barren and unfamiliar landscapes as potentially fecund Christian analogues for theologizing the unhomelikeness of depressive experience. Harkening back to the imagery of depression narratives and the dreams of my own depression, I argue that, perhaps for some of us, depression is a wilderness experience.

In what follows, I first introduce a brief account of the meanings and uses of this landscape imagery across the Christian tradition, beginning with the Bible itself. Second, I elaborate on how this biblical imagery can provide correlates for depression, an argument that returns us to the narrative-phenomenological description of depression that I proposed in chapter 1. Third, using the work of biblical theologian Walter Brueggemann, I tease out the variant theological implications of reading depression as a wilderness experience. I suggest that the theological plurality and ambiguity of Christianity's wilderness imagery makes it an especially fecund resource for sufferers striving to interpret their condition from a Christian perspective.

To clarify my proposals and highlight their possible theological implications, I at times emphasize points of similarity and difference between them and the theological principles that shape existing popular theologies of depression. Highlighting points of contrast is not intended to dismiss or downplay the potential validity of these popular theologies when they are appropriated in the first person; that would constitute the kind of overreach I have discounted in the previous chapter by way of Kilby's work. Rather, identifying differences across potential theologies of depression could serve the interests of depression sufferers as they discern how best to interpret their own conditions before God. Motivating my proposals is a desire to expand, not constrain, possibilities for Christians who seek to interpret their depression.

Wilderness in the Sacred Scriptures and Christian Theology

Like depression narratives, the Christian Scriptures abound with stories of dislocation into "unhomelike" places. Indeed, so plentiful is this imagery in the scriptural canon that Walter Brueggemann characterizes the Bible as "primarily concerned with the issue of being displaced and yearning for a place."[1] He labels the Israelites a "landless folk" and "God's homeless people" because of the frequency with which they are unmoored from home and immersed in a harsh and unfamiliar place.[2]

Readers witness this from the very start of the canon, which begins with Adam and Eve's forced migration from paradise into an unruly

---

1. Walter Brueggemann, *The Land: Place as Gift, Promise, and Challenge in Biblical Faith*, 2nd ed. (Minneapolis: Fortress, 2002), 2.

2. Brueggemann, *Land*, 5. In the preface to the second edition of *The Land*, Brueggemann admits that in the book's original edition, he was not sufficiently attentive to the ideological violence that has resulted from Israel's identification with land in the ancient world and on through today. Our needful attention to the imperial violence imbued in Israel's identity with land does not nullify Brueggemann's point about its centrality in the ancient Israelites' identity, however. On the contrary, it evinces the fact of Israel's attachment to the land, regardless of whether one judges that right or wrong. The ideological inflections of the Israelites' relationship to land require that we consider what right relation to space—literal and symbolic—might be.

land (Gen 3). Then when Cain, the son of the mythical first humans, murders his brother, God condemns him to a life of itinerancy away from the safety and comforts of his family and their homeland (Gen 4). Later in the Genesis narrative, God commissions Abram (later Abraham) from his familiar terrain into foreign land: "Go from your country and your kindred and your father's house to the land that I will show you" (Gen 12:1). Harsh landscapes permeate the famous story of Moses too. Upon the liberation of the Israelites, Moses leads them into the desert where they wander for forty years (Exod 13–40). Through perseverance and conquest, the Israelites eventually reach and establish a new home in the land of Canaan (Josh). Yet, the powerful kingdoms they construct there are in time overtaken by the Assyrian and Babylonian Empires (2 Kgs, 1–2 Chr, Ezra). Reflecting on the period of exile that follows, the writings of many of the prophets convey the severity of their displacement.

Important themes of place and the predominance of movement between homelike and inhospitable landscapes persist throughout the gospels and other New Testament writings, too, where authors, drawing on the sacred stories of Judaism, reflect their practiced attention to place. For example, early in all three Synoptic Gospels, John the Baptist emerges from the wilderness to begin his ministry (Matt 3:1; Mark 1:4; Luke 3:2). Soon after, Jesus is led to the wilderness where he is tempted by "Satan" (Mark 1:12-13) or "the devil" (Matt 4:1-11, Luke 4:1-13). The gospels report that while Jesus traverses the lands of first-century Palestine during his ministry, he regularly retreats to isolated places to pray (e.g., Mark 6:46, Luke 6:12).

Contemporary Bible scholars emphasize the geographical and cultural differences among the Bible's literal landscapes as well as the linguistic distinctions that surface in ancient authors' descriptions of them. However, Christian thinkers throughout history have not always been attentive to the same ancient details that concern today's Bible scholars. Reflecting on interpretations of the Hebrew Bible's terms *midbar, arabah, tsiyyah, tohu, chorbah, yeshimon*, theologian George Williams observes, "Although in their literal sense they designated different kinds of terrain—sandy and rocky desert, steppe, and forest—there appears to have been no significant difference among them in their successive non-literal or theological applications."[3] Theologians have often grouped stories featuring these diverse landscapes and referred to them more generally as tales of the "wilderness"—a label Bible scholars more strictly associate with the terms *midbar* in the Hebrew Bible and *eremia* in the New Testament.

This practice of grouping variant biblical landscapes together as "wildernesses" is not entirely disconnected from understandings of wilderness in the ancient world, however. According to Robert Barry Leal, what ultimately distinguished the wilderness from other places in the ancient world was its relationship to humankind: A wilderness was a place that was difficult to domesticate in service of human nourishment and flourishing.[4] Accordingly, Leal argues that the Bible's ancient authors present a portrait of the wilderness as a landscape of precarity, unfamiliarity, isolation, and danger to human flourishing—even danger to human life itself.[5] A wilderness is not only a difficult place, as we will see, but it is always at least this. It is precisely the human struggle engendered by this place that makes it a wilderness. Employing a more capacious understanding of wilderness than what is referred to as *midbar* and *eremia* in the biblical text, subsequent Christian interpreters usually retain the basic understanding of wilderness as a landscape that persistently threatens human flourishing, be it a barren desert or a violent sea. Thus, whether narrowly or more broadly construed, wildernesses have been seen as difficult landscapes for human living. It is in this broad sense that I reflect on wilderness in this chapter.

The fact that ancient landscapes were defined relative to human experience positioned them as useful vehicles for symbolic expression. Commenting on this point, Brueggemann says of biblical geographies, "Land is never simply physical dirt but is always physical dirt freighted

---

3. George Williams, *Wilderness and Paradise in Christian Thought: The Biblical Experience of the Desert in the History of Christianity & Paradise Theme in the Theological Idea of the University* (Eugene, OR: Wipf & Stock, 1962), 12 and 12n4.

4. Robert Barry Leal, *Wilderness in the Bible: Toward a Theology of Wilderness* (New York: Peter Lang, 2004), 36–39.

5. See Leal, *Wilderness in the Bible*, 65–95.

with social meanings derived from historical experience."[6] For instance, the so-called "promised land" is not merely the literal place of Canaan. It also functions in the text as a symbol of God's covenant and blessing. In this example and elsewhere in the Scriptures, the dual meanings of land—literal and symbolic—are interrelated.[7]

Because the literal wilderness was demarcated for its inhospitality to human life, biblical authors employed the wilderness as a symbolic image for conditions of precarity, struggle, and even fatality (Isa 51:3; Jer 4:26; Ps 107:33-35). In the New Testament, Ulrich Mauser observes, "In the majority of cases, whenever the wilderness is mentioned, the thought of the New Testament writers is not directed to the geographical disposition of the country, but to the memory of the basic action of God which took place in the wilderness in the course of Israel's history."[8] Thus, while the Bible depicts "actual earthly turf," or what Brueggemann sometimes calls "literal land," the coexistence of symbolic representations of land in the text enriches its interpretative potential. As Alec Gilmore puts it, "the geographical wilderness underlies and brings out the emotional wilderness."[9]

It is no surprise, then, that over the course of Christian history, religious teachers and writers have read biblical stories of "literal" untamed lands as meaningful analogues for the struggles of the present day, including those with little to nothing to do with literal land. Susan Bratton observes the influence of such biblical stories in the colorful hagiographies of the early Christian desert monastics. For example, "The story of the crows feeding Paul the hermit is similar to the account of Elijah at wadi Kerith, where ravens brought him bread and meat (1 Kgs 17:1-6)."[10] In the referenced passage from 1 Kings, the land is experiencing severe drought, and Elijah's survival hinges on his exile to an isolated ravine and the miraculous provision

6. Brueggemann, *Land*, 2.

7. Brueggemann, *Land*, 2.

8. Ulrich W. Mauser, *Christ in the Wilderness: The Wilderness Theme in the Second Gospel and its Basis in the Biblical Tradition* (London: SCM, 1963), 14.

9. Alec Gilmore, "Wilderness in the Bible and the Wild Places of Earth," *Journal of European Baptist Studies* 7, no. 1 (2006): 45.

10. Susan Bratton, *Christianity, Wilderness, and Wildlife: The Original Desert Solitaire* (Scranton, PA: University of Scranton, 2009), 163.

of these birds. Hearers of the hagiography would have understood Paul the hermit's biblical allusion as a likening of the hermit's ascetic existence to Elijah's precarious but blessed experience in the literal desert of the biblical narrative.

In George Williams's study of mystical theology in the late Middle Ages, he identifies yet another correlation between the deserts of the Scriptures and the figurative wilderness experienced by Christians during the Middle Ages. The mystical sense of wilderness during this era "made it possible for [Meister] Eckhart boldly to extend the meaning of *Wüste* [wilderness] as a technical term of apophatic theology."[11] Namely, Eckhart describes the human mystical experience of God as "desert," writing:

> In this barren Godhead, activity has ceased and therefore the soul will be most perfect when it is thrown into the Desert of the Godhead where both activity and forms are no more, so that it is stuck and lost in this Desert where its identity is destroyed and it has no more to do with things than it had before it existed. Then it is dead to self and alive to God. What is dead in this sense has ceased to be so that that soul will be dead to self which is buried in the Godhead-desert.[12]

Other mystical theologians similarly engaged the wilderness during the medieval and early modern era, including Richard of St. Victor, Hildegard of Bingen, Mechthild of Magdeburg, and John of the Cross.[13]

Symbolic interpretations of geographical displacement continued throughout the Protestant Reformation and the rest of the modern era. In 1520, Martin Luther penned *The Babylonian Captivity of the Church*, a diatribe against the Catholic Church and its sacramental practices and theologies.[14] Luther utilizes the story of the Israelites'

---

11. Williams, *Wilderness and Paradise*, 53.

12. Cited in Williams, *Wilderness and Paradise*, 53. See Meister Eckhart, *Meister Eckhart: A Modern Translation*, ed. Raymond B. Blackney (New York: Harper and Brothers, 1941), 200.

13. Williams, *Wilderness and Paradise*, 51–57. For additional examples, see also Andrew Louth, *The Wilderness of God* (Nashville: Abingdon, 1991), 71–130.

14. Martin Luther, *The Babylonian Captivity of the Church, 1520*, Annotated Luther Study ed. (Minneapolis: Fortress, 2016).

experience of occupation and exile under the Babylonian Empire as an extended metaphor for the captivity of the contemporary laity under the cruel authority of the church's hierarchy. In the seventeenth century, Baptist author John Bunyan drew on the Bible's symbolic imagery of harsh landscape in a number of writings. His 1687 classic, *The Pilgrim's Progress*, combines scriptural allusions to the Books of Job, Jeremiah, and Revelation to present a journey through what George Williams summarizes as the "wilderness of the religious and political turmoil of the English seventeenth century."[15]

These historical examples show how people of faith have read sacred stories of the wilderness not merely as tales of a past, literal geographical reality but also as figurative stories that speak to the experiences of a present, very different historical moment. They have drawn on the tradition's wilderness imagery as a correlate for the disorientation, spiritual and existential precarity, isolation, entrapment, struggle, aimlessness, and death that marred their contemporary lives. And in the process, they made new meaning of the trying realities of their lives, often emphasizing not only the difficulty of the wilderness but also the good work of God that unfolds in otherwise desolate circumstances. This process of bringing these ancient texts to bear on contemporary experience in service of drawing out new interpretations and implications is grounded in the Christian belief that biblical memories of the land are never mere retellings of a historical place and time. These inspired stories also always have the potential to reveal something timeless about the nature of God's creation, including human beings, as well as valuable truths about how the God of All relates to them, past and present. The question of what the Bible's ancient tales could reveal for those enduring depression is therefore but a new and particular version of a longstanding question of Christian faith.

Indeed, already some contemporary Christians have associated wilderness with experiences of psychological distress. We find one

---

15. Williams, *Wilderness and Paradise*, 85. Williams offers a concise overview of the wilderness motif in Bunyan's writings in *Wilderness and Paradise*, 84–86. See also John Bunyan, *The Pilgrim's Progress*, 11th ed., ed. Roger Pooley (New York: Penguin Classic, 2009).

example in Andrew Louth's study of two nineteenth-century spiritual companions, Saint Charles de Foucauld and his longtime spiritual director, Abbé Huvelin. Louth argues that both of their lives were shaped by deserts, albeit deserts of differing kind. Foucauld, the "desert saint," was drawn willingly into the literal desert as a young man and regularly returned throughout his vocational journey through religious life and the priesthood. For him, the desert wilderness was "a place of solitude, of hiddenness, a place of being alone with God in prayer. It is a place of presence: the purifying presence to oneself of solitude, and the still more purifying presence of God."[16]

The lesser-known Abbé Huvelin played a central role in Foucauld's conversion to Christianity as a young man, and Huvelin continued to serve as his confessor and spiritual director in the years that followed, even across the saint's lengthy stays in the desert. Louth argues that for Huvelin, "his desert was no literal desert of sand—he lived all his life in Paris—but an inner desert of mental anguish."[17] Because of this, Louth suggests, "he too can be considered a desert saint, one who dwelt in the desert, only for him it was not a literal desert but the inward wilderness of desolation of his own mind."[18] Louth elaborates further on Huvelin's wilderness condition:

> His letters and diary reveal one who knew endless misery, and often found his thoughts turning toward death—as release, and suicide as the means. The enormous demands of preaching, teaching, caring for the sick and dying, hour after hour in the confessional, added to the continual burden of suffering, physical and mental, the encroachment of despair and depression: all this produced an intense weariness. Weariness, nothing more, he said to himself, not the suffering of reparation, of sharing Christ's suffering: a weariness that seemed to undermine his reason and threaten to topple him over into madness.[19]

Huvelin's public writings affirm the potential spiritual gains of suffering, but according to Louth, "his own suffering seemed rather to

16. Louth, *Wilderness of God*, 21.
17. Louth, *Wilderness of God*, 14.
18. Louth, *Wilderness of God*, 26.
19. Louth, *Wilderness of God*, 28.

drive him to the brink of madness and despair."[20] Huvelin's personal writings include intriguing doodles, which inform Louth's observation. "The obsessive, anguished character of these doodles seems to point to the genuine sense of inner desolation, verging on madness and a depressive longing for annihilation. It seems to suggest that Huvelin lived in an inner wilderness, a desert within, that—like the literal desert—afforded him no sense of security, no place of comfort. It suggests we should see Huvelin as a desert saint struggling in a barren place, inhabited by demons quite as terrifying as any St. Anthony faced."[21]

This is just one example of how contemporary Christians have interpreted psychological distress in light of the wilderness imagery that finds its roots in the Scriptures.[22] The work of Louth and others invites depression sufferers to participate in the theological tradition of exploring what Christian wilderness tales might reveal about this contemporary condition.

Depression as a Wilderness Experience

Informing explorations of how the Bible's wilderness imagery might serve sufferers striving to theologize their depression is the observation from chapter 1 that many depression sufferers already draw on similar imagery to represent their suffering. I recognize this organic intuition as a worthy starting point for theological reflection, and what I aim to demonstrate in this chapter is that this recurring imagery across depression narratives is indeed ripe with theological possibility.

---

20. Louth, *Wilderness of God*, 29.

21. Louth, *Wilderness of God*, 30.

22. For another contemporary example of Christians connecting wilderness imagery and psychological distress in a theological key, see Jean Vanier, "From Wilderness towards Home," in *Wilderness: Essays in Honor of Frances Young*, ed. R. S. Sugirtharajah (London: T&T Clark, 2005), 167–174. On February 22, 2020, L'Arche International, an organization founded by Vanier, reported that he engaged in coercive sexual relationships with multiple adult women under his spiritual guidance. I decry this abuse and join others in wrestling with its implications for Vanier's legacy, particularly because such abuse can contribute to the very mental-health challenges to which he speaks in the writings cited here. For the report, see https://www.larche.org.uk /Handlers/Download.ashx?IDMF=139bf786-3bbc-45f5-882a-9f78bfbc99e9.

Recall from chapter 1 how, amid the struggle to capture and convey this elusive condition, sufferers frequently turn to the spatial imagery of harsh landscapes to represent their dislocation into the encompassing, isolating, and often meaningless state of unhomelikeness: Depression is a dark wood, an alien place. It is unfamiliar, unhomelike terrain. Sufferers' use of this figurative imagery invites a consideration of biblical landscapes as lifeworlds: Just as depression sufferers—and all people—always occupy some world (*Umwelt*) that is constituted by one mood or another (*Stimmung*), the people of the Bible always occupy some landscape that conditions their experiences.

Like phenomenological lifeworlds, conditioning each biblical landscape are the possibilities it affords or lacks. Whether a place abounds with the resources for human flourishing—water, bountiful soil, edible plant and animal life—or it shrivels in drought and decay affects the possibilities of human experience there. As in depression narratives, we see in the stories of the people of Israel that some places are homelike not only because they are physically comfortable but also because of the experiences that the Israelites have there. These are places where the Israelites feel "landed," as Walter Brueggemann puts it, because these landscapes are familiar or laden with meaning, affording inhabitants a sense of belonging. Such lands facilitate relative safety and stability. Phenomenologically, these places correlate to the at-home-ness or everydayness of most people's ordinary experience.

Yet we know, too, that the Israelites are often far from the familiar landscapes of home, dwelling in places that leave them feeling "landless," as Brueggemann puts it; that is, they are unknown and uncomfortable places. Frequently, the people of Israel are isolated in foreign lands, arid places, and life-threatening landscapes. Being that the wilderness is a difficult setting for human life—a place defined by the possibilities for human life that they lack—the possibilities it affords are unfamiliar and less than ideal, and it lacks other possibilities to which the ancient community would have been accustomed. The wilderness is an engrossing world of discomfort and isolation, precarity, and struggle. Experientially, the untamed and difficult landscapes of the Scriptures share characteristics with the unhomelikeness of depression.

Correlating the imagery of depression narratives to those of the Sacred Scriptures invites what Sandra Schneiders, drawing on philosophical hermeneutics, calls a "fusion of horizons," where the unhomelike world of the depression sufferer "fuses with the horizon of the world projected by the text."[23] Like the world of the sufferer, the wildernesses of the Scriptures are difficult and inhospitable to human life. Yet, in contrast to many experiences of depression, the Bible's tales of desolate places often project a world abundant with theological meaning. How the people of Israel find themselves in and out of these places, how they experience them, and how God, in turn, interacts with sufferers there can afford contemporary depression sufferers an array of possibilities for interpreting their own conditions.

That said, not all efforts to bring together the world of the sufferer and the world of the biblical text will result in a "fusion of horizons" or what Schneiders terms an "appropriation" of the text. Building on the argument of chapter 4, this is but another reason why imposing meaning onto the suffering of others is a misguided pursuit. One simply cannot force a sufferer to see her depression through one or another wilderness tale from the Scriptures. A transformative encounter with the biblical text, one "by which we appropriate the meaning of the text by a fusion of horizons with the world the text projects,"[24] ultimately hinges on a sufferer's "genuine dialogue" with the Scriptures.[25] "For the believer . . . this dialogue is rooted in the faith that this text is a mediation of transformative divine revelation."[26] It follows that what may result from such a dialogue is a sufferer's conclusion that the wilderness depicted in a particular biblical scene is *not*, in fact, a story that helps her interpret her condition before God. This dissonance, too, can be revealing. What can also result, however, is a transformative encounter with the text that affords the sufferer ways of interpreting her condition in relation to God and the truths of the Christian faith. This may address that second, religious displacement that often accompanies the phenomenological dislocation of depression.

---

23. Sandra M. Schneiders, *The Revelatory Text: Interpreting the New Testament as Sacred Scripture*, 2nd ed. (Collegeville, MN: Liturgical Press, 1999), 172.

24. Schneiders, *Revelatory Text*, 174.

25. Schneiders, *Revelatory Text*, 177.

26. Schneiders, *Revelatory Text*, 177.

Before looking more closely at the biblical narrative to consider the worlds of meaning it offers depression sufferers for their consideration, I note that the prospect of correlating the harsh landscapes of Scripture to depression, though not unprecedented in the Christian tradition, is distinct from how many contemporaries engage Scripture in their interpretations of depression. When adherents to popular theologies of depression draw from Scripture to support their interpretations, they frequently read depression into the Scriptures in a literal fashion. They identify the lamentations of Jeremiah as "depression," for example, suggesting that the prophet experienced the same condition that many people do today.[27]

In addition to presenting some historiographical problems, these literal engagements with biblical narratives have other limitations.[28] First, this approach narrows the relevance of biblical texts to only scenes of sadness and misery. While such scenes are not uncommon throughout the canon, they constitute but one rather limited possibility for bringing depression into correlation with the Scriptures. Second, this approach reinscribes the common reduction of depression to sadness, which many depression sufferers have identified as discordant with the fundamental features of their experience. For sufferers who resist the identification of their depression with sadness, this approach to Scripture may not suffice. Thus, correlating depression to wilderness imagery has the potential, first, to expand possibilities for interpreting depression with the biblical narrative and, second, to extend more resources to sufferers who resist or find themselves unsatisfied by the identification of depression with sadness alone.

The Theological Plurality of the Bible's Treacherous Landscapes

In addition to offering representations of suffering that might resonate with experiences of depression, biblical wilderness narratives

27. David Murray, *Christians Get Depressed Too: Hope and Help for Depressed People* (Grand Rapids, MI: Reformation Heritage, 2010), 2–3.

28. See chapter 1 for more on the risks of anachronism when identifying past instantiations of psychological distress with contemporary depression.

present differing interpretations of suffering and depictions of God. Variations in why the Israelites find themselves in difficult territory, how they experience these places, and how God responds to them suggest an array of theological implications for interpreting depressive experience. While some of these wilderness narratives lend themselves to theologies of God and suffering not unlike the popular theologies of depression that already prevail among U.S. Christians today, others can expand possibilities for theologizing depression.

Brueggemann's look at some biblical tales of harsh landscape offers a heuristic for recognizing the various worlds of meaning that sufferers encounter across the Bible's wilderness imagery. Focusing on the early Hebrew Scriptures, Brueggemann studies three particular "memories of landlessness"—memories of *sojourn*, of *exile*, and of *wandering*. Each discloses distinct theological possibilities for interpreting wilderness experiences in general and experiences of depression in particular. This is because, as I noted earlier, Brueggemann emphasizes the entanglement of literal and symbolic meaning in the Bible's geographical narratives. This is reflected in his term, "landlessness," which denotes not a state of being outside of place and time but rather the ancient Israelites' experience of separation from places that ground their identity. To be landless is to be away from home, from familiarity, and from the place where the Israelites experience community and belonging—all qualities that resonate with common descriptions of depression.

Brueggemann associates the Israelites' first memory of landlessness, *sojourn*, with the stories of Abraham, Isaac, and Jacob, which unfold across Genesis 12–50. Characteristic of their sojourns are free choice and a strong sense of direction.[29] They are "pilgrims," filled with anticipation, Brueggemann observes.[30] Although the discomforts of landlessness are not ideal for the patriarchs and their communities, their journeys are animated by faith in Yahweh and hope for themselves in the land that God has promised to them, despite instances when they doubt. Motivated by the divinely commissioned destination of their travels, their driving hope informs their experi-

29. Brueggemann, *Land*, 6.
30. Brueggemann, *Land*, 6.

ence of difficult and unfamiliar landscapes. Brueggemann notes that the sojourner of these tales "can be observed as placeless, but he knows of a promised place, and that changes his sojourn."[31] This also distinguishes stories of sojourn from the other two images of landlessness that Brueggemann identifies.

Though the interpretive possibilities of the Scriptures are manifold, it is easy to see how memories of sojourn could serve interpretations of depression that cast suffering as a condition to be embraced for some higher, divine purpose. Taking Abraham's sojourn through unfamiliar and inhospitable lands as an analogue for depression, one might identify depression as a journey toward a "better place" that God intends. Because depression sufferers do not typically describe themselves as having chosen their suffering in the conscious way that Abraham chooses to respond to God's call to Canaan, however, this depiction of suffering does not map onto every dimension of contemporary depression in an obvious way. Some depression sufferers, especially those who view depression as a privileged site of divine instruction, may nevertheless be drawn to the example of Abraham as one who embraces the trials of his wilderness experience as part of God's plan and in anticipation of the blessings his suffering will supposedly engender.

The Babylonian *exile* is, for Brueggemann, representative of another of the Israelites' memories of landlessness. As a literal geographical place, Babylonia was not a treacherous landscape, and while there, "[t]he exiled Jews were not oppressed, abused, or imprisoned," explains Brueggemann. Nevertheless, the exiled Israelites "were displaced, alienated from the place that gave identity and security."[32] It is in this sense that the exile constitutes a profound dislocation. Under conditions of separation not only from the city of Jerusalem but also from the religious rituals and institutions that had rooted the identity of the Jewish people at this time, the Israelites question God. And while the Israelites wait in hope of God's faithfulness throughout this period, their experience of the unfamiliar lands of the exile take on a different, more distressed tone than what we

---

31. Brueggemann, *Land*, 6.
32. Brueggemann, *Land*, 7.

witness in tales of sojourn. "This event of landlessness evoked rage and anger (see Ps 137) but also yearning pathos (Lam 1:2, 3, 6, 21)," writes Brueggemann.[33]

The circumstances that occasion this exilic dislocation distinguish it from Brueggemann's other memories of landlessness too. These differences are of significant theological consequence. The exilic memories of the prophets, especially Jeremiah, who Brueggemann calls "the poet of the land par excellence," suggest that the Israelites are complicit in their exilic landlessness.[34] Under the governance of their monarchy—which was established against the initial wishes of God (1 Sam 10:17-24)—the people of Israel had become comfortable, taking for granted the securities and well-being of their community. In such circumstances, Jeremiah saw exile as inevitable. Landlessness would come. "His message to Israel, who thought it was ultimately secure and at home, is the coming ultimate homelessness," writes Brueggemann.[35]

Memories of exile lend themselves to another theological perspective on wilderness experience, one that might also resonate with one of the existing popular theologies of depression. Prophetic calls to repentance echo across the writings of the exilic era, and their messages are clear: The people of Israel have strayed from right relationship with God, sinning against God and betraying their fellow creatures. Indeed, Jeremiah pronounces God's reasoning for the Israelites' displacement as follows: "Because your guilt is great, because your sins are so numerous, I have done these things to you" (Jer 30:15). Consequently, the Israelites' only hope for rescue from foreign occupation hangs on repentance for its wrongdoing and appeal to the mercy of God. This tale of exilic landlessness is a story of suffering that results from one's own sinfulness. Reading the experience of exile as a correlate for depression—that is, as expulsion from at-home-ness because of one's sinfulness and for the sake of purgation—would suggest that depression sufferers are morally culpable for their suffering and should in turn repent if they are to ever escape this harrowing condition. This, of course, aligns with

---

33. Brueggemann, *Land*, 8.
34. Brueggemann, *Land*, 101.
35. Brueggemann, *Land*, 102.

what many U.S. Christians claim by identifying depression as a sin or as the result of some other sinful aspect of a sufferer's life.

The Israelites' third memory of landlessness, *wandering*, is characterized by a lack of direction and a scarcity of necessary means for survival. Brueggemann lifts up Exodus 16–18 as a paradigmatic example of this. This biblical text narrates the Israelites' decades-long period in the wilderness after escaping slavery in Egypt. Relatively early in their forty years of desert wandering, they beg their leaders for food. So desperate are the Israelites that they implore Moses and Aaron, "If only we had died by the hand of the Lord in the land of Egypt, when we sat by the fleshpots and ate our fill of bread; for you have brought us out into this wilderness to kill this whole assembly with hunger" (Exod 16:3). Desperation for mere survival persists throughout their wilderness trek, notes Ulrich Mauser:

> At several points of the journey the desert provides no means to quench the thirst of the wandering people. In the wilderness of Shur, they have no water for three days, at Marah the water is bitter so that it cannot be used (Ex 15:22-23), and again in the wilderness of Sin no water can be found (Ex 17:1; Num 33:14). There are other narratives which tell about the lack of food (e.g., Ex 16:3). The way through the wilderness imposes on Israel a life full of difficulties and miseries. The most basic human needs—food and drink—are barely ensured.[36]

Their hopelessness and struggle for basic survival typify the experience of wandering.[37] Distinct from sojourn is the absence of any apparent purpose for this wilderness wandering. The lamentations of the wandering Israelites reveal that they do not dwell in the wilderness of their own volition. Theirs is an unwilled displacement.

Different from exilic memories of the landlessness, Brueggemann's paradigmatic tale of wandering, Exodus 16–18, does not attribute the suffering of the Israelites to their own sinfulness. Some commentators emphatically distance the wilderness wandering of Exodus from sin through a comparison to another biblical wilderness narrative, the one found in the Book of Numbers, which picks up shortly after

36. Mauser, *Christ in the Wilderness*, 22.
37. Brueggemann, *Land*, 7.

the Israelites' reception of the Ten Commandments at Mount Sinai. Of the Israelites' landlessness in Numbers, commentators write, "Continuities with the wilderness stories in Exodus 15:22–19:1 are seen in the gifts of quail and manna, the ongoing complaints, and military victory; but discontinuities are also there, evident especially in sin and judgement."[38] Elsewhere, they similarly note, "Many of these narratives [in Numbers] mirror Exodus 15:22–18:27: manna, rocks producing water, battles with desert tribes, and nonstop complaints. . . . But Numbers is different: the people are sharply identified as rebellious, against both God and Moses and Aaron."[39] The comparison emphasizes that the wilderness wandering of Exodus is not attributed to the sin of the people. This not only distances the wandering of Exodus 14–16 from the story of landlessness of Numbers but also the landlessness of the Babylonian exile.

If sin does not the occasion the wilderness wanderings of Exodus 16–18, then what does? The Exodus narrative invites this question, when in 13:17-18 the author notes, "When Pharaoh let the people go, God did not lead them by way of the land of the Philistines, although that was nearer; for God thought, 'If the people face war, they may change their minds and return to Egypt.' So God led the people by the roundabout way of the wilderness toward the Red Sea." Why this roundabout way? What is God's purpose for the suffering that awaits them on this difficult journey? According to Exodus 14:1-4, the aimless wandering of the Israelites serves the glorification of God. Yet, at various points in Exodus 15–22, the text suggests that this roundabout route through the wilderness, which would stretch on for forty years, was God's way of "testing" the people of Israel through its trails in the wilderness.[40] The Exodus text thus offers multiple answers, but all point to the existence of some ultimate

---

38. Michael D. Coogan, ed., *The New Oxford Annotated Bible*, fully rev. 4th ed. (New York: Oxford University, 2010), 186.

39. Coogan, *New Oxford Annotated Bible*, 203; note concerning Numbers 10:11–25:18.

40. On God's testing of the people of Israel and its implications for theologies of suffering, see Cornelis Houtman, "Theodicy in the Pentateuch," in *Theodicy in the World of the Bible*, ed. A. Laato and Johannes Cornelis de Moor (Leiden, Netherlands: Brill, 2003), 155–156.

divine purpose for the Israelites' suffering in the wilderness, albeit a purpose unknown to the wandering sufferers themselves.

This consideration of the Israelites' memories of wilderness wandering further evinces the diverse theological implications that could follow from correlating these biblical tales to contemporary depression. The depiction of a God who ordains suffering for some higher purpose unknown to those who endure it aligns with what many contemporary Christians believe about their suffering when they theologize it as a privileged site of divine instruction. Though this wilderness wandering may feel aimless, the authors of the biblical text retrospectively assert that this suffering is in some way worthwhile because of some benevolent purpose it serves. Likewise, those who espouse interpretations of depression as divine instruction insist that the aimless suffering experienced by depression sufferers is, in fact, purposeful. Furthermore, those who hold this view claim to know that this suffering serves some divinely ordained higher good. Yet, unlike the story of Abraham's sojourn, which also resonates with theologies of depression as divine instruction, this tale of wilderness wandering features a consistently despairing community. The desperation and doubt of these wanderers may resonate especially well with depression sufferers who struggle to interpret their condition in view of the Christian worldview.

What the Wilderness's Theological Plurality Affords

Brueggemann's taxonomy of Israel's movements between and relationship to land in the Hebrew Bible highlights the diversity of this imagery and its myriad implications for theologizing wilderness experiences. To correlate depression to the biblical image of the wilderness, then, does not imply *one* set of theological conclusions about why depression comes about, how one should relate to and escape from it, or how God relates to it. Insofar as this correlation suggests a common message, it is that depression, as a wilderness, is a difficult place for people to inhabit. For those who understand the inherent precarity and difficulty of wilderness living, there is no saying, "Cheer up! Look on the bright side! This is not so bad!" Bringing depression and biblical wilderness narratives into conversation thus resists these common dismissals of depression.

The theological associations and implications of inhabiting this difficult condition, however, vary dramatically according to which biblical wilderness one associates with depression. So while bringing together biblical tales of the wilderness and depression can afford an opening for sufferers to locate their harrowing experiences within Christianity's Sacred Scriptures, doing so does not necessarily settle all the pressing questions of meaning with which many sufferers grapple. Rather, exploring depression as a wilderness experience invites the question, "*Which* wilderness is this?" because the occasion in which one finds oneself in the wilderness, God's relationship to the situation, and how and whether the experience is resolved differs notably across the Bible's wilderness narratives.

Scholars frequently speak of the "ambiguity" or "ambivalence" of the wilderness in the Scriptures as a means of conveying the plural and even contradictory theological associations that I point to here. "Wilderness in the Bible is not all vastness, nothingness, horror and disaster, though all these elements are there," observes Alec Gilmore. "It is rather a very diverse arena—a cauldron—in which all of life takes place. . . . It is an image capable of arousing and nurturing the most diverse emotions, and the location of some of the most startling encounters between a human being and God."[41] Noting the "varied connotations of wilderness" throughout the Christian tradition, Keith Innes notes that "the ambiguity of this concept runs deep."[42]

More often than not, when theologians speak of the ambiguity of the wilderness, they point to a particular, fundamental "ambiguity" or "ambivalence" that joins even the theologically diverse examples of wilderness narratives examined so far. It is one that the above quote from Gilmore alludes to as well. Innes explains, "In the Old Testament narrative the wilderness is . . . a place of alienation and terror. Yet it is also the place where Yahweh meets with people, is made known to them, provides for them and rescues them."[43] This ambiguity, according to Innes, persists in representations of the wilderness beyond the Bible and throughout the Christian tradition:

41. Gilmore, "Wilderness in the Bible," 46–47.
42. Keith Innes, "Aspects of Wilderness," *Theology* 110, no. 854 (March 1, 2007): 110.
43. Innes, "Aspects of Wilderness," 114.

Towards the end of the third century CE Antony of Egypt retired to the Egyptian desert to live a life of simplicity, renunciation and prayer. . . . The desert was thus both the place where demons were encountered, and also a setting for the pursuit and attainment of holiness. In later periods, when the language of wilderness was often interpreted in a purely symbolic sense, its ambiguity remained. George Williams, writing of the medieval period, shows how in some traditions the wilderness was viewed negatively as an experience of darkness and testing; in others as a positive state of "emptiness" enabling total surrender to God. . . . Among the first European settlers in America the ambivalent perception of wilderness continues.[44]

Innes proceeds to point to representations of the wilderness in the African American spiritual tradition as another expression of this ambiguity within the Christian tradition. Delores Williams famously explores this in her classic, *Sisters in the Wilderness*, where she shows how African Americans' lived experiences of the ambiguity of the wilderness landscapes of the United States shaped the hermeneutic that they brought to biblical tales of the wilderness, especially the figure of Hagar whose story I explore in forthcoming chapters.[45]

The ambiguity of the Bible's wilderness narratives affords a basic theological understanding of the wilderness even amid its diversity: The wilderness is an unquestionably harsh place for human living and even survival, but it is also often a place where people encounter God in transformative ways. It is a difficult place where God is. Thus, to correlate depression with the biblical image of the wilderness, in general, is to affirm from a Christian perspective that depression is a tremendously difficult condition of living, though one not necessarily absent from the presence of God. What the Hebrew Bible's tales of sojourn, exile, and wandering make clear, however, is that God appears to relate to sufferers enduring these spaces in myriad ways.

For those who seek to recognize their experiences within the authoritative sources of the Christian community and to do without

---

44. Innes, "Aspects of Wilderness," 114. Louth also highlights the ambivalence of the desert in early monastic writing in *Wilderness of God*, 12.

45. Delores Williams, *Sisters in the Wilderness: The Challenge of Womanist God-Talk* (Maryknoll, NY: Orbis, 1993).

identifying depression with mere sadness, this general association between depression and the biblical wilderness may be a welcome possibility. What this correlation will not necessarily do is neatly resolve all the other theological questions that depression sufferers bring to the Christian tradition—such as "what is this?" and "why me?" and "what should I do?" and "what will come of this?" The multiple and variant theological implications of wilderness imagery resist any simple or simplistic response to such inquiries, for the expanse of biblical wilderness imagery offers multiple responses to these questions. As I have shown, some biblical wilderness narratives could attribute depression to the sinfulness of those who suffer in the wilderness, whereas others could attribute it to God's wish to test the faith of those who wander there. The theological plurality of the image of the wilderness in the Scriptures may, for some, seem a sign that this biblical image is rather unhelpful one. Yet there is also reason to believe that this multivalence is precisely what renders biblical wilderness imagery such a fecund resource for depression sufferers seeking to interpret their conditions. I offer three reasons why.

First, the theological plurality of wilderness imagery is an alternative (and even a corrective) to the exclusive prescriptions of meaning that are often imposed onto suffering, preemptively constraining other possibilities for meaning making and belying the mystery of suffering about which I wrote in previous chapters. For a sufferer who begins to explore how her suffering is and is not akin to the wilderness suffering of the Scriptures, she will find not one set of theological claims to accept or reject but rather a panoply of theological possibilities to explore in and through the wilderness stories of the Bible. Some depression sufferers may engage wilderness narratives and interpretations of them that reinscribe popular theologies of depression. Others may not. Whatever the case, opening up multiple theological possibilities and this variety of considerations could be a valuable offering to depression sufferers and those who accompany them in the process of theologizing depression.

Likewise, for Christian communities that strive to actively and openly address mental-health conditions, likening depression to a wilderness experience may serve as a way to represent the condition without perpetuating the imposition of meaning that often spreads from pulpits and Christian self-help books. To invite Christians to reflect on depression as a wilderness does not necessarily imply that it is sinful or the result of sin (or not), that it is a blessing from God for one's own good (or not), or that it necessarily holds some other alternative theological status (or not). Suggesting that depression is a wilderness experience is not to suggest that it means something. The theological multiplicity of wilderness experiences lends itself to how theologians and other Christians should relate to the suffering of others. It reflects the persistent mystery of a confounding condition like depressive suffering. At the same time, what this invitation to theological reflection entails at the most basic level is an affirmation of the difficulty and precarity of depressive experience and God's relation to it in a general sense.

Second, the theological plurality of biblical wildernesses could potentially accommodate some of the phenomenological and interpretative shifts that frequently occur across the course of living with chronic and recurring depression. David Karp's work shows that the meanings sufferers assign to their depression may resonate and serve them for a time, but a need for alternative interpretations sometimes emerges as their condition and context shift.[46] Throughout this book, I have noted that these shifts often amount to moments of profound crisis when one's belonging to a faith community is thrown into question or when the very possibility of any meaning in one's life seems entirely imperceptible. It is conceivable that the wilderness imagery of the Scriptures is capacious enough to accommodate these shifts. For, just like the Israelites who as one community had multiple wilderness experiences and various interpretations of them, so too the wilderness that a depression sufferer initially identifies with may not be the one she always associates with as her experience or interpretations of depression shift. It is conceivable that an image as theologically multivalent as the wilderness may be able to accommodate some of these fluctuations, remaining relevant to a sufferer even as she weighs different interpretations of her condition.

Third, just as the plurality of wilderness imagery may be a refreshing alternative to a religious context where Christians tend to

---

46. David Karp, *Speaking of Sadness: Depression, Disconnection, and the Meanings of Illness*, updated and expanded ed. (New York: Oxford University, 2017).

impose meaning, this multiplicity may also be an appealing resource in a broader social context where mental-health conditions such as depression are maligned and stigmatized. Building on the work of Susan Sontag, Richard Arrandale notes how discourse about depression in church and society tends to characterize it as "an enemy that is hostile towards us, and that needs to be overcome and destroyed."[47] Though some depression sufferers certainly characterize their own depression this way—and some do so quite literally, identifying their depression as the work of the devil—Arrandale cautions that the prevalence of this perspective in society imposes limitations on sufferers' perceived possibilities for interpreting and responding to their conditions. Arrandale is naming how narrative and metaphorical language can shape and limit one's perception of mental illness, and in the case of society's prevalent antagonistic metaphors for mental-health conditions, he argues that they have the power to perpetuate stigmatizing, negative moralizations of consideration like depression: "If we dwell in the language of the negative and the military [think: enemy] there is a serious danger that this will set the agenda for the people language is used for/against."[48]

In response, Arrandale suggests, "A more positive and theological language might enable people to break free from the chains and fetters with which they have been bound. Such a language, exorcised of negativity and value-judgements may allow people with mental health problems to be brought back into the kingdom from which they can feel alienated."[49] The biblical image of the wilderness is what Arrandale points to as an alternative, and it is precisely its theological plurality and ambiguity that make it ideal. "The desert, as a metaphor, is not a single concept and it has been used in various ways, thus allowing it to have a variety of meanings and applications," he explains. "However the wilderness is viewed, it is a place which is on the edge of periphery of life, geography and experience." Unlike the enemy language that perpetuates the negative moralization of mental-health conditions throughout society, speaking of depres-

---

47. Richard Arrandale, "Madness, Language and Theology," *Theology* 102, no. 807 (1999): 197.

48. Arrandale, "Madness, Language and Theology," 197.

49. Arrandale, "Madness, Language and Theology," 197.

sion as a wilderness need not bring with it these inherently negative moral and theological associations, he suggests. In fact, the Bible is full of wilderness experiences wherein a person "blossoms," where one "meet[s] God in a new way."[50] The multivalence of wilderness imagery, with its range of moral associations, is therefore a potentially significant corrective to the overwhelming negativity of society's prevailing view of depression and other mental-health conditions.

Moving Forward

In this chapter, I have shown how exploring resonances between depression and the wilderness imagery of the Scriptures as well as the long theological tradition of interpreting contemporary experiences in light of it can serve as a resource for depression sufferers seeking to interpret their condition with the Christian faith. Exploring this correlation will not automatically resolve some of the theological questions that sufferers bring to Christianity as they grapple with their conditions, but the plurality and ambiguity of the tradition's wilderness imagery may in fact be an asset for theologizing depression.

Along the way, I have also demonstrated how particular wilderness stories, when taken up and brought into dialogue with depression, can lend themselves to certain theological perspectives on this condition. Some of these theological perspectives mirror those that already circulate in U.S. Christian communities as popular theologies of depression. I turn next to one wilderness narrative—the story of Hagar—that could open up another set of theological perspectives on depression for depression sufferers. Unlike popular theologies of depression, the wilderness experiences of Hagar do not incline us to presume meaning of suffering. On the contrary, her story confronts us with a sacred possibility of meaningless suffering and, in so doing, offers depression sufferers another way of inhabiting the Christian worldview amid the senseless unhomelikeness of their condition.

---

50. Arrandale, "Madness, Language and Theology," 200.

Chapter 6

Depression as an Hagaric Wilderness

At the turn of the twentieth century, English sculptor Albert Toft applied his acclaimed realism to a representation of Hagar.[1] Featured on the left, she kneels naked, her vulnerability apparent. Her raised arms clutch her head in distress. Her closed eyes and arched body evince a consuming interior life that has collapsed her attention inward. Atop this sculpture pedestal and surrounded by empty space, Hagar's isolation is striking. With this, Toft poignantly captures the desperation of this biblical foremother. Seeing this sculpture today, it could just as well be a depiction of someone struggling with depression.

I noted in the last chapter that the most commonly translated word for "wilderness" in the Hebrew Scriptures is *midbar*, and in the order of the biblical canon, readers first encounter it in the story of Hagar (Gen 16, 21). Hagar appears as an enslaved Egyptian woman in the clan of Abraham, Brueggemann's exemplary sojourner. Hagar's movements from "home" to harsh landscape are unlike the hopeful journey of her counterpart in many ways, however, no doubt because of her social position in the world of the text. Yet Hagar's harrowing wilderness experiences are no less theologically rich. In this chapter, I explore

---

1. Albert Toft, "Hagar," from *Art at the Royal Academy, 1897,* special issue of *The Studio, Internet Archive* digitized from a copy in the University of Toronto Library, accessed May 6, 2020: http://www.victorianweb.org/sculpture/toft/13.html.

what a theological reading of her story might offer depression sufferers striving to connect their experiences to the Christian tradition.

In chapter 5, I pointed to biblical wilderness narratives as potentially resonant and fecund resources for depression sufferers. I demonstrated the theological plurality of these wilderness tales, showing how some lend themselves to theological claims already commonly associated with suffering in the U.S. Christian community, including popular theologies of depression. I also suggested that the Bible's wilderness narratives could disclose theological frameworks for depression that are not yet common in the Christian community. It is my interest in these stories—stories that disclose a theological world different from others already at hand—that occasions this closer look at Hagar's brief and often-overlooked story.

When we read Hagar's story analogically and with an eye toward contemporary experiences of depression, we encounter a theological world with different implications for depressive suffering than others examined thus far. Hagar's story of suffering is a tragic one that is phenomenologically resonant with contemporary depression in many ways. Like so much depression, it is also without any apparent reason and resolution. Nevertheless, Hagar's wilderness is one where God is. Following a summary of Hagar's story in the Book of Genesis, I draw out these features in the Bible's telling of her life, particularly its presentation of Hagar's second wilderness experience in Genesis 21. My analysis shows that her story withholds claims to some originating coherence or retroactive justification for suffering, and, in so doing, it extends to depression sufferers an additional set of theological possibilities with which to dialogue.

Hagar's Life in the Wilderness

Hagar's story unfolds in two scenes. While Bible scholars attribute each to distinct authorial traditions from differing periods in the history of Israel, the canon presents them sequentially as parts of the continuous story of Abraham and his family.[2] First, in Genesis

---

2. For more on the redaction history of Hagar's story, see Philip Y. Yoo, "Hagar the Egyptian: Wife, Handmaid, and Concubine," *Catholic Biblical Quarterly* 78 (2016): 215–235.

16, the barren Sarah (then Sarai) gives the enslaved Hagar to her
husband Abraham (then Abram) as a wife for the purpose of con-
ceiving offspring. Upon the conception of what will become Hagar's
son, Ishmael, Sarah jealously turns against Hagar, dealing with her
"harshly" (v. 6). The pregnant Hagar runs away to the wilderness,
where she encounters God. There, God instructs her to return to
Sarah, but not before God discloses that Hagar will bear a son. "I
will so greatly multiply your offspring that they cannot be counted
for multitude," promises the angel of the Lord (v. 10). Astonished,
Hagar names the Lord, *El-roi*—the "God Who Sees"—and returns
to Sarah and Abraham to bear her son. This event makes Hagar the
first figure in the Bible to name God. Chapter 16 concludes with the
birth of her child, Ishmael.

In Genesis 21, we meet Hagar again. She has returned to life
with Abraham and Sarah. By this point in the story, Sarah, too, has
birthed a son, Isaac. The sight of young Ishmael and Isaac together
provokes Sarah to demand Hagar's expulsion. "She said to Abraham, 'Cast out this slave woman with her son; for the son of this
slave woman shall not inherit along with my son Isaac' " (v. 10).
Abraham, troubled by the request, seeks further instruction from
God, who tells him, "Do not be distressed because of the boy and
because of your slave woman; whatever Sarah says to you, do as she
tells you, for it is through Isaac that offspring shall be named for
you. As for the son of the slave woman, I will make a nation of him
also, because he is your offspring' " (vv. 12-13). Abraham complies,
sending Hagar and her child to "wander about in the wilderness of
Beer-sheba" (v. 14).

Having been given very little water, Hagar and Ishmael soon find
themselves in death-bound circumstances. Hagar, despairing, "casts
her child under one of the bushes. Then she went and sat down opposite him a good way off, about the distance of a bowshot; for she
said, 'Do not let me look on the death of the child.' And as she sat
opposite him, she lifted up her voice and wept" (vv. 15-16). Rosalyn
F. T. Murphy notes, "Hagar's weeping at the prospect of watching her
son dying of thirst underscores the Jewish tradition whereby tears
are openly expressed signifying anguish due to approaching death
(2 Kgs 20:5; Isa 38:5; Ps 39:12; 116:8; Heb 5:7). Weeping for a loved
one is customary in the Old Testament, particularly in the Book of

Genesis."[3] Hagar's tears thus communicate to readers not only her personal anguish but also the severity of the wilderness conditions that surround her and her son. This is a life-threatening landscape.

God hears the cries of Ishmael and calls to Hagar in turn. "What troubles you, Hagar? Do not be afraid; for God has heard the voice of the boy where he is. Come, lift up the boy and hold fast with your hand, for I will make a great nation of him" (vv. 17-18). Then, the God of Seeing opens Hagar's eyes to a well of water. In the biblical account, Hagar's story ends there in the wilderness as the text gives way to Ishmael's story: "God was with the boy, and he grew up; he lived in the wilderness, and became an expert with the bow. He lived in the wilderness of Paran; and his mother got a wife for him from the land of Egypt" (vv. 20-21).

Reflecting on this story, Phyllis Trible calls Hagar "a fleeting yet haunting figure in scripture."[4] Hagar's memory haunts because of the horrors that befall her under God's watch and the purview of a couple of the faith's forbearers. Consequently, Trible has classified Hagar's story as one of the Bible's "texts of terror." Contending with this terror, scholars have responded in different ways. Some have advocated that Christians reject this story rather than straining to redeem its characters through liberative reinterpretation.[5] In contrast, and precisely because of the suffering Hagar experiences, others have identified with her story and interpreted it as a generative narrative in support of their lives. Speaking of scholars such as Delores Williams and Elsa Tamez, Amanda Benckhuysen observes, "By reading from the margins, these [women] redeem Hagar's suffering and draw on her story to strengthen, convict, and comfort their respective communities."[6]

---

3. Rosalyn F. T. Murphy, "Sista-Hoods: Revealing the Meaning in Hagar's Narrative," *Black Theology* 10, no. 1 (2012): 88–89.

4. Phyllis Trible, *Texts of Terror: Literary-Feminist Readings of Biblical Narratives* (Philadelphia: Fortress, 1984), 27.

5. See Renee K. Harrison, "Hagar Ain't Workin', Gimme Me Celie: A Hermeneutic of Rejection and a Risk of Re-appropriation," *Union Seminary Quarterly Review* 58, nos. 3-4 (2004): 45.

6. Amanda Benckhuysen, "Reading Hagar's Story from the Margins: Family Resemblances between Nineteenth- and Twentieth-Century Female Interpreters," in *Strangely Familiar: Protofeminist Interpretations of Patriarchal Biblical Texts*, ed. Nancy Calvert-Koyzis and Heather Weir (Atlanta: Society of Biblical Literature, 2009), 19.

The following consideration of Hagar's story advances the hermeneutical legacy of the latter group, exploring the links between Hagar's suffering to that of contemporary depression sufferers for the sake of generating potentially life-giving theological insights. Yet this approach cannot come at the cost of eliding the story's horrors and perplexities—the very qualities that lead so many people of faith to reject it. Ignoring the terror of this text would not only undermine the integrity of the sacred story itself, but it would also risk deadening the theological challenge mediated through Hagar. And, as Trible asserts, "To neglect the theological challenge she presents is to falsify faith."[7] Indeed, it is precisely the suffering and theological challenge of Hagar's story that makes it potentially valuable for depression sufferers, particularly those looking for theological alternatives to the justifications of suffering that prevail in the U.S. Christian context. My hope is that a clear-eyed reflection on Hagar's story will aid contemporary sufferers in their determination of whether it warrants rejection or appropriation in their own lives.

A Resonant Wilderness

In Hagar's dislocation into the lonely and precarious wilderness of Beer-sheba, we can recognize similarities with the depressive suffering described by many individuals who live with depression today. This is not to say that Hagar was herself depressed. Though she clearly and understandably experiences immense psychological distress throughout her story, this alone need not lead us to conclude that her tears and desperate pleas are manifestations of what we today call depression. Rather, Hagar's suffering and contemporary depressive suffering—worlds apart as they may be—share certain experiential qualities, including many that depression sufferers often identify as some of the most significant features of their suffering. By way of these common features of experience, contemporary depression can be seen as analogous to Hagar's wilderness suffering.[8]

---

7. Trible, *Texts of Terror*, 29.

8. Nyasha Junior surveys the reception of Hagar's story throughout history, including influential analogical interpretations. See *Reimagining Hagar: Blackness and Bible* (New York: Oxford University, 2019). See also Christopher Heard, "On the Road

Among the similarities between Hagar's suffering and that of contemporary depression sufferers is isolation. The very etymology of Hagar's name conveys to readers her isolation. The root *gēr* means "resident alien" or "foreigner."[9] Her name thus signals her position as one set apart—*alienated*—from others, even when she lives among the community of Abraham's house. During her time in the wilderness, Hagar wanders alone with the exception of her vulnerable young son, who accompanies her during her second wilderness experience. There, Ishmael appears too young to understand and console Hagar in her distress and too helpless when their journey begins to assist her in making the wilderness a sustainable habitat for them. And even the companionship of this young dependent is precarious under the threat of their severe dehydration. Especially during the scene where Hagar abandons Ishmael, her loneliness is apparent (Gen 21:15-16).

The isolation Hagar endures is a pronounced feature of her story relative to many other wilderness narratives, including those examined in the previous chapter, where the people of Israel struggle collectively, commiserate about their hunger and thirst, and help one another as they suffer. Hagar's isolation is all the more striking when we consider the risks of isolation in the ancient context of the text, where a life of such isolation was rare and also life-threatening. Drawing on the work of Bible scholar Roland de Vaux, Delores Williams explains that "Even for the slave, 'to be without family is to be without protection.'"[10] The isolation of Hagar and Ishmael renders them "not only without economic resources; they were without protection in a nomadic culture where men ruled the families, tribes and clans. As mother and child wander off into the desert of Beersheba, we cannot help but wonder how their survival will be

---

to Paran: Toward a Christian Perspective on Hagar and Ishmael," *Interpretation* 68, no. 3 (2014): 270–285; and John L. Thompson, *Writing the Wrongs: Women of the Old Testament among Biblical Commentators from Philo through the Reformation* (New York: Oxford University, 2001), 17–99.

9. Yvonne Sherwood, "Hagar and Ishmael: The Reception of Expulsion," *Interpretation* 68, no. 3 (2014): 291 and 300.

10. Delores Williams, *Sisters in the Wilderness: The Challenge of Womanist God-Talk* (Maryknoll, NY: Orbis, 1993), 28.

secured. . . . [The desert or wilderness] is hardly a place where a lone woman and child ought to be wandering without sustenance, shelter or protection."[11]

Hagar's isolation both distinguishes her suffering from that of many other biblical wilderness tales and aligns her suffering with that of contemporary depression sufferers. Recall from chapter 1 that depression sufferers commonly report feelings of isolation, disconnection, and the absence of possibilities for belonging. Testifying to this, Daphne Merkin writes of her own depressive state, "She feels isolated, stuck in a cave of grief, of ancient and permeant sorrow."[12] In addition to this disconnection, sufferers' sense of isolation is often magnified and complicated by mental-health stigma, an experience that David Karp perceives from sufferers' earliest experiences of depression and onward. Karp observes that the feelings of self-hatred and disconnection common to depression frequently compel sufferers to withdraw from social interactions, reinforcing their sense of isolation and anguish.[13] Social withdrawal then magnifies isolation and self-hatred, making the urge to withdraw more powerful. He calls this "a truly vicious cycle."[14] Even though the beginning of this cycle typically precedes an official diagnosis of depression, sufferers report an awareness of stigma attached to their feelings. One recalls, "It never occurred to me to talk to anyone about it. . . . I had this idea that it just wouldn't be acceptable. . . . I think there's something of a taboo against talking about bad things or bad feelings. . . . I had to maintain a façade so that people would treat me with respect."[15] Here, we glimpse how the perception of a socially "respectable" self, which grounds social stigma, intersects with the symptoms of early depression to engender what Karp describes as "an ongoing and mutually reinforcing double

11. Williams, *Sisters in the Wilderness*, 28.

12. Daphne Merkin, *This Close to Happy: A Reckoning with Depression*, 1st ed. (New York: Farrar, Straus and Giroux, 2017), 9.

13. David Karp, *Speaking of Sadness: Depression, Disconnection, and the Meanings of Illness*, updated and expanded ed. (New York: Oxford University, 2017), 103–105.

14. Karp, *Speaking of Sadness*, 105.

15. Karp, *Speaking of Sadness*, 120. The internalization of this stigma can lead to what psychologists call "self-stigma." See Philip T. Yanos, *Written Off: Mental Health Stigma and the Loss of Human Potential* (New York: Cambridge University, 2018).

stigmatization—by self and society"[16] Were depression only an experience of entrapment, hopelessness, meaninglessness, and diminished
agency, it would be sufficiently difficult to endure. The fact that it is
also radically isolating—an experience absent of the belonging that the
person ordinarily takes for granted in the world—makes it all the more
difficult. Doubly stigmatized by self and by society, these depression
sufferers endure a profound experience of isolation as they live with
depression, just as Hagar does in her story.

Though in both Genesis 16 and 21 Hagar experiences the distress
and precarity of the wilderness in relative isolation, some features
of her second wilderness experience lend it to phenomenological
correlations with depression more than her first. Hagar's wilderness
experiences differ in their portrayal of Hagar's self-determination.
Recall that Hagar's first wilderness experience is an active flight
from oppression. She willfully—though desperately—chooses the
danger and isolation of the wilderness as an alternative to the terrible
circumstances in which she lives. Conveying this, Delores Williams
describes Hagar's flight from slavery in Genesis 16 as "self-initiated
liberation."[17] Hagar's self-possession is evident throughout her story
in Genesis 16 when, at God's direction, she chooses to leave the
wilderness and return to slavery. Though we ought not overstate her
freedom amid the very real constraints of her social situation, Hagar
clearly exercises what agency she has. With that in mind, her willful
movement between home and harsh landscape in Genesis 16 does
not resonate with the unexpected and often perplexing imposition
of depression that so many sufferers describe.

Indeed, Gillian Marchenko reminds us that depression sufferers
do not experience themselves as freely opting in and out of their
conditions: "When depression comes, I can never figure out how it
gets here. What are my triggers: stress with the kids? too much stuff
at church? friendships? my relationship with [my husband] Sergei?
I have no idea. Depression comes and go [*sic*] as it pleases."[18] Elsewhere, she characterizes the unwilled and mysterious circumstances

---

16. Karp, *Speaking of Sadness*, 121.

17. Williams, *Sisters in the Wilderness*, 24 and 25.

18. Gillian Marchenko, *Still Life: A Memoir of Living Fully with Depression* (Downers
Grove, IL: InterVarsity, 2016), 14–15.

of depression this way: "I watch depression approach. It rolls closer, dark, ominous, like the Great Nothing from the 1980s movie *The Neverending Story*. One day my life is a clean sheet of white paper, and then a tiny bottle of ink gets knocked over. Do I knock it over? Does someone else? These questions nag in little pockets of light, and then the blackness spreads and seeps."[19] Daphne Merkin also reflects on the condition's mysterious imposition, explaining, "You lie there in the sludge, no longer bothering to flail around, marooned in a misery that is no less easy to bear because there is nothing wildly terrible to point to in the circumstances of your own life—on the surface, at least—to account for it."[20]

To say that Hagar's first wilderness experience differs significantly from the descriptions of suffering presented by many with depression is not to say that circumstances of oppression such as those from which Hagar flees are irrelevant to depressive suffering. On the contrary, a growing body of multidisciplinary research tracks how social oppression contributes to and compounds mental-health struggles. Yet, to the extent that social oppression contributes to depressive suffering today, it does not set up sufferers to choose depression as an alternative to their oppressive circumstances like we witness in Genesis 16. The relationship of social oppression and depression is more elusive and complex, and depression's comings and goings evade the volition of sufferers in a way unrepresented in the story of Hagar's first wilderness experience.

In this regard, the experienced helplessness that sufferers such as Marchenko and Merkin describe is more akin to the forced dislocation that occasions Hagar's second wilderness experience. Hagar, like depression sufferers, helplessly finds herself amid this trying landscape. She does not flee; she is forced. And the text indicates that Hagar's helplessness endures once there. Trible notes that, in contrast to Genesis 16, in Hagar's second wilderness experience she is said to "wander" (v. 14). "The verb *wander* (t`h) connotes uncertainty, lack or loss of direction, and even destitution."[21]

---

19. Marchenko, *Still Life*, 30–31.
20. Merkin, *This Close to Happy*, 4.
21. Trible, *Texts of Terror*, 23.

Hagar's wilderness wandering in Genesis 21 resonates experientially with the world of depression in another way, too, particularly in contrast to her wilderness experience in Genesis 16. During Hagar's first wilderness experience, we do not see a woman frightened for her survival and well-being in light of her recent self-initiated liberation. Even as she is pregnant, there is no indication that she perceives her situation in the wilderness to be fatal. In fact, God finds Hagar near a spring of water, a vital natural resource in this otherwise inhospitable terrain. Though she is "afflicted" (v. 11)—presumably because of Abraham and Sarah—this water source would be an asset for her isolated endurance in the wilderness.

Hagar's proximity to this spring and the absence of any apparent worry on her part stand out in contrast to her second wilderness experience. Trible notes, "Unlike the region of Shur,"—where Hagar's first wilderness experience takes place—"the territory of Beersheba provides no water at all. Furthermore, it does not border Egypt," Hagar's homeland.[22] "Receiving Hagar in forced exile rather than voluntary flight, this wilderness is an arid and alien place. It offers a deathbed for the child," Trible explains.[23] "While the wilderness she chose in [Genesis 16] was hospitable, yet fleeting, the wilderness imposed upon her in [Genesis 21] is hostile, yet enduring."[24]

While Trible emphasizes the material differences between the wildernesses of Genesis 16 and 21, other scholars note that Hagar's first wilderness experience was profoundly dangerous as well, albeit for different reasons than Genesis 21. Elsa Tamez suggests that giving birth alone in the wilderness would have been a dire risk to Hagar and her child, which may explain why God tells Hagar to return to slavery and life with Abraham and Sarah in Genesis 16.[25] Considering the relative dangers of both of Hagar's wilderness experiences, the difference in *her* experiences of these wildernesses stands out.

22. Trible, *Texts of Terror*, 24.
23. Trible, *Texts of Terror*, 24.
24. Trible, *Texts of Terror*, 25.
25. Elsa Tamez, "The Woman Who Complicated the History of Salvation," in *New Eyes for Reading: Biblical and Theological Reflections by Women from the Third World* (Bloomington, IN: Meyer Stone, 1987), 14–15. See also Williams, *Sisters in the Wilderness*, 20.

This difference resides in Hagar's perception—her sense of whether or not survival is possible. Genesis 16 does not indicate that Hagar perceives this imminent danger, especially compared to her expressions of acute precarity in Genesis 21, where, without water, she weeps in despair.[26] She does not perceive any means of survival for her and her son, and she says as much.

Like Hagar who desperately cries out to God without any perception of how she and her son will survive this wilderness suffering, so too many who live with depression struggle to perceive any means of survival or improved quality of life amid their condition. Recall from chapter 1 that, for many, depression is characterized by the diminishment or loss of possibilities for change. Combined with the fluctuations in sufferers' overall temporal experience, this frequently results in an inability to perceive any possibilities for an end to their entrapment in the world of depression. Again, this may be why so many depression sufferers characterize their condition with images of hell or purgatory: The condition truly *feels* eternal, unchanging, and all-encompassing. Amid this aimless suffering, survival is not taken for granted. It can even appear impossible from the vantage of a sufferer. As such, both the Hagar of Genesis 21 and many contemporary depression sufferers find themselves stuck and without perceived possibilities for surviving their situation.

A last phenomenological similarity between Hagar's second wilderness wandering and that of many depression sufferers concerns the persistence of suffering. The Genesis text provides no indication that Hagar's suffering in the wilderness ends, no reassurance of her escape from this difficult life in a desolate landscape. Though God is with her and her son, there is no offer of rescue, no revelation of a divinely charted escape route from their precarious circumstances. Rather, we learn that Hagar survives at least long enough to raise her son and find him a wife, indicating, at the very least, many years of persistent struggle in this inhospitable environment (v. 21).

---

26. For more on the significance of the biblical motif of water in the wilderness, see Frances Klopper, "Aspects of Creation: The Water in the Wilderness Motif in the Psalms and the Prophets," *OTE* 18, no. 2 (2005): 253–264.

Delores Williams's commentary on Hagar's second wilderness experience highlights this distinctive aspect of the story: "There were some rules peculiar to nomadic life that might finally have alleviated the poverty and homelessness of Hagar and Ishmael. These rules had to do with hospitality and asylum. Roland de Vaux says: 'Nomadic life . . . gives rise . . . to a law of asylum. In this type of society it is impossible and inconceivable that an individual could live isolated, unattached to any tribe. Hence, if a man is expelled from his tribe . . . for any reason . . . or he leaves it . . . he has to seek the protection of another tribe.' "[27] The ancient rules of nomadic life in this region would lead readers to assume that Hagar and her son should have been able to escape their solitary and difficult plight in the wilderness by finding welcome from a new community. "Information in the biblical text, however, suggests that Hagar and Ishmael might not have become attached to another family or tribe. One is led to believe that with the aid of God, Ishmael and Hagar maintained an autonomous existence," notes Williams.[28] "Hagar's autonomy is manifested in the last act she performs in the Genesis 21 narrative. Assuming a role ordinarily prescribed for males in most ancient Near Eastern households, Hagar gets a wife for Ishmael from Egypt (verse 21b)."[29] Thus, against the social customs of the day, Hagar and Ishmael's life in this difficult landscape stretches on.

Further distinguishing the persistence of Hagar's suffering in Genesis 21 from some other wilderness narratives, Delores Williams famously contrasts Hagar's suffering from the wilderness wandering of the Exodus narrative. In the Exodus narrative, divine intervention culminates in an end to both oppression and wilderness wandering, whereas, in Hagar's story, suffering persists even in the wake of God's presence. This differentiates it not only from the wandering of the Exodus, as Williams notes, but also from the sojourn of Abraham and his sons, which concludes when their clan settles in the Promised Land. The continuation of Hagar's suffering also differs from Israel's exile under the Babylonian Empire, which diminishes when

---

27. Williams, *Sisters in the Wilderness*, 28.
28. Williams, *Sisters in the Wilderness*, 29.
29. Williams, *Sisters in the Wilderness*, 30.

the Persian Empire grants the Jewish people permission to return to their holy city and rebuild what will become the Second Temple. Though Hagar's suffering is not the only tale of persistent suffering in the Scriptures, it is a distinctive feature relative to some other wilderness tales that we encounter there.

The persistence of Hagar's suffering in the wilderness is, again, a feature that makes it a representation of the wilderness that is potentially resonant with depression sufferers, for it mirrors the experiences of many who live with this commonly chronic and recurring condition.[30] Though the suffering of depression fluctuates over time for many who experience it as a persistent condition, and though strides in the treatment of this condition have enabled many to live longer and better with it than in previous times, there remains no cure. Speaking to this, Andrew Solomon comments that, even when he was relatively well, he knew "that episodes of pain might lie ahead, that depression is cyclical and returns to afflict its victims over and over."[31] Many who live with it therefore characterize depression as a persistent presence that enduringly shapes their lives, not unlike the difficulties of wilderness living that continued to shape Hagar's.

What's more, the altered perception of time that often constitutes depression can make even a single episode seem endless. This returns us to the significance of subjective perception in the stories of Hagar and of depression sufferers. A depression of a few weeks can feel like a lifetime of desolation. Amid depression, "it is *life* that seems too long, endless. A clock ticks somewhere in the silence of your apartment, empty second after empty second, reminding you that time hangs heavy when you have lost your way, like a vise around your neck," recounts Merkin.[32] Rod Steiger echoes, "When you're depressed, there's no calendar. There are no dates, there's no day, there's no night, there's no seconds, there's no minutes, there's nothing. You're

30. See Daniel N. Klein and Anna E. S. Allmann, "Course of Depression: Persistence and Recurrence," in *Handbook on Depression*, 3rd ed., ed. Ian H. Gotlib and Constance L Hammen (New York: Guilford, 2014), 64–83.

31. Andrew Solomon, *The Noonday Demon: An Atlas of Depression* (New York: Scribner, 2015), 78.

32. Merkin, *This Close to Happy*, 4.

just existing in this cold, murky, ever-heavy atmosphere."[33] Depression is thus not only persistent from the vantage of onlookers who observe the long suffering of those with this condition. Depression is also experienced as persistent. "One definition of depression, I read, is an inability to construct a future," explains Marchenko.[34] For those in this state, then, depression can be an endless present—a seeming lifetime of wilderness wandering, like Hagar's.

An Unreasonable Wilderness

For depression sufferers who recognize analogues of their experience in the story of Hagar, this text also offers theological insights. The first theological affordance of this wilderness narrative once again sets it apart: The telling of Hagar's second wilderness wandering resists the theological rationalizations for suffering to which many other biblical wilderness narratives lend themselves. Free of the kinds of theological explanations that commonly justify suffering today, Hagar's enduring struggles in Genesis 21 are presented as unjustified suffering—what John Thiel would call "innocent suffering."[35]

Revisiting the common comparison between Hagar's story and the Exodus story puts into focus the inexplicably of Hagar's situation and its theological implications. Several Bible scholars note parallels between the stories of Moses and Hagar.[36] Both intimately knew the realities of human slavery. Following Trible, Delores Williams notes that "the harshness of the force Sarai exerts upon Hagar is indicated in the passage of the verb (*'nh*), which is also used in Exodus to indicate the suffering experience of all the Hebrews when they

---

33. Kathy Cronkite, *On the Edge of Darkness: Conversations about Conquering Depression* (New York: Delta, 1994), 46.

34. Marchenko, *Still Life*, 41.

35. See John Thiel, *God, Evil, and Innocent Suffering: A Theological Reflection* (New York: Herder and Herder, 2002).

36. See Thomas B. Dozeman, "The Wilderness and Salvation History in the Hagar Story," *JBL* 117, no. 1 (1998): 29–32; Andrea D. Saner, "Of Bottles and Wells: Hagar's Christian Legacy," *Journal of Theological Interpretation* 11, no. 2 (2017): 202–211, esp. 202n12; Trible, *Texts of Terror*, 9–35.

were slaves in Egypt."[37] Both Hagar and Moses have two wilderness experiences. Early in their stories, each experiences a temporary, self-initiated stay in the wilderness wherein they encounter God, who offers them instructions. Thomas Dozeman notes,

> Each character responds to the changed situation by fleeing (*barach*) to a well in the wilderness in order to escape oppression (Hagar in Gen 16:6 and Moses in Exod 2:15b). Once the journey is made, each character undergoes the same sequence of action: (1) Each encounters the messenger of God in the wilderness (Hagar in Gen 16:7 and Moses in Exod 3:2); (2) each is commanded to return to the threatening situation from which they fled (Hagar in Gen 16:7–14 and Moses in Exod 3:10); and (3) each receives a word of promise and leaves the wilderness with a special name for God (Hagar names God as El Roi in Gen 16:13 and Moses receives the name Yahweh).[38]

Later in their stories, both figures have a second and far more treacherous experience of the wilderness, and for both this experience extends through the remainder of their lives. Concerning these second wilderness experiences, David Daube observes another commonality: Both are preceded by situations of oppression—Sarah's oppression of Hagar and Pharaoh's oppression of the Israelites—and both Sarah and Pharaoh "drive them out" into the wilderness (Gen 21:10; Exod 12:39).[39] Dozeman notes that, "In each case, however, God indirectly orchestrates and sanctions the expulsion. . . . Thus, in both instances, expulsion is an act of liberation for the one being driven out, signifying release from slavery. The salvific character of expulsion for Hagar is made explicit when she receives a divine oracle of salvation in Genesis 21:17, with the stereotyped formula that she 'not fear.' The content of liberation is ambiguous, however, for both Hagar and Moses, since the act of expulsion leads to the second episode of the wilderness."[40] While Dozeman frames the occasion

37. Williams, *Sisters in the Wilderness*, 19. See also Trible, *Texts of Terror*, 13–14.

38. Dozeman, "Wilderness and Salvation History," 30.

39. David Daube, *The Exodus Pattern in the Bible* (London: Faber & Faber, 1963), 23–38. See also Trible, *Texts of Terror*, 13–14.

40. Dozeman, "Wilderness and Salvation History," 30–31.

for their second wilderness experiences quite positively—in terms of "liberation"—he also concedes that "[t]he wilderness becomes a more threatening setting in the second episode for both characters. As a result, what has been a place of escape and safety for the heroes in the original flight becomes a potentially more sinister location in the act of expulsion."[41]

Against the backdrop of these similarities, some theological differences between the stories of Hagar and Moses stand out. Though Dozeman rightly observes that the wilderness wanderings of Hagar and Moses mark an end to their direct oppression and that God has an indirect hand in that both cases, these stories differ in the reasons they present for the decades of wandering that subsequently unfold. As I noted in the previous chapter, the wilderness experience of Exodus 16–18 is variously attributed to the higher purposes of God. Consequently, the purpose of this suffering can be understood as a justification for the harrowing wilderness wanderings of Moses and the rest of the Israelites: It is initiated, at least indirectly, by God for the community's spiritual edification.

In contrast, descriptions of Hagar's second wilderness experience include neither the justification of a higher purpose nor some other theological reason to account for the onset of her lifetime of struggle in the wilderness. Sarah asks Abraham to "cast out" Hagar (Gen 21:10). God instructs a distressed Abraham to do as Sarah says, noting that great nations will come from the offspring of both mothers, though only Sarah's will be named for the patriarch (vv. 12-13). Abraham obeys, sending Hagar and Ishmael off. Across these events, the text offers no rationalization for the initiation and endurance of Hagar's struggles in the wilderness. The closest we come to an explanation of this sort is in the exchange between God and Abraham that precedes Hagar's eviction to the wilderness (Gen 21:12-13). Even there, however, God does not indicate a purpose for the lifetime of wilderness wandering that will ensue. Rather, God simply offers assurance that Abraham's lineage will endure through his son Isaac in accordance with God's covenantal promise—a fact already affirmed by the text.

---

41. Dozeman, "Wilderness and Salvation History," 31.

As Hagar's story continues and readers glimpse God again, we continue to be left without any theological justification for what she endures. Hagar grieves her situation and cries out to the God of Israel in lament, pleading, "Do not let me look on the death of the child." The text recounts that "as she sat opposite him, she lifted up her voice and wept" (Gen 21:16). Like Job who grieved, despondent in his own spiritual wilderness, there are no theological justifications that could sufficiently explain the reason for Hagar's suffering.[42]

Unlike the Exodus account of the Israelites' wandering, there are no indications that Hagar's expulsion into the wilderness is necessary for serving some higher purpose of spiritual edification, even one that is opaque to the figures in this biblical tale but known to God and the reader. What's more, in contrast to the suffering of the Israelites' exilic experience, which is presented as purgation for the Israelites' sin, the suffering of Hagar's second aimless and endless spell in the wilderness has no particular theological prompt or apparent purpose. Sarah is jealous, and she wields the upper hand of privilege against the vulnerable Hagar and her son. And furthermore, Abraham, who has power over both women, wields it with cowardice—here and elsewhere in the larger biblical narrative. Though, on a human level, these serve as explanations for the occasion of Hagar's second wilderness experience, neither explains why, on a theological level, God permits such treacherous behavior among humans or allows the wilderness wandering that unfolds for Hagar and her son.[43]

42. Though my analysis here focuses on the inexplicability of Hagar's expulsion into the wilderness for the remainder of her life, it is worth noting that the text also withholds any justifications for the suffering she experiences as an enslaved woman in the house of Abraham. Delores Williams speaks to this, noting: "Hagar's story in the Bible does not provide enough information for us to respond to the 'why' of her enslavement. The Bible does not tell how or why the Egyptian woman Hagar came to be the slave of a Hebrew woman—given Egypt's overwhelming power and leadership in antiquity and the Hebrew people's relative obscurity and powerlessness." See *Sisters in the Wilderness*, 75.

43. The distinction I draw between inter-human dynamics and divine-human dynamics in the text is analogous to the distinction that Delores Williams draws between "horizontal encounters" and "vertical encounters" in her commentary on the realities that concern and shape Black liberation theologies. See *Sisters in the Wilderness*, 136.

Admittedly, it is concerning that God does not chastise Sarah's jealousy toward Hagar and Ishmael or intervene in the plan that would place Hagar and her son in life-threatening circumstances. With John Waters, we might rightly wonder, "Why does Yahweh not offer her some kind of protection? . . . Would it not be in the best interest of God to have Abraham demonstrate some humane treatment to Hagar and his son?"[44] In view of the Hebrew Bible's stories where justifications for suffering are otherwise prevalent, it is telling that the text neither explains Hagar's suffering with a claim of divine intent, nor does it explain God's inaction. God does not stop Hagar's expulsion to the wilderness, but God does not justify the occasion of her suffering either. With regard to theological questions of *why* Hagar was left to live in the wilderness, the text is silent. It simply leaves readers horrified and confounded at the senselessness of her situation.

On this note, one might wonder whether it would be right to say that Hagar's suffering results from the moral evil of others and is thus justified theologically. This could support the claim that what her second wilderness experience projects is not a world of senseless suffering but a world like the one described by free-will theodicists—one where God withholds God's involvement in creation in order to preserve human free will, which, in this case, is the will of Sarah and Abraham. Though it is correct that their unjust actions cause Hagar's suffering, the text does not support the free-will theodicist's explanation for why God does not intervene to stop Hagar's suffering. First, the text does not depict an uninvolved or indifferent deity like what we encounter in free-will theodicies. Leading up to and throughout Hagar's second wilderness experience, God is remarkably involved. This is not the absent, onlooker God of modern theism. Second, the text does not provide any explanation for how God does or does not relate to Hagar's suffering in this regard. We simultaneously witness in Genesis 21 a God who is present, who does not prevent Hagar's wilderness wandering, and who does not justify this divine inaction

---

44. John W. Waters, "Who Was Hagar?," in *Stony the Road We Trod: African American Biblical Interpretation* (Minneapolis: Fortress, 1991), 200. Delores Williams also offers a litany of unanswered theological questions that arise in response to Hagar's expulsion. See *Sisters in the Wilderness*, 175.

with an explanation. Again, on why God relates to her suffering, this text is silent. Why Hagar is consigned to live the rest of her life amid the precarious landscape of the wilderness is unclear. Hagar's long suffering has no apparent rationalization within the logic of God's cosmos, no alleged purpose. Thus, while readers witness how myriad social and interpersonal circumstances coalesce to contribute to Hagar's suffering, including actions of undeniable wrongdoing and injustice, the story resists the kind of theological justification characteristic of theodicies and the other biblical wilderness narratives examined thus far.

Not only does the theological world of this text differ from other examined wilderness narratives but also from those disclosed in popular Christian interpretations of depression. In the previous chapter, I demonstrated theological parallels between some biblical wilderness tales and popular theologies of depression. Though Israel's memories of sojourn and the wilderness wandering of the Exodus are experientially quite distinct, they are commonly justified in the biblical text by their outcomes: In both cases, the suffering endured is allegedly warranted as a means to some higher good. This is also the theological reasoning that underlies the popular Christian interpretation of depression as divine instruction. In Brueggemann's example of Israel's exile, where the text justifies the people's displacement and struggle as punishment for betraying their faithfulness to God, we encounter another theological justification for suffering at work: Their suffering is warranted as the logical and just consequence of its source. Suffering is a fitting consequence of the sufferers' sinfulness, for example. This is of course the theological reasoning that underlies the popular theologies of depression as a self-imposed moral evil. These wilderness narratives and popular theologies of depression suggest that the suffering at hand, no matter how harrowing, is nevertheless justified before God. The story of Hagar's wilderness experience in Genesis 21 does not.

As such, Hagar's story offers sufferers a representation of potentially resonant suffering that is also free of any theological justification. Without clarity concerning *why* the suffering of Hagar and of contemporary depression comes about, we are left with a theological mystery. Based on the text itself, Hagar's remaining lifetime of wilderness suffering cannot be justified as an inherent good, something worthwhile for the spiritual edification it promises. Nor can it be explained as a punishment for sin, when there is no mention of anything about her sin. Furthermore, recognizing that her suffering results from the sinfulness of others does not explain why God relates to Hagar's suffering as God does, permitting it and withholding rescue from life in this harsh landscape. As far as anyone can tell, this suffering is, in itself, meaningless.

A Tragic Wilderness

Another way to frame this distinctive feature of Hagar's story—with its absence of theological justifications for the woman's enduring and isolated struggle in the wilderness—is to recognize Genesis 21 as a tragedy in the classical sense. In recent decades, some theologians have applied the contrasting narrative frameworks of comedy and tragedy to elucidate the features of particular theological worldviews in this way.

To clarify the tragic theological qualities of Hagar's wilderness experience, I first introduce the contrasting features of a comedic narrative. Theologians note that comedic storylines are distinguished by their "U" structure: They commence from a state of peace, which is disturbed by a central conflict and the unfortunate consequences that follow from it. In time, however, the plotline's central problem is resolved, and peace is restored as a consequence. This happy resolution of conflict and struggle is emblematic of comedies. Across the high points and valleys of the comedic plotline is a consistent logic: The audience recognizes suffering and struggle as the logical consequence of the story's driving problem; though difficult, comedic suffering is sensible in this regard. It is explicable, justifiable. A comedy's resolution brings to fruition the logical coherence of this storyline. In a narrative world of orderly cause-and-effect relations, it is only fitting that upon the resolution of the plot's central conflict—the story's problematic source of the suffering—struggle and strife will cease.

According to theologian Flora Keshgegian, the classic Christian story is "relentlessly comedic: all's well that ends well for the redeemed. And all will end well because God is in charge."[45] Like all comedies, this classic Christian story presents an orderly world where all that unfolds—the good and the bad, including even the most horrendous suffering—is presented as having some logical explanation. Suffering is a consequence of sin, and sin is a consequence of human freedom, the story goes. Or suffering serves some higher purpose in the order of God's cosmic scheme. Comedy's etiological presentation of suffering, wherein all events stem from some discernable and justifiable cause within God's providential gaze, leads Wendy Farley to associate it with theodicy. Theodicies, such as those featured in previous chapters, assume a comedic worldview insofar as they are predicated on a rational, orderly world that affords the possibility of a logical justification for all suffering.[46]

While theodicies have distinctively modern features, it is easy to read the ancient texts of the Christian tradition, including its tales of wilderness suffering and its resolution, in service of this modern mindset. I have already demonstrated this, suggesting how Abraham's sojourn or Israel's exile can be read to confirm the theological justifications for suffering that theodicies forward. Read comedically in this classical sense, the theological world projected by these stories is scarcely different from those that constitute existing popular theologies of depression, wherein suffering is said to unfold according to an overarching, cosmic coherence.

Hagar's is a different kind of story—a tragic one. Unlike comedic narratives that proceed and conclude according to some encompassing logic, tragedy "does not attempt to penetrate the opacity of evil by providing justification of suffering. It recognizes that certain kinds of suffering are irredeemably unjust," explains Farley.[47] Tragic suffering is nonsensical; it has no warrant in the life of the sufferer or her community. It serves no apparent purpose. As such, tragic suffering "baffle[s] one's capacities to understand, control and restore

---

45. Flora A. Keshgegian, *Time for Hope: Practices for Living in Today's World* (New York: Bloomsbury, 2008), 158.

46. Wendy Farley, *Tragic Vision and Divine Compassion: A Contemporary Theodicy* (Louisville, KY: Westminster John Knox, 1990), 51–52.

47. Farley, *Tragic Vision*, 22.

the situation to a better level."[48] Farley remarks that the injustice of tragic suffering is often most apparent when it befalls a protagonist of clear goodness and innocence. In such instances, "[t]here is nothing to appeal to which would make this suffering meaningful. It is antithetical to even the crudest notions of justice since it cannot be traced to punishment. It is not pedagogical since it cannot strengthen or purify the person. . . . The suffering is raw, unmediated by justice or utility."[49]

Recognizing Hagar's suffering and its analogue, depressive suffering, as inexplicable or tragic suffering opens additional theological possibilities for sufferers grappling with their depression. For Christians who long to understand their suffering in relation to God and the Christian faith but who do not or will not adopt the proposed justifications for suffering required by the prevailing popular theological perspectives on depression, Hagar's story offers another way. Hagar's suffering matters to God. God is present to it. And yet the telling of her story presents no theological justification for this suffering. In so doing, the biblical narrative invites depression sufferers to consider whether their meaningless suffering, too, might be significant to the benevolent God of the Christian faith—the God who is profoundly concerned with and attentive to the suffering and the distraught.

This is another possible response to the double displacement that many Christian depression sufferers experience, as I recounted in chapter 2. Dislocated phenomenologically into the unhomelikeness of depression, some sufferers concomitantly find themselves unable to locate their experience within the parameters of their Christian worldview. They long for the comfort and reassurance of interpreting their suffering in relationship to God and the broader Christian worldview, but they see no way to do so. As I have demonstrated, many other biblical wilderness narratives and Christian popular theologies of depression offer some map by which these sufferers might situate depression in the Christian worldview, but they do so by means of justifying suffering, rationalizing it, assigning suffering a necessary purpose and place in God's plan. Hagar's suffering, in

---

48. Kristine Rankka, *Women and the Value of Suffering: An Aw(e)ful Rowing toward God* (Collegeville, MN: Liturgical Press, 1998), 162.

49. Farley, *Tragic Vision*, 24.

contrast, is significant to God even as it appears to have no inherent purpose or meaning, no "justice or utility" that it serves. Might this be the case for depressive suffering too?[50]

It is important to note that the inexplicability of the suffering of both Hagar and of depression sufferers today does not negate the relevance of other efforts to analyze or explain what this suffering is or how it comes about. As I indicated in chapter 1, scholars and healthcare providers across a range of fields have developed their own accounts of his condition—its origin, its course, corresponding treatments and potential remedies. Many of these scholars are engaged in debates—sometimes quite contentious ones—about whose etiological account of depression is correct. If these debates are someday settled, then it may be possible to offer an empirical explanation for depression. That is, it may be possible to justify it from a scientific or cultural perspective. Even so, this would not negate the claim that, from a theological perspective, depressive suffering often appears nonsensical. It is tragic, and this analogy to Hagar's suffering may help Christians represent and reflect on it as such. Existing and potential empirical explanations for depression do not address the theological questions that this experience raises: Why would God allow this? Why doesn't God rescue me from it? Why do I persist in this difficult landscape of depression? While reflecting on depression with Hagar's suffering in the wilderness does not afford answers to these questions, it can offer one theological lens through which to interpret the confounding suffering of depression in relation to God while these unanswered questions remain.

An Unresolved Wilderness

Another feature of Hagar's story aligns it with the tragic worldview and resists the theological justifications common to other Christian narratives, including many biblical wilderness tales, theodicies, and popular theologies of depression. This feature concerns

---

50. For another exploration of depressive suffering as tragic suffering, see Jessica Coblentz, "Depressive Suffering as Tragic Suffering: Theological Insights and Trajectories," in *Suffering and the Christian Life*, ed. Karen Kilby and Rachel Davies (London: T&T Clark, 2020), 155–162.

the irresolution of Hagar's suffering. Along with the persistence of her suffering itself—a characteristic that is continuous with a great deal of depressive experience, as noted above—there is a theological irresolution in the telling of what Hagar endures: The conclusion of her story does not resolve questions about the purpose of her struggles. Readers are left with that unrelenting *why*—"Why does Hagar suffer so?" As a result, Hagar's suffering remains unjustified across the course of this tale.

To understand the significance of this theological irresolution— both in Hagar's story and, potentially, for theological reflection on depression—a closer look at how narrative resolutions contribute to justifications of suffering is necessary. Here, again, classical narrative frames are illustrative, as the resolution of suffering or lack thereof is a characteristic that distinguishes comedic narratives from tragedies. As noted, comedies are known for the "U" structures of their plot-lines, which culminate in the resolution of a story's central conflict and with it a restoration of peace. The inevitability of this resolution follows from the orderly worldview of the comedic narrative: Because suffering is justified—it has a clear source and purpose within this orderly narrative universe—a path towards its resolution is always latent. Fix the problematic source of suffering or bring the purpose of suffering to its fruition and this comedic suffering will be resolved.

There is, in contrast, uncertainty that follows from unjustified suffering, from suffering that resists explanation, that obeys no reason. Unlike comedic suffering, tragedy "does not offer deliverance into a utopian promised land," Keshgegian explains.[51] It has no clear course. To the point, "At the end of a Shakespearean tragedy, there is more dissolution than resolution. Death abounds. . . . The outcomes do not seem commensurate with the flaws or mistakes" of those who suffer.[52] This is not to say that the experience of suffering never ends in tragic narratives. Consider, for instance, the tragic ending of Shakespeare's *Romeo and Juliet*. The culminating death of the star-crossed lovers ends their suffering, but this ending brings no resolution; it bears no revelation as to why their struggles necessarily

51. Keshgegian, *Time for Hope*, 114.
52. Keshgegian, *Time for Hope*, 111–112.

unfolded as they did. Their suffering remains confounding. Its conclusion offers no retrospective justification. Whereas the resolution of comedic narratives round out the logical coherence of the comedic narrative world, the conclusion of a tragic narrative confronts the audience with the illogic of the suffering it witnesses. Hagar's story is a tragedy in this regard.

The tragic end of Hagar's story comes into greater focus when considered alongside Kristine Rankka's tragic reading of Job, one of the Hebrew Bible's famous sufferers. Of Job's ending, Rankka observes, "God does not *explain* in these final speeches what has happened (by giving reasons for Job's suffering), or reveal an underlying motive for Job's testing (perhaps, to see if his piety was based on a genuine service and love for God as God). Nowhere does God pronounce Job to be guilty of specific misdeeds, but neither does God acquit him of fault or guilt."[53] Like the Book of Job, the end of Hagar's story in Genesis 21 gives no indication that her struggle somehow serves a special purpose after all. There is no repentance from sin or flight from evil that brings resolution to it all. No spiritual achievement or encounter with God brings an end to her precarious situation and suffering. God is present to her pain. God even intervenes in support of the survival of Hagar and her son. But a resolute rescue from the harsh landscape of the wilderness is not what God's intervention brings, and what God brings does not unveil a justification for the wilderness suffering she endures. God's intervention does not explain why she has suffered or goes on suffering. The irresolution of Hagar's story resists the imposition of theological coherence. Even to its end, we cannot make sense of this.

In this way, Hagar's story offers a theological worldview that is not only a departure from some other biblical wilderness tales but also from popular theologies of depression, where claims about the resolution of suffering, promised or realized, logically follow from the explanations they put forth. When, according to interpretations of depression as self-imposed moral evil, one's sin is the occasion for one's suffering, and one's suffering will cease when one repents and the purgative purpose of suffering is fulfilled. Likewise, if suffering

---

53. Rankka, *Women and the Value*, 189–190.

serves some higher purpose, such as facilitating spiritual maturity or spiritual intimacy as in the case of interpretations of depression as divine instruction, then some will assume that suffering will cease once this purpose is accomplished. In both scenarios, a promise of depression's end follows from its justifying purpose. These lines of theological reasoning sometimes work in reverse, too: When one's depression ceases, some Christians adopt one of these popular explanations for their suffering in retrospect, as if to claim some explanation for why their depression finally came to an end.

In contrast, Hagar "experiences exodus without liberation, revelation without salvation, wilderness without covenant, wanderings without land, promise without fulfillment, and unmerited exile without return."[54] As such, her story has the potential to both affirm the experienced irrationality and irresolution of depression and, in so doing, withhold any imposition of intellectual coherence onto it. Her story projects a theological world where suffering is as tragic as depression often feels. Hagar's story reminds us that the persistent senselessness and the unresolved questions of tragic suffering are not antithetical to the Christian worldview. The experienced tragedy of depression need not distance sufferers from their Christian faith—though it may distance them from certain interpretations of Christianity that presume the world to be logical, consistent, and always transparent to human reason.

A Wilderness Where God Is

While Hagar's story of suffering in the wilderness withholds both theological justification and resolution, it does offer a portrait of a personal and life-giving God who is concerned with those who suffer. To depression sufferers, then, Genesis 21 offers the possibility of divine presence amid tragedy. In contrast to classic theodicies and popular theologies of depression, her story does not reconcile the seeming illogic of a good God's personal concern for Hagar's suffering, on one hand, and the persistence of her wilderness experience, on the other. It simply affirms that *it is so* and validates

54. Trible, *Texts of Terror*, 28.

that even tragic suffering, such as depression, is not antithetical to a perspective of faith: Sometimes wilderness suffering is as senseless as it feels, and a good and powerful God sees it and responds as it persists without inherent purpose.

Rather than distancing sufferers from God by withholding answers to the myriad questions of "why" that suffering often rouses, the tragic worldview of stories like Hagar's can actually orient Christians beyond the limits of their own understanding toward the transcendent God. "What a tragic vision of reality . . . helps us recognize is that we cannot approach some of our deepest experiences with rationality and reliance on our virtue alone," Rankka contends.

> It encourages in us, at times, a willingness to relinquish explanation and a desire to find cause or fault when they no longer enlighten our suffering or move us to make concrete changes to alleviate our own or others' suffering. In so doing, a tragic vision can move us into an approach toward suffering that incorporates ambiguity, paradox, and mystery. Such a view of reality can lead, paradoxically, away from despair when all one's best efforts fall short and can lead to placing one's trust and hope in something beyond this radical contingency.[55]

To be clear, Rankka does not claim that a turn to the transcendent necessarily follows from a confrontation with the senselessness of tragic suffering. Certainly, not all depression sufferers have this response to their own suffering, even when they see it as tragic. But against critics who see tragedy as antithetical to the Christian worldview because of its inability to rationally account for how God makes good on suffering or to rationally reconcile a benevolent God with the persistence of inexplicable pain, Rankka affirms other valid, Christian theological possibilities engendered by representations of tragic suffering.

Thus, rather than resigning sufferers to double displacement, seeing depressive suffering as tragic suffering—seeing it as suffering akin to Hagar's in the wilderness—can "[lead] one to recognize, acknowledge, and accept one's insufficiency [when it comes to understanding

---

55. Rankka, *Women and the Value*, 199.

suffering] and therefore, one's need for the transcendent, for God. In so doing it opens us to the activity of God's grace in our lives in new ways."[56] That is, instead of erasing, denying, or simplifying the senselessness of suffering, naming depressive suffering as tragic suffering can broaden the Christian theological worldview to include the coexistence of a benevolent God and meaningless suffering. In the process, "Tragedy can move us, perhaps, to reflect ever more concretely and deeply about our images, metaphors, and experiences of God in our particular historical realities and social locations, and to weave these into a tapestry that includes all aspects of life as we know it."[57]

Is this not, in fact, what unfolds for Hagar? Amid senseless circumstances that she is helpless to understand or navigate by her own means, Hagar, like many tragic sufferers, turns to God. Of Genesis 21, Tamez observes: "She cries desperately, without the slightest hope. God speaks to her from the heavens (Elohistic style), and asks her: What is the trouble Hagar? God didn't ask her about the past, or the future"—as God does in Genesis 16—"only the present."[58] Tamez continues, "Her present is agony, anxiety and desperation. . . . Now she is in the desert, alone, with her dying child, without the possibility of returning to the tribe, because she had been thrown out, and there is no spring from which to drink. For this reason, at this moment, this hour, the present, she cries in desperation. She is not thinking of the past or the future, only of the desperate need of the present."[59] Tellingly, notes Tamez, "Hagar doesn't answer, perhaps because God gave her no opportunity to speak, or perhaps because the situation said everything, and silence speaks more loudly."[60] Hagar's bafflement and desperation are not met with an explanatory reply. God's response does not bestow understanding or justification. The story extends no theological resolution.

What God does bestow is presence, and with that presence, Hagar gains the perception of possibilities previously unrecognized. "God,

56. Rankka, *Women and the Value*, 204.
57. Rankka, *Women and the Value*, 202.
58. Tamez, "Woman Who Complicated," 15.
59. Tamez, "Woman Who Complicated," 15–16.
60. Tamez, "Woman Who Complicated," 16.

in solidarity, comforts her. . . . Before giving her water God gives her courage, spirit, and hope," suggests Tamez.[61] Still, God's attention leaves unresolved both the theological questions that accompany Hagar's distress as well as much of the difficulty of the situation itself. Yes, "God succeeds in instilling hope in Hagar. She revives. God opens her eyes (v. 19a), and she becomes capable of seeing a well of water (v. 19b). She fills her wine-skin with water and gives it to her son to drink (v. 19c)."[62] God "makes a way out of no way," as Dolores Williams famously puts it. But, in doing so, God does not rescue Hagar from this desolate landscape. Rather, as Tamez explains, "Hagar simply has to stop crying, in spite of everything. She has to pick herself up, pick up the child and teach him to struggle against the hardships of the desert. She has to take hold of the hand of the child forcefully, that is to say with strength, and courage."[63] Hagar's life-saving action appears tied to her encounter with God. Even so, it does not resolve the theological perplexities of her situation nor relieve her of a precarious life of wilderness wandering. God's response to her suffering does not bestow understanding or justification. Why Hagar? Why stranded here? We do not know, but we do see that the God who is beyond comprehension attends to Hagar's struggle and opens her and her son to unforeseen possibilities for survival.

In sum, Hagar's story represents God's attention to and concern for the one who suffers innocently in the harsh and lonely landscape of the wilderness. God's presence is not understood in light of any justifications or promised resolutions. This is who God has revealed Godself to be: As Hagar put it, this is "the God Who Sees."

Depression as a Hagaric Wilderness

Seeing one's suffering in and through the theological lens of Hagar's suffering may strike some depression sufferers as unsatisfying precisely because it leaves unresolved the perennial question of why this suffering has come about. For others, this could be the appeal of the theological world disclosed in her story: It represents, rather

61. Tamez, "Woman Who Complicated," 16.
62. Tamez, "Woman Who Complicated," 16.
63. Tamez, "Woman Who Complicated," 16.

than elides, this confounding struggle and the theological challenge that depressive suffering presents. Unlike other theologies of suffering—including popular theologies, modern theodicies, and even those that can be garnered from other biblical tales of the wilderness—Hagar's narrative represents suffering in a Christian frame without justifying it before God. This suffering *just is*.

Parker Palmer reflects on the significance of affirming unjustified suffering for some who struggle with depression. He recalls a conversation he had with a woman seeking his spiritual counsel. Speaking of depression, she asks, "Why do some kill themselves yet others get well?" she inquired. *Why?* Palmer recounts:

> I knew that her question came from her own struggle to stay alive, so I wanted to answer with care. But I could come up with only one response. "I have no idea. I really have no idea." After she left, I was haunted by regret. Couldn't I have found something more helpful to say, even if it were not true? A few days later, she sent me a letter saying that of all the things we had talked about, the words that stayed with her were "I have no idea." My response had given her an alternative to the cruel 'Christian explanations' common in the church to which she belonged—that people who take their lives lack faith or good works or some other redeeming virtue that might move God to rescue them. Not knowing had freed her to stop judging herself for being depressed and to stop believing that God was judging her. As a result, her depression had lifted a bit.[64]

Again, not everyone will welcome representations of depression as inexplicable suffering, and certainly not everyone will experience the accompanying relief of symptoms that this woman did upon encountering this view. But for those whose experiences and theologies clash with the theological justifications for depressive suffering that prevail in the U.S. Christian context, they may welcome a biblical representation of wilderness suffering that answers our "why?" with a response like Palmer's: I really have no idea. Similarly, Rankka tells us, "a tragic sensibility keeps the question of 'why suffering?'

---

64. Parker Palmer, *Let Your Life Speak* (San Francisco: Jossey-Bass, 1999), 59.

open, and reduces the possibilities of doctrinal triumphalism and claims to absolute truth that do less to help a radical sufferer than to shore up rational justifications for violence, self-sacrifice, passive acceptance, and silence."[65]

Palmer notes how countercultural it is to entertain the possibility that depressive suffering is unjustified—that it is inexplicable before God and humankind:

> Depression demands that we reject simplistic answers, both "religious" and "scientific," and learn to embrace mystery, something our culture resists. Mystery surrounds every deep experience of the human heart: the deeper we go into the heart's darkness or its light, the closer we get to the ultimate mystery of God. But our culture wants to turn mysteries into puzzles to be explained and problems to be solved, because maintaining the illusion that we can "straighten things out" makes us feel powerful. Yet mysteries never yield to solutions or fixes—and when we pretend that they do, life becomes not only more banal but also more hopeless, because the fixes never work.[66]

The truth of Hagar's suffering—and of the struggle of depression—may be that there are simply no apparent theological reasons or purposes for them, despite how badly we long for such justifications in the context that Palmer describes. Recognizing the persistent theological incoherence of depressive suffering invites a different theological perspective than the one we witness in the Christian justifications of depression that we have examined so far. As I have shown in this chapter, reading the Hagaric wilderness experience as a scriptural analogue for depression engenders one such alternative, for it brings this contemporary experience of suffering into a Christian milieu, both phenomenologically and theologically, without eliding the enduring mystery of this condition's reason for being.

65. Rankka, *Women and the Value*, 203.
66. Palmer, *Let Your Life Speak*, 60.

Chapter 7

God and Salvation in the Wilderness of Depression

Early in chapter 2, I noted Richard Sparks's observation that Christian reflection on suffering "involves one's concept of human nature (anthropology) as well as one's image of God (theology). For Christians, one also incorporates the message and person of Jesus (christology) and one's notion of redemption (soteriology)."[1] In other words, realities of suffering concern the whole Christian theological enterprise. My analyses of existing popular theologies of depression, the critiques brought against them, and various stories of harsh landscapes from the biblical canon, including that of Hagar, have demonstrated some of these interconnections. These analyses have also revealed how theological claims about suffering hinge on implicit and sometimes explicit claims about who God is, how and why God acts in relation to suffering, and how sufferers and those who accompany them ought to respond to this suffering in turn.

This chapter and the next continue to examine the interconnections of suffering and various Christian theological loci. Whereas chapter 6 centered on how a tragic theological reading of Hagar's story can support a Christian interpretation of depression that

---

1. Richard Sparks, "Suffering," in *The New Dictionary of Catholic Spirituality*, ed. Michael Downey (Collegeville, MN: Liturgical Press, 1993), 950.

withholds justifications of suffering and the imposition of meaning onto it, these chapters develop this interpretation of suffering in relation to three other intersecting theological topics, demonstrating how reflection on depression as a Hagaric wilderness can further expand and develop the Christian theological landscape available to sufferers and other people of faith. First, in this chapter, I reflect further on the representation of God's presence to and concern for suffering in Hagar's story and consider its potential pertinence for ongoing theological reflection among those living with the perceived endlessness, isolation, and helplessness of depression. Second, with the aid of Delores Williams, I explore an image of salvation that emerges from Hagar's wilderness experience and its repercussions for hope amid the wilderness of depression. Third, in chapter 8, I consider the implications of Hagar's story for the practice of Christian discipleship among those who accompany depression sufferers. Altogether, my reflection on these overlapping theological topics fill in the tragic theological worldview projected by Hagar's story, which I offer for the ongoing consideration of depression sufferers and those who accompany them. For that reason, the narratives of depression sufferers continue to shape this theological reflection.

The God Who Sees

What is the significance of the image of God in the Hagar story for ongoing theological reflection on depression? In the previous chapter, I highlighted God's presence and concern for Hagar's tragic suffering and emphasized what this image of God is *not*. Namely, it is not a depiction of God that imposes a justification for the suffering that God attends to. Here, I reflect further on what this representation of God might afford to sufferers who endure the unhomelikeness of depression and who often concomitantly struggle to interpret this experience in light of the Christian faith.

Recall how, in Genesis 16, the God of the Israelites finds Hagar weeping in the wilderness. The Lord speaks of her pregnancy and instructs Hagar to name her son "Ishmael," which means "God hears." In turn, Hagar declares, "You are El-roi," meaning, "the God who sees." In this exchange, God reveals Godself in word and deed as one who personally attends to Hagar and her offspring, as one who hears and sees them. In naming God and in naming her son Ishmael, Hagar affirms that this is indeed what her encounter with God reveals. It should not surprise us, then, that amid Hagar's senseless suffering and despair in Genesis 21, she cries out to this God who she has already come to know as attentive and concerned. She pleads for the life of her child, who is on the verge of death. God once again responds with reassurance, and, more still, God "opened her eyes and she saw a well of water. She went, and filled the skin with water, and gave the boy a drink" (v. 19). Though the figure of Hagar fades into the background of the story as the chapter concludes (as often happens to women in the Scriptures), the text assures us that "God was with the boy" as he grows up alongside his mother in the desolate landscape of Paran (vv. 20-21).

Delores Williams observes that representations of God's presence differ slightly between Genesis 16 and 21 due to their distinct authorship: "Unlike the Yahwist narrative (Genesis 16), the Elohist narrative (Genesis 21) does not present an image of an immanent deity. Rather, in Genesis 21, God is transcendent, calling down to Hagar from heaven."[2] Nevertheless, God's attention to and care for the suffering Hagar and Ishmael remains consistent across these accounts. God is with Hagar and then with the pair as they live on in the wilderness.

In the previous chapter, I noted that this revelation already differentiates God's character from depictions of the divine forwarded in theodicies and popular theologies of depression. Theologies that cast depression as a self-imposed moral evil present a distant and uninvolved deity whose indifference to suffering is predicated on the original justice of God's creation. In such a world, humans get what they deserve, so God can rightly look on unconcerned. This is not the God revealed in Hagar's story, the God who sees and hears. Likewise, the God Who Sees is not the "sadist God" of theologies that cast depression as a necessary site of divine instruction. In those theologies, God's presence serves to justify suffering, to explain it

---

2. Delores Williams, *Sisters in the Wilderness: The Challenge of Womanist God-Talk* (Maryknoll, NY: Orbis, 1993), 29.

for some higher purpose. Because God is involved, the suffering is presumed to be good. No such justification accompanies the revelation of the God Who Sees, and God's contribution to the survival of Hagar and her son does not validate or sacralize her suffering. Her suffering remains illogical, and God is nevertheless present and working for good in their midst. The latter does not negate the former, as in theologies of depression as divine instruction.

The Unmoored God

Though this image of God is distinct from those in popular theologies of depression, it aligns with affirmations of God's presence and concern for creation that can be found throughout Scripture and the Christian theological tradition. Paul Crowley captures these divine characteristics in his reflections on "the unmoored God," a description that uniquely speaks to the spatial imagery of depression narratives and the story of Hagar. According to Crowley, the Hebrew Scriptures reveal that "this God who has heard the cries of his people will be located in the midst of their suffering, not in a fixed place." He continues, "God dwells with his people, and in fact emphasizes that this belongs to his nature: the chosen people come to know this God by letting him enter into the depths of their suffering as they wander through the desert."[3] These stories of God's indwelling are remarkable in view of God's simultaneous Otherness relative to creation. All throughout the Scriptures, we witness how God traverses this ontological distance to be with God's people. The presence of the Holy Spirit at work in the world—from the *ruah*, the "breath" or "spirit," that hovers over the deep in the creation narrative of Genesis 1 to the sending of the Spirit in Acts 2 and beyond—is but another iteration of God's elected dislocation for the sake of dwelling with and among God's creation. In Christ, "[t]he Christian story recalls that God has voluntarily undertaken a divine dislocation, captured in the Christian doctrine of the Incarnation of the Son," writes Crowley.[4] Here again, he frames the divine *kenosis* of the Incarnation in

---

3. Paul Crowley, SJ, *The Unmoored God: Believing in a Time of Dislocation* (Maryknoll, NY: Orbis, 2017), 34.

4. Crowley, *Unmoored God*, 51.

resonant spatial terms as God's willful dislocation for the sake of presence to and reconciliation with all of creation.

That God in God's very nature enters into creation's suffering and dwells among those who wander in the wilderness is revealed in the incarnation but also in the specific actions of Jesus Christ during his life. There are numerous examples of Christ's willingness to traverse literal and figurative boundaries to be present with those who suffer. Ronald Rolheiser points us to one example in his reflections on suicide. Alluding to resurrection appearances in the Gospel of John where the resurrected Christ walks through walls (20:19, 26), Rolheiser writes, "Jesus assures us . . . that God's love can go through locked doors and into broken places and free up what's paralyzed and help that which can no longer help itself. God is not blocked when we are. God can reach through."[5]

Finding Comfort in Images of Divine Presence

Among those who find themselves helplessly trapped in a world closed off from others, one that appears without possibilities for escape, the image of a God who is present and concerned for their suffering—like a God who meets Hagar in the wilderness, or the unmoored God who dwells among those who find themselves senselessly suffering and helpless to escape their situation, or the person of Jesus, who walks through walls to dwell among those who are scared and distraught—might resonate among sufferers who strain to find some sense of connection and personal belonging to remedy the radical isolation of their condition. Though such an affirmation of divine presence will not register with the experiences or longings of all depression sufferers, it may be amenable to those in search of a representation of divine presence that does not entail claims about suffering's necessity and meaning.

Indeed, some depression memoirs evince the significance of this portrait of God. The significance of God's presence to and concern for suffering is central to the memoir of theologian Monica Coleman, for example. As I noted in chapter 2, Coleman's experience with depression

---

5. Ronald Rolheiser, *Bruised and Wounded: Struggling to Understand Suicide* (Brewster, MA: Paraclete, 2018), 21.

exemplifies the double displacement that many people of faith experience as they struggle not only with depressive suffering itself but also with its unsettling implications for their previous vision of God as Christians. Coleman's memoir charts her journey from theological loss to a discovery of a God of radical presence. Of her early struggles with depression, she recounts, "Inside . . . I was gray. Listless and groundless. The faith that believed that God would deliver dissipated over. I had gotten in the habit of turning to God. . . . But all of sudden, I couldn't. It's not that I didn't want to. I just couldn't. I didn't trust God to take care of me. I didn't trust God to hear me. And I didn't trust the church to understand."[6] However, Coleman's perception of how God relates to her suffering shifts after her encounter with process theology in graduate school. "Process thought talks about a God who is radically present. It explains that God is present with everyone at all times in all things. God is not just present with us but knows us better than anyone else. God knows us from the inside out."[7] For Coleman, this image of God was part of what restored and sustained her authentic experience of faith amid depression, and it supported her ability to persist amid the challenges of her condition. She testifies, "If I can believe—in the midst of my most wordless, painful, razor-shiny moments—that God isn't doing this to me, then that is an act of faith. If I can believe that God hears me, knows me, loves me, and rocks me, then that is a leap of faith. I don't need more than that. . . . The leap to believe that God does not abandon me is all I need."[8]

Similarly, David Finnegan-Hosey writes of the significance of the image of a present and caring God during his hospitalizations for depression. Like Coleman, Finnegan-Hosey juxtaposes an image of divine presence to other perceptions of God that seemed irrelevant in his suffering state:

> A mighty yet distant king was of no use to me in the psych ward. I already felt disconnected and distant. . . . The image of God as a

---

6. Monica Coleman, *Bipolar Faith: A Black Woman's Journey in Depression and Faith* (Minneapolis: Fortress, 2016), 182.

7. Coleman, *Bipolar Faith*, 202.

8. Coleman, *Bipolar Faith*, 342.

distant king, or even a rarely available doctor, only worked to exacerbate my suffering. But God as a companion, healer, or caretaker? All of these images, in both biblical and modern-day forms, were able to get in underneath my pain and shore up my fragile sense that I was not alone and that I might even be able to survive at all.[9]

Finnegan-Hosey connects this image of divine presence and concern to his need for a sense of belonging as he struggles to survive depression, and suicidologists tell us that addressing this need is crucial. Thomas Joiner argues that helping sufferers rediscover a sense of belonging is one of the most lifesaving measures one can extend to someone struggling with a desire for death. "The fact that those who die by suicide experience isolation and withdrawal before their deaths is among the clearest in all the literature on suicide," he explains.[10] This dangerous experience of isolation is at least partially objective in that actual interactions with others are crucial for sustaining a sense of belonging.[11] Ultimately, though, one's sense of belonging hinges on whether these interactions are satisfying for the sufferer, on whether they leave one feeling cared about.[12]

To the point, Finnegan-Hosey writes that for as helpful as perceptions of divine presence were for him, such images of God cannot be imposed by others as a fix for the theological displacement and personal doubts that many sufferers experience amid their depression.[13] "Had visitors shared their intellectual or even their initial emotional responses, they would have gone unheard. 'But David,' people could have said, 'God is always with you, even in this difficult time.'. . . But, from within the storm of mental illness, I could not always hear that truth."[14] Finnegan-Hosey's warning calls to mind the methodological parameters of chapter 4, reminding us that images

---

9. David Finnegan-Hosey, *Christ on the Psych Ward* (New York: Church Publishing, 2018), 84–85.

10. Thomas Joiner, *Why People Die by Suicide* (Cambridge, MA: Harvard University, 2005), 122.

11. Joiner, *Why People Die by Suicide*, 96–97.

12. Joiner, *Why People Die by Suicide*, 97.

13. Finnegan-Hosey, *Christ on the Psych Ward*, 38.

14. Finnegan-Hosey, *Christ on the Psych Ward*, 38.

of divine presence such as the one we encounter in the Hagar story should not be imposed for moral reasons and also for the practical reason he states here.

At the same time, the significance of these images for depression sufferers such as Coleman and Finnegan-Hosey suggests that it is important to find proper avenues to introduce sufferers to these images of God for consideration on their own terms. Both Coleman and Finnegan-Hosey encountered some of these theological resources in their formal, graduate-level theological education—a formative spiritual and educational opportunity unavailable to most Christians. Extending such resources beyond the academy is imperative, especially in view of Joiner's charge that one ought to do what one can to help those who are suicidal to restore a sense of belonging to their lives. For Christian sufferers, the revelation of God's persistent presence and concern for Hagar amid her senseless suffering, along with other images of divine presence, may be part of this. For some, they could serve as an invitation to encounter a God who cares—a God who sees and hears those who suffer in the wilderness of depression.

The Metaphysics of Divine Presence

Theologians may note from the examples of Coleman and Finnegan-Hosey that distinct metaphysical claims about God inform their discussions of divine presence. Coleman's understanding of divine presence is grounded in the Whiteheadian metaphysics of process theology. More radically than most Christian theological traditions, process theology describes God as not only present to human suffering but also suffering in and through human sufferers. Furthermore, God's suffering in and through human suffering changes God's own self.[15] Finnegan-Hosey does not align himself with process theology, but divine compassion remains a central feature of the image of divine presence in his theological reflection on depression. Joining some other theologians who emphasize divine transcendence more than process thought but who nevertheless affirm divine passibility, Finnegan-Hosey asserts the significance of encountering a God

---

15. Coleman, *Bipolar Faith*, 202–203.

who suffers in solidarity with those who suffer depression, which he expresses through repeated applications of Jürgen Moltmann's theology to the context of depression.[16] There are still others who might affirm God's presence to and concern for suffering while diverging from Coleman's process theology as well as Finnegan-Hosey's suggestion of divine passibility.

Christian claims about divine presence and care are not exclusive to a single position on divine metaphysics, and the witness of these depression sufferers indicates that what is consistently and personally significant for them traverses a range of theological positions. It is the underlying affirmation of divine presence and care for sufferers that these individuals ultimately endorse. Thus, as between the Yahwist and Elohist representations of divine presence in Genesis 16 and Genesis 21, these examples affirm God's presence and concern as a central feature of God, regardless of how exactly God is metaphysically involved with those who suffer in the wilderness.

That these depression memoirs suggest a range of views on how, metaphysically, God is present and concerned with suffering does not mean rigorous theological reflection on issues such as divine passibility are necessarily irrelevant to depression sufferers who reflect on God's relationship to their suffering. For some sufferers, staking out a particular position on the metaphysics that inform their affirmation of divine presence and concern may be important and generative.[17] However, theologians who accompany sufferers in reflection on the nature of God's presence and concern for their suffering should beware of the tendency of theologians to slip into theodical thinking and second- and third-person impositions when it comes to this topic. Karen Kilby notes that these metaphysical debates are often (though not always) occasioned by the demands

---

16. Finnegan-Hosey, *Christ on the Psych Ward*, 26, 36–37.

17. For example, some argue that claims of divine passibility can result in the imposition of meaning onto suffering, for locating suffering within God's own nature inadvertently valorizes human suffering, thus undermining the tragic affirmation of suffering's meaninglessness. Theologians, for ethical and methodological reasons, and sufferers, for the sake of working out their own interpretations of God and suffering, may be interested in wading into these debates.

of modern theodicy, and positions on whether and how God suffers with those who suffer are regularly presented as responses to questions of *why* God permits suffering at all.[18] This need not be the case, however, and it should not be the case for Christians who are exercising the theological restraint that Kilby exhorts.

Salvation in the Wilderness[19]

The revelation of God in Hagar's story is not limited to God's presence and concern for suffering. It also discloses a God at work in Hagar's situation of suffering. God's presence results in new possibilities for life when God opens Hagar's eyes to a well of water in Genesis 21:19. Whereas previously Hagar did not perceive this vital resource, the opening of her eyes allows her to hydrate her dying son and presumably continue to live in the difficult terrain of the wilderness.

This glimpse of God's work in a context of tragic suffering has implications for how Christians might conceive of salvation in contexts of depressive suffering. Broadly speaking, salvation is the process by which God in Jesus Christ and through the Holy Spirit brings creation into right relationship with Godself. That God does this is a central tenet of Christianity; how God does this is and always has been a matter of theological dispute, however. At the origin of Christianity's soteriological diversity is an array of scriptural images that theologians have drawn upon to convey God's transformative work, including images of redemption, atonement, reconciliation, sacrifice, expiation, justification, sanctification, regeneration, and liberation, among others.[20] Theologians draw upon these images of God's saving work to develop doctrinal theories, which Robin Ryan characterizes in terms of "first-level" and "second-level" reflection: "The images

18. See Karen Kilby, "Evil and the Limits of Theology," *New Blackfriars* 84, no. 983 (January 2003): 20.

19. Parts of this section are adapted from Jessica Coblentz, "The Possibilities of Grace amid Persistent Depression," *Theological Studies* 80, no. 3 (September 2019): 554–571.

20. Gerald O'Collins, *Jesus Our Redeemer: A Christian Approach to Salvation* (New York: Oxford University, 2007), 3–10.

and metaphors of first-level language 'show' God's redeeming action, while theories attempt to 'explain' God's redeeming action."[21]

Delores Williams on Salvation as Survival

What does the story of Hagar reveal about the salvific effects of God's loving presence in the context of depressive suffering? Delores Williams's *Sisters in the Wilderness* engages the story of Hagar to make a pivotal contribution to theological reflection on how salvation manifests in history. Williams's most famous soteriological argument from this book concerns Hagar's role as a forced surrogate for Sarah. Drawing on the Hagar narrative and the history of African American women's roles as forced and hired surrogates for white women, Williams critiques the theory of substitutionary atonement, one of the more prevalent "second-order" soteriologies in Christian history.[22] However, it is another soteriological contribution from Williams's project—one concerning "first-order" images of salvation—that I lift up as a potentially rich starting point for reflection on salvation and depressive suffering.

Williams's argument begins with her observations about the state of soteriological reflection in Black liberation theology. Writing in 1993, Williams observes that Black liberation theology had focused on "liberation" as the primary image for God's saving work in history. This emphasis focused scholars on biblical stories and promises of salvific liberation for the oppressed, stories in which male characters are often central. Though Williams affirms the history and importance of God's liberating work in the biblical narrative and in the African American community, she argues that its predominance in Black liberation theology elides other critical images of salvation, including those lifted up by Black women throughout African American history.[23] In addition to the liberation tradition of African American biblical appropriation, Williams observes a second tradition that "emphasized female activity and de-emphasized male

---

21. Robin Ryan, *Jesus and Salvation: Soundings in the Christian Tradition and Contemporary Theology* (Collegeville, MN: Liturgical Press, 2015), xvi.

22. Williams, *Sisters in the Wilderness*, 143–151.

23. Williams, *Sisters in the Wilderness*, 1–2, 128–143, 173–176.

authority. . . . For more than a hundred years Hagar—the African slave of the Hebrew woman Sarah—has appeared in the deposits of African-American culture."[24]

Williams proceeds to argue that salvation in the story of Hagar is not manifest in divine liberation from suffering, as in the Exodus narrative at the center of so much Black theology, but rather in God's enduring presence amid persistent suffering and in the divine gift of possibilities for survival and for improvements in one's quality of life. In the wilderness, which, for Hagar and so many Black women, is "a near-destruction situation," God gives "personal direction to the believer and thereby helps her make a way out of what she thought was no way."[25] In the case of Hagar, "God gave her new vision to see survival resources where she saw none before."[26] In so doing, "God's response to Hagar's (and her child's) situation was survival and involvement in their development of an appropriate quality of life, that is, appropriate to their situation and their heritage."[27]

Salvation as Survival: An Affirmation of Black Women's Experiences

Reclaiming this image of salvation is important to Williams because it reflects the discernable work of God amid African American women's own suffering throughout history. African American women long identified with Hagar's story in part because their own senseless suffering, like Hagar's, persists without liberation. As long as Black liberation theology focuses on liberation alone, it misses not only aspects of God's salvific work in the Scriptures but also the experiences of Black women, past and present. "In black consciousness, God's response of survival and quality of life to Hagar is God's response of survival and quality of life to African-American women and mothers of slave descent struggling to sustain their families with God's help," explains Williams.[28] "Many black women have

---

24. Williams, *Sisters in the Wilderness*, 2.
25. Williams, *Sisters in the Wilderness*, 96.
26. Williams, *Sisters in the Wilderness*, 29–30.
27. Williams, *Sisters in the Wilderness*, 5.
28. Williams, *Sisters in the Wilderness*, 5.

testified that 'God helped them make a way out of no way.' They believe God is involved not only in their survival struggle, but that God also supports their struggle for quality of life, which 'making a way' suggests."[29] In this, we find an example of the ambivalence that has often characterized Christian theological reflection on the wilderness: The harrowing realities of suffering persist, yet God sometimes works for some good in their midst.

Exploring Williams's image of salvation as survival/quality of life in the context of depression is not necessarily a departure from her original proposal. Like many other womanist theologians, Williams is attuned to and concerned for the profound psychological distress endured by Black women, whose distinctive experiences of oppression can engender and magnify experiences of trauma, anxiety, and depression. Williams notes this explicitly at times, linking this history of psychological suffering to the importance of her soteriological proposal: "Several black scholars have suggested a bond in black American heritage between the survival/quality-of-life struggle and the community's belief in God's presence in the struggle. Historian John Blassingame points to this reality in the slave community when it claims that . . . 'In short religion helped him preserve his mental health. Trust in God was conducive to psychic health insofar as it excluded all anxiety-producing preoccupations by the recognition of a loving presence.' "[30] Bringing Williams's account of God's salvific work into conversation with contemporary experiences of depression is thus an affirmation of Williams's original insight that this image has already resonated with Black women who experience conditions such as depression. It is furthermore an invitation to individuals and communities of all races to learn from and engage this theological insight born of Black women's experiences and theological reflection: Sometimes God's saving work manifests in the expansion of possibilities for survival and improved quality of life.[31]

29. Williams, *Sisters in the Wilderness*, 5.

30. Williams, *Sisters in the Wilderness*, 5–6.

31. Williams points to theologians in other marginalized communities who have likewise explored survival as an instantiation of God's saving work, including Ada Maria Isasi-Díaz and Yolanda Tarango. See *Sisters in the Wilderness*, 264n29.

Salvation, Not Liberation; Incorporation, Not Cure

Though I point to the potential relevance of Williams's critique of liberation soteriology and her proposal of salvation as survival/quality of life for depression sufferers, this is not to say that sufferers do not wish for liberation from their depression, to be sure. Vividly reminding us of this, Andrew Solomon remembers a difficult episode of depression, when, "In the tightest corner of my bed, split and racked by this thing no one else seemed to be able to see, I prayed to a God I had never entirely believed in, and I asked for deliverance."[32] Liberation is precisely what Solomon and many sufferers request of God. David Karp argues that social factors inform sufferers' focus on deliverance from suffering as the necessary means by which they can go on living a good life—or go on living at all. In his research on depression sufferers in Boston, he observes how modern medicine bolsters an often-singular focus on liberation from depression, for it unequivocally pathologizes suffering and strives for its elimination, mostly by way of medicinal remedy. Medicine teaches sufferers that depression, like other medical conditions and diseases, are the enemy of the body from which the embattled sufferer requires rescue. And though modern medicine offers a decidedly secular framing of depression, Karp and some of his interviewees link its framework to Christian interpretations of suffering that likewise address suffering, and thus depression by implication, as an enemy of the body from which humans require liberation.[33]

Depression sufferers often desire liberation—by medicine, or by God, or by anyone—and understandably so. Yet while many sufferers turn to modern medicine determined to "fix" the "problem" of their suffering, many never experience a decisive cure, and accord-

---

Articulations of non-liberative soteriologies that are in some ways compatible with Williams's description of salvation as survival include Ivone Gebara, *Out of the Depths: Women's Experience of Evil and Salvation* (Minneapolis: Fortress, 2002); Shelly Rambo, *Spirit and Trauma: A Theology of Remaining* (Louisville, KY: Westminster John Knox, 2010); and Serene Jones, *Trauma and Grace: Theology in a Ruptured World*, 3rd ed. (Louisville, KY: Westminster John Knox, 2009).

32. Andrew Solomon, *The Noonday Demon: An Atlas of Depression* (New York: Scribner, 2001), 19.

33. David Karp, *Speaking of Sadness: Depression, Disconnection, and the Meanings of Illness*, updated and expanded ed. (New York: Oxford University, 2016), 242–245.

ing to Karp, "even among those who experience[e] a 'miracle' and [feel] 'saved' by medication, several eventually have other episodes of depression and become *disenchanted* with drugs."[34] Consequently, many reach the conclusion that liberation from their suffering may not materialize. "As the reality of pain's permanence sinks in, the goal shifts from eradicating depression to living with it," Karp notes.[35] This occasions a "new approach" to suffering that "involves fighting against depression as best they can while constructing a life premised on its continuing presence."[36] This often initiates a process of opening oneself to something other than liberation from depression, unideal as any alternative may be.

For example, one of Karp's interviewees recalls her "wanting to get out" of depression "and realizing that you can't get out." "That to me is like a tragic realization," she explains. "That you can't get out. And that's the way the cookie crumbles, as they say. Why you and not someone else, I don't know. And that leaves me with a feeling of real sadness and disappointment in life. And that's what I tried to make sense of. . . . I don't believe that, you know, I'll ever be a happy person. And, when I stopped believing that is when I started to get better."[37] In the case of Karp's interviewee, accepting that she would "never be a happy person" led to an alternative self-understanding and vision of hope for her life. She explains, "I believe that people hobble along, and you can learn to limp gracefully and nobly, or you know, you can scream about it."[38] This image of limping "gracefully and nobly" highlights a crucial dimension of this transformative shift, which Karp calls "incorporation." Sufferers are not only accepting the limitations of depression but also affirming that possibilities of dignity, meaningfulness, and goodness might be compatible with it—possibilities previously unforeseen when they were singularly invested in liberation from their condition. He observes that incorporation "involved a cognitive and attitudinal shift from the medical

34. Karp, *Speaking of Sadness*, 181.
35. Karp, *Speaking of Sadness*, 236.
36. Karp, *Speaking of Sadness*, 242.
37. Karp, *Speaking of Sadness*, 239–240.
38. Karp, *Speaking of Sadness*, 239–240.

language of cure to the spiritual language of transformation" amid the continuing presence of depression.[39]

Beyond Karp's study, other depression sufferers testify to the life-giving effects of this shift in perception. Daphne Merkin explains, "I once dreamed of conquering my depression for good, but I have come to understand that it is a chronic condition, as much a part of me as my literary bent."[40] She continues, "If I can't quite declare victory over my depression, I am giving it a run for its money, navigating around it, reminding myself that the opposite of depression is not a state of unimaginable happiness but a state of approximate contentment, of relative all-right-ness."[41] Merkin's reflection mirrors a shift across many narratives of chronic and recurring depression, where sufferers recount the realization that what actually facilitates an improved quality of life is not the absolute eradication of their suffering but the expansion of possibilities that one experiences amid enduring depression. In other words, living with depression is not a matter of liberation, but survival and improved quality of life.

Offering another example, Monica Coleman writes,

> I remember the day my therapist asked me to stop thinking of depression as an enemy. I cut my eyes at her and scowled. *Are you joking? Something inside of me can take me out, and I'm not supposed to fight it?* Author and teacher Parker J. Palmer writes of this cogently in his book *Let Your Life Speak*. He recalls a therapist saying, "You seem to look upon depression as the hand of an enemy trying to crush you. . . . Do you think you could see it instead as the hand of a friend pressing you down to ground on which it is safe to stand?" "Friend"? Could a depressive condition be a friend? Could it be a part of myself to explore, to understand, and accept? It's taken me years to stretch my original understanding of depression to one that refuses to go to war against my own body.[42]

---

39. Karp, *Speaking of Sadness*, 242.

40. Daphne Merkin, *This Close to Happy: A Reckoning with Depression* (New York: Farrar, Straus & Giroux, 2017), 282.

41. Merkin, *This Close to Happy*, 283.

42. Monica Coleman, *Not Alone: Reflections on Faith and Depression* (Culver City, CA: InnerPrizes, 2012), 149. Coleman is citing Parker Palmer, *Let Your Life Speak: Listening for the Voice of Vocation*, 1st ed. (San Francisco: Jossey-Bass, 1999), 66.

Her therapist's suggestion helped her to entertain possibilities of living with depression beyond the mindset that her suffering was merely an enemy from which she required liberation. The suggestion of a meaningful alternative other than mere escape from depression was a revelation.

This brings us back to Williams's incisive soteriological reflection on the story of Hagar. Without downplaying the human yearning for liberation from suffering and without negating the validity of liberation as an image of God's saving work, Williams demonstrates the importance of recognizing multiple representations of God's salvific relationship to suffering. Furthermore, she demonstrates that non-liberative images of God's saving work can be especially important for those who endure situations of seemingly endless struggle and need assurances of God's presence and benevolent work to ground their hope in otherwise seemingly hopeless circumstances. This is the case for African American women, argues Williams, including those who have long endured psychological suffering such as depression. The witness of depression sufferers beyond women in the Black community indicates that non-liberative images of salvation may also resonate with the experiences of God's saving work among other depression sufferers as well. Depression sufferers may be inclined to recognize God's saving work in the expansion of possibilities for survival and improved quality of life more so than in the relatively rare or merely temporary liberations from depression. That is, salvation may manifest in the realization of possibilities for incorporation rather than liberation, and Williams's soteriological framework can aid sufferers in recognizing this and naming it in a Christian frame.

Some Salvific Possibilities in the Wilderness of Depression

Like the well of water that appeared to Hagar in the wilderness, depression memoirists identify examples of emergent possibilities for survival and improved quality of life that they have experienced amid persistent depression. Though such possibilities understandably vary across accounts of depression, some patterns appear across first-person narratives. For instance, a number of sufferers attest to the emergence of previously unperceived possibilities for what I call "small agency." Because a major difficulty of depression is the loss of certain kinds of possibility, of which possibilities of agency are one, even the most mundane, seemingly insignificant actions can become difficult, if not impossible. "The force of gravity around me has tripled," describes sufferer Martha Manning. "It takes so much effort just to lift an arm or take a step."[43] Often, a sufferer like Manning does not simply feel apathetic about getting out of bed; the very possibility of getting out of bed is no longer available to her. The latter is far more disabling, and it puts into perspective the profound significance of recovering even the smallest possibilities of agency amid depression—when, once again, a person perceives that she might maintain basic personal hygiene, like showering and washing clothes, or she discovers the capacity to concentrate long enough to read an article, if she so chooses. Such possibilities can constitute "a way out of no way"—a path for survival in the ongoing wilderness of life with depression.

From David Finnegan-Hosey, we glimpse the reemergence of small agency, which he characterizes as small "victories" amid depression: "In the hospital, I developed the habit of verbally assigning small happenings to what I called 'the victory column.' Got out of bed in the morning? One for the victory column. Finished a meal? Took a shower? Victory column. Occasionally, one or two of my ward-mates would pick up on the practice. It was a way of naming aloud the small wins that, in normal times, might not even be noticed, but seemed to us like the overcoming of insurmountable obstacles."[44] Finnegan-Hosey associates these victories with the grace of God and likens them to "manna in the desert"—another biblical wilderness image (Exod 16:1-36; Num 11:1-9). "It will often feel scarce. It is a miracle in a minor key. . . . It doesn't seem like much, but it might be just enough."[45] Among those who identify God's saving work with possibilities for survival and improved quality of life, Finnegan-Hosey's association of small agency with grace—God's love presence in the world—makes good theological sense.

---

43. Martha Manning, *Undercurrents: A Life Beneath the Surface* (New York: Harper-One, 1994), 104.

44. Finnegan-Hosey, *Christ on the Psych Ward*, 70.

45. Finnegan-Hosey, *Christ on the Psych Ward*, 70.

Frequently accompanying the emergence of small agency is a realization of new possibilities for meaningful action as well. We witness this in the stories of sufferers who, amid enduring depression, awaken to new possibilities of compassionate service to others. Anastasia Scrutton helps us recognize evidence of this in the writings of the late Catholic spiritual writer Henri Nouwen. She explains, "Nouwen writes that his experience of depression was 'fertile ground' for a kind of spiritual and moral transformation, enabling him to love unconditionally."[46] Nouwen writes, "My heart, ever questioning my goodness, value, and worth, has become anchored in a deeper love and thus less dependent on the praise and blame of those around me. It also has grown into a greater ability to give love without always expecting love in return."[47] Nouwen clarifies for readers that "none of this happened suddenly." It was "gradually, hardly perceptible" that "I discovered that I was no longer the person who had left the community in despair."[48] Furthermore, he notes that this does not mean that he was free from anguish. "There is hardly a day without some dark clouds drifting by."[49] And yet, for Nouwen, "what once seemed such a curse has become a blessing."[50]

Williams's image of salvation as survival/improved quality of life affirms that such experiences might rightly be interpreted by depression sufferers as part of God's saving work, mediated in and through the particularities of the wilderness of depression. As in the story of Hagar, the trying circumstances of depression ultimately do not dissolve entirely—depression persists and ebbs and wanes—but sufferers' capacity to live with depression can sometimes change for the better. It happens that many perceive possibilities for living a meaningful life in the wilderness of depression, possibilities that they previously had not seen. In view of this, one can affirm that the

46. Anastasia Scrutton, "Two Christian Theologies of Depression: An Evaluation and Discussion of Clinical Implications," *Philosophy, Psychiatry, & Psychology* 22, no. 4 (December 2015): 280.

47. Henri Nouwen, *The Inner Voice of Love: A Journey Through Anguish to Freedom* (New York: Image, 1998), 116.

48. Nouwen, *Inner Voice of Love*, 116.

49. Nouwen, *Inner Voice of Love*, 117.

50. Nouwen, *Inner Voice of Love*, 117.

God Who Sees is a god who saves—albeit sometimes, on this side of heaven, only in the form of mere survival and improved quality of life.

Surviving Persistent Meaninglessness

There is an important caveat to these possible affirmations of salvation in the midst of depression: The emergence of possibilities for meaningfulness experienced by Nouwen and other sufferers should not be interpreted as a revelation that, thanks to God's presence and saving work, depression is inherently meaningful. Such a conclusion presumes the *theo*-logic operative in interpretations of depression as divine instruction and would only serve to imposingly reconcile Christians to this harrowing condition. Though some sufferers do adopt such a view of depression upon the discovery of possibilities of meaning, many—including Nouwen—appear to be naming a different experience, one that Scrutton helpfully names and which nuances the proposed image of salvation as survival.

Scrutton differentiates between what she calls, on the one hand, "spiritual health" perspectives on depression—which, like theologies of depression as divine instruction, see the condition as "an indication (and means of furthering) holiness or closeness to God"—and, on the other hand, "potentially transformative" perspectives, "where depression (along with many other instances of suffering) is inherently bad and undesirable, but can become the occasion for the person's spiritual growth (e.g., compassion, insight, appreciation for beauty)."[51] In contrast to spiritual health perspectives and theologies of depression as divine instruction, potentially transformative perspectives do not assign to the condition an inherent purpose and meaning. Potentially transformative perspectives see depression as undesirable and negative but *potentially* meaningful, as this label suggests.[52] Whether or not one's suffering is meaningful is at least partially contingent upon the sufferer's response to it along with other factors, including whether or not a sufferer even experiences possibilities for meaning making at all. Scrutton points to Nouwen as someone whose writings about depression and meaning making

---

51. Scrutton, "Two Christian Theologies," 275.
52. Scrutton, "Two Christian Theologies," 281.

reflect this perspective. It is this potentially transformative interpretation of depression, with its emphasis on the possibility and
contingency of meaning making, that is compatible with the tragic
reading of Hagar in chapter 6 and the soteriology that Williams
forwards based on her reading of the text.

Thus, affirming as a potential site of salvation the experiences of
those who discover possibilities for meaning making amid depression
does not mean that all depression inherently possesses yet-uncovered
meaning. Nor does it suggest that all depression sufferers will experience salvation as survival and improved quality of life. Still more, it
does not follow that an expansion of possibilities for meaning making
is the only marker of salvation and God's loving presence amid depression. Rather, it recognizes that, from a context of suffering that often
appears to have no inherent meaning, some sufferers discover possibilities for meaning making where there previously were none, and
for some this is a salvific revelation. Like lifesaving water discovered
in the wilderness, possibilities of meaning can be a means of survival
amid the desolate landscape of depression, and Williams offers us
the theological resources to affirm this from a Christian perspective.

In keeping with Christian theology's wilderness tradition, the
sketch of salvation that results from bringing Williams's Hagaric
soteriology into conversations with experiences of meaning making and meaninglessness amid depression is an ambivalent one:
Though possibilities for survival and improved quality of life can be
vital relative to the desolation of depressive experience, they do not
resolve all the persistent difficulties of depressive suffering, nor do
they afford solutions to the theological conundrums of this tragic
suffering. That some survive depression—that some can even live a
better life than they once thought they could with depression—does
not resolve the theological question, "Why me?" It does not explain
why depression persists under the purview of a benevolent, personal,
and concerned God. Survival and even possibilities for meaning making do not necessarily reveal depression to be worthwhile in God's
grand scheme. This view of salvation also does not resolve why some
sufferers never experience the lifesaving possibilities that Hagar and
many depression sufferers eventually perceive. It does not explain
why some do not survive.

Salvation and a Reason for Hope in the Wilderness

Delores Williams identifies another reason why it is important to affirm salvation as survival/improved quality of life, and it is one to consider while keeping in mind the inexplicable absence of salvation in some experiences of depression. Williams argues for the importance of this soteriological image not only because it affirms how many Black women have already experienced God's saving work but also because it introduces a possible image of hope for those who continue to suffer in the wilderness, often struggling to perceive a course of survival for themselves.

Just as God opens Hagar's eyes to the previously unseen and lifesaving well of water, Williams suggests that biblical stories themselves can facilitate a salvific expansion of vision among contemporary sufferers. For Williams, God's salvific work is a matter of perception, which is, for instance, afforded in the person of Jesus Christ whose life provides a vision for the way of life that God calls us to. When readers encounter in Hagar's story an account of God "giving individuals the vision to see the resources that promote their survival, quality of life, and right relations with the self, the world, and God," the inspired text may itself afford a salvific vision, one that introduces to sufferers potentially unforeseen resources in their own lives.[53] Indeed, Hagar's story suggests that one's inability to perceive "a way out of no way" is not in fact an indication that there will *never* be possibilities for survival or improved quality of life in one's circumstances. It invites sufferers to hope against hope—to *hope that* salvation will come even when they cannot possibly perceive *what* salvation will look like. It introduces the possibility of hope for those who cannot perceive exactly what they are *hoping for*.

This distinction between *hoping that* and *hoping for* comes from Linn Tonstad's reading of Karen Kilby, who cautions against concrete claims about what a sufferer can *hope for*—that is, about what, exactly, the fruition of salvation will look like—out of concern for how over-determined eschatological claims about suffering can inadvertently

---

53. Monica Coleman, *Making a Way Out of No Way: A Womanist Theology* (Minneapolis: Fortress, 2008), 24.

impose meaning and purpose onto the suffering of others.[54] "[T]o have a richly imagined eschatology, a concrete depiction of what it might be that would allow us to say that all things are well, would once again entail a failure in the proper 'apophatic' stance before suffering," Kilby argues.[55] Kilby calls Christians to *hope that* some goodness and meaning might come from suffering even as they refrain from making claims about *what* one can *hope for*.

As I see it, hope in Hagar's story is a vision of *hoping that*—one that sufficiently obviates the overdetermined eschatology that Kilby warns against. Williams names a hope that God will make "a way out of no way"—that God will make something possible that is utterly impossible to human perception in the present. It is hope that out of utterly meaningless, nonsensical, and dehumanizing suffering, God will nevertheless reveal possibilities for survival and even the generation of meaning. To hope that I will soon or someday perceive the possibility of connection with others from within a state where this kind of possibility is utterly absent is a radical hope. To hope that I will soon, someday perceive possibilities for meaningful action in a state where this kind of possibility is profoundly diminished is a radical hope. Recognizing the radicality of this hope in the particular context of depression shows this hope to be something other than the positive valuation of depressive suffering that Kilby rightly cautions against.

Admittedly, my inclusion of various anecdotes about the kinds of unforeseen possibilities that emerge with some regularity in the stories of depression sufferers and that support their survival and improved quality of life may cross a line that Kilby would draw between *hoping that* and *hoping for*. I have presented these concrete accounts of kinds of salvific possibilities in the same spirit as the diverse and even conflicting scriptural images of suffering and salvation that I affirmed in chapter 5. Insofar as these concrete images of salvation amid depression accompany a clear-eyed affirmation that sometimes salvation does not look like this—and sometimes

54. Linn Tonstad, "Response to Kilby," *Modern Theology* 36, no. 1 (January 2020): 106.

55. Karen Kilby, "Negative Theology and Meaningless Suffering," *Modern Theology* 36, no. 1 (January 2020): 104.

salvation never appears to come at all in this life—then I believe I avoid an overdetermined eschatological vision. At the same time, naming these diverse images of salvation amid depression expands the resources for envisioning the hope amid depression for which many sufferers yearn and on which some sufferers may even depend.

That said, Kilby also expresses concern about how a realized eschatology such as this might inadvertently valorize suffering. "[I]f theology is not to slide into a positive valuation of suffering, it needs to maintain a genuine hope that there is a time—however impossible to imagine—when what has been promised in the resurrection will be made good. . . . There must be a hope for a world radically different from what we now see and know."[56] Kilby suggests that it is only in placing our hope in a radically different world that we fully acknowledge the utter meaninglessness of suffering in the present. When we hope for any goodness latent in present suffering, we signal that we do not really think the suffering at hand is all that bad. In Williams's soteriology, however, I think we encounter a realized eschatology that meets this concern. Without negating the significance of a transcendent eschatology, Williams's realized eschatology suggests hope in a reality beyond our comprehension. Though it is a material hope, it is one that transcends the reality of so many depression sufferers: To hope that God will help me perceive possibilities for survival when I am in the midst of depression is a radical hope. It is radical because this hope is hardly "realistic" for me in the midst of my depressive despair. The fact that depression sufferers die by suicide, often partially because their present experience of the only one they can fathom—that dangerous word, "only"—is further evidence of how radical it is to hope that life can be different from within the wilderness of depression.

When There Is No Sign of God and Salvation in the Wilderness

Williams's emphasis on salvation/improved quality of life as *one* among many valid images of God's saving work is another strength of her soteriological proposal for theologizing depression. Her aim

56. Kilby, "Negative Theology," 104.

is to affirm and represent the realities of salvation in the history and present of many African American women, not to impose a single soteriological destiny onto the suffering of her community. Accordingly, I emphasize that what I have explored in this chapter are not the only visions of who God is and how God works in the wilderness, including the wilderness of depression. For some sufferers, God does not appear to be present and acting for good at all, no matter how sincere their cries for divine rescue. Some are not gifted a well of water and a miraculous expansion of perception in the wilderness like Hagar was given, and I do not know why. "I do not understand why others are able to find new life in the midst of a living death, though I am one of them," Parker Palmer confesses. "I can tell you what I did to survive and, eventually, to thrive—but I cannot tell you why I was able to do those things before it was too late."[57] Neither can I. But that these and other images of God and salvation might aid the hope and endurance of at least some depression sufferers who find themselves doubly displaced in the wilderness is reason to offer them for consideration here.

57. Palmer, *Let Your Life Speak*, 58.

Chapter 8

Discipleship alongside Depression Sufferers

The previous chapter explored images of God and salvation grounded in a tragic theological reading of Hagar's story, which, as I have argued, offers depression sufferers resources for a distinctive Christian interpretation of this condition. Building on these explorations of depression, this chapter reflects a third, intersecting theological trajectory—the life of discipleship to which all Christians are called. I consider: What does the tragic reading of Hagar's wilderness experience suggest about how Christian communities should live? How might fellow Christians support the actualization of salvation—that is, the expansion of possibilities for survival and improved quality of life—among those who struggle with depression? How can churches do this without imposing meaning and their own agendas onto depression sufferers? And if a depression sufferer invites her faith community to understand her suffering as a Hagaric wilderness, what demands might this make on the church?

Chapter 7 commenced with a reminder about the interconnections of the Christian theological enterprise. Focused on discipleship, this chapter showcases more of these interconnections. Discipleship is a matter of following in the way of one's leader or teacher, and for Christians, it is an effort to imitate the God who became human in the person of Jesus and who generously empowers this imitation through the Holy Spirit. To be a Christian disciple, then, is to aspire to emulate God—the God Who Sees—and to do what God does in the world—namely, to expand possibilities for survival and improved quality of life, especially for the vulnerable among us who struggle the most.

Mediating Divine Presence

Depression narratives abound with examples of individuals who support those living with this difficult condition. Sufferers frequently lift up friends, family members, and caretakers who accompany them, not imposing purpose or demanding a cure but simply staying with them amid the disconnection and debilitation of depression. Andrew Solomon's memoir offers a glimpse into the role that loved ones play in surviving depression, especially during periods marked by the absence of agency and other kinds of possibility. At the depth of his most severe depression as a young adult, Solomon moved back into his father's apartment. Illustrating the dramatic effects of depression and his utter dependence on his father, Solomon recounts his inability to shower during this time. When he occasionally garners the effort to get himself out of bed for a shower, he usually collapses in tears before completing the twelve steps required to move himself into the shower. He describes experiences of lying on the floor between the bed and the bathroom: "I couldn't turn over again, until a few hours later, when my father or a friend would come in and help to hoist my feet back up onto the bed."[1] During this time,

> I would feel unable to eat, but I could get up and sit in the dining room with my father, who canceled all other plans to be with me. . . . I tried to explain what it was like. My father nodded, implacably assured me that it would pass, and tried to make me eat. He cut up my food. I told him not to feed me, that I wasn't five, but when I was defeated by the difficulty of getting a piece of lamb chop onto my fork, he would do it for me. . . . Some evenings, my father read to me from the books he had read me when I was a child. I would stop him. "Two weeks ago, I was publishing my novel," I would say. "I used to work

1. Andrew Solomon, *The Noonday Demon: An Atlas of Depression* (New York: Scribner, 2001), 53.

twelve hours and then go to four parties in an evening, some days. What happened?" My father would assure me, sunnily, that I would be able to do it all again, soon. He could as well have told me that I would soon be able to build myself a helicopter out of cookie dough and fly on it to Neptune, so clear did it seem to me that my real life, the one I had lived before, was now definitely over.[2]

I have yet to encounter a tale of depression that does not include figures like Solomon's father, who provides both material support and accompaniment that directly enable a sufferer's survival.[3] Similarly, Monica Coleman recalls reaching out to her friends during a period of difficult depression in college. "They trudged through the snow, one by one, to the little building behind Cabot House. Over the weeks, Keith came, Doug came, Kevin came, Ray came. Within ten minutes, I fell asleep. But if they left while I slept, I woke up and couldn't get back to sleep. I begged them to stay the night on the couch. They never asked me anything. They just sat there."[4] When sufferers like these find themselves unable to live by their own will and ability, these caretakers often help to make a way out of no way for them.

In keeping with the image of God's care and concern from the previous chapter, some depression sufferers explicitly link examples of lifesaving accompaniment like these to divine presence. Parker Palmer offers one such example:

> Blessedly, there were several people, family and friends, who had the courage to stand with me in a simple and healing way. One of them was a friend named Bill who, having asked my permission to do so, stopped by my home every afternoon, sat me down in a chair, knelt

---

2. Solomon, *Noonday Demon*, 54.

3. These narratives of familial care are often incredibly moving. However, I am grateful to a colleague who urged me to recognize the difficulties that familial care responsibilities can place on the children of depressed parents. Caring for a parent can lead to difficult and sometimes age-inappropriate "role reversals," as Amy Simpson puts it. For this reason, we must account for familial power dynamics and our differing responsibilities to one another within family and social units as we reflect on discipleship practices of presence. See Amy Simpson, *Troubled Minds: Mental Illness and the Church's Mission* (Downers Grove, IL: IVP, 2013), 68–69.

4. Monica Coleman, *Bipolar Faith: A Black Woman's Journey with Depression and Faith* (Minneapolis: Fortress, 2016), 88.

in front of me, removed my shoes and socks, and for half an hour simply massaged my feet. He found the one place in my body where I could still experience feeling—and feel somewhat reconnected with the human race. Bill rarely spoke a word. When he did, he never gave advice but simply mirrored my condition. He would say, "I can sense your struggle today," or, "It feels like you are getting stronger."[5]

Palmer explicitly identifies Bill's support with God's love. Yet he notes, "it is a love in which we represent God's love to a suffering person, a God who does not 'fix' us but gives us strength by suffering with us."[6] His description of God's love, mediated by his friend, mirrors God's saving work in Delores Williams's reading of the Hagar story. Neither Bill nor the God whose presence is seen to be mediated through him brings about a fix to the suffering at hand. Nor does either deliver a justification for the depression that persists. Rather, Bill, and God through him, are present to this suffering amid its enduring incoherence and inexplicability. Like the God Who Sees and Hears but does not explain, so too Bill and many other individuals who accompany depression sufferers bear forth God's presence to them.[7]

In Jessica Kantrowitz's reflection on those who accompanied her through the difficulties of her depression, she also emphasizes the difference between individuals who mediated God's presence and others who imposed theodical explanations in response to her suffering:

> We try to find explanations for suffering to create a safe structure of moral order and explain bad things as the result of abandoning that

5. Parker Palmer, *Let Your Life Speak: Listening for the Voice of Vocation* (San Francisco: Jossey-Bass, 2000), 64.

6. Palmer, *Let Your Life Speak*, 64.

7. There is no indication in these depression memoirs that loved ones somehow fail to live up to their role as participants in God's saving work if a depression sufferer does not survive depression. I am certainly not suggesting this, just as I am not suggesting that God's loving presence does not extend to those who do not survive depression. A compelling exploration of these matters is Elizabeth L. Antus's " 'The Silence of the Dead': Remembering Suicide Victims and Reimagining the Communion of Saints," *Theological Studies* 81, no. 2 (2020): 394–413, where she addresses through the doctrine of the communion of saints both the responsibilities of Christians who accompany the suicide dead and the wide-saving mercy of God.

moral order. It would be easier, in some ways, if God were just a system of rules that we had to follow where good behavior was rewarded and bad behavior punished. But God is something different than that, [Frederick] Buechner says. "God is not an answer man can give, God says. God himself does not give answers. He gives himself, and into the midst of the whirlwind of his absence gives himself." God doesn't answer our questions, but instead gives us God's presence. And that is what we need from each other too: Not answers, just presence—understanding, listening, acceptance, and presence.[8]

Again, a striking feature of her links between divine presence and individual, human presence is their congruence with the image of God forwarded in the Hagar story. If, as Kantrowitz suggests, God "does not give answers" but rather "gives himself," then discipleship—a way of life in imitation of God—should look similar: "Not answers, just presence—understanding, listening, acceptance, and presence." Looking to God as a model can dispose Christian disciples for the work of bearing with this tragic suffering without imposing meaning or explaining it away.

Cultivating a Tragic Imagination

Offering presence while exercising proper theological restraint can be difficult, especially for Christians who have been socialized to justify and explain human suffering. Thus, part of the work of Christian discipleship in a world of tragic suffering should entail the cultivation of a disposition that enables this kind of unimposing accompaniment—whether in the form of sheer presence or in accompanying a sufferer as she discerns an interpretation of her own condition.

Rowan Williams indicates that the cultivation of a "tragic imagination" may ready Christians for such work.[9] He argues that tragedies, as arresting contemplations on nonsensical suffering, afford

---

8. Jessica Kantrowitz, *The Long Night: Readings and Stories to Help You through Depression* (Minneapolis: Fortress, 2020), 146.

9. Kilby points to Rowan Williams's work to this end in "Negative Theology and Meaningless Suffering," *Modern Theology* 36, no. 1 (January 2020): 104n49. That said, she also raises critical questions about Williams's proposals in 104n51.

knowledge of realities that contemporary Western society often otherwise elides through sheer denial or through the theodical theories that attempt to justify suffering that is unjustifiable. In contrast to these prevailing dispositions toward suffering, tragedies cultivate in audiences an ability to face those realities of human suffering that are "unspeakable," that are irreconcilable and thus should not be reconciled to. "Our stillness in the face of represented pain becomes a forced acknowledgement of our habits of avoidance and denial and a confrontation of the helplessness in the presence of catastrophe that we regularly experience and avoid reflecting about," Williams argues.[10] Tragedy uncovers "not so much the unknown as the *fact* of our not-knowing. . . . [I]ts task is to persuade us that at some significant level we have *never* really known it"—that our tidy explanations for why suffering is or isn't were, in fact, always utterly insufficient.[11] In so doing, tragedies afford an aesthetic training in a "particular kind of imagining that *stays with* the risk of returning to familiar and apparently unresolved narratives of suffering and pacification and asking them new questions by finding new voices in which to tell or, better, realize the stories."[12] Increased immersion in tragic narratives—whether classical Greek dramas, the story of Hagar, or many of the stories of depression sufferers themselves—may cultivate in Christian disciples a greater capacity to *stay with* depression sufferers who wrestle with their own suffering. It could foster in Christians a greater capacity for the theological restraint to which Kilby calls those who accompany depression sufferers.

Though the contemplation of tragic suffering can be pursued individually, Williams urges Christians to reclaim the original collectivity of Greek dramas. Tragic dramas were performed publicly in and for the *polis*. Over and over again, the community gathered for a collective contemplation of tragic suffering—which was often familiar suffering, their *own* communal memories of suffering. This gave tragic dramas a liturgical quality, suggests Williams. They were—

10. Rowan Williams, *The Tragic Imagination* (New York: Oxford University, 2016), 37.

11. Williams, *Tragic Imagination*, 27.

12. Williams, *Tragic Imagination*, 10.

and are—a "liturgical showing-forth" in and through and for the gathered community. The cultivation of the tragic imagination was thus a communal undertaking and an occasion for collective "conversion," he explains. "[T]o think in terms of liturgy connects it with more overtly religious language about 'conversion,' in the biblical sense of a radical change of perception. It is a reminder of why a dramatic representation that shows us what disaster does not silence or exhaust might be called a showing of the sacred, that excess of unearned, unexpected life that sustains us in going on speaking and thinking."[13] This invitation to a conversion of perception suggests that it is not only depression sufferers who are often in need of a salvific expansion of vision. In order to live a Christian life in support of those who suffer, Christians who are not in immediate pain also often require a holy expansion of vision.

Williams's call to contemplate unresolved suffering evokes Pope Francis's reflections on the centrality of mourning in contemporary discipleship. In the pontiff's apostolic exhortation on the call to holiness in today's world, *Gaudete et Exsultate*, he observes how often "[t]he worldly person ignores problems of sickness or sorrow in the family or all around him; he averts his gaze . . . it would rather disregard painful situations, cover them up or hide them."[14] Yet holy persons "are unafraid to share in the suffering of others; they do not flee from painful situations." Rather than avoiding the inexplicable suffering of others, "[t]hey sense that the other is flesh of our flesh, and are not afraid to draw near, even to touch their wounds. They feel compassion for others in such a way that all distance vanishes."[15]

If the ability to "mourn" and "draw near" to the suffering of others is central to the way of holiness in today's world, as Pope Francis suggests, then cultivating a tragic imagination that enables Christians to "stay with" unresolved suffering is imperative. Sitting with stories such as Hagar's and doing so in a way that "contemplates"

---

13. Williams, *Tragic Imagination*, 27.

14. Pope Francis, *Gaudete et Exsultate* 75 (March 19, 2018), https://www.vatican.va /content/francesco/en/apost_exhortations/documents/papa-francesco_esortazione -ap_20180319_gaudete-et-exsultate.html.

15. Francis, *Gaudete et Exsultate* 76.

its theological incoherence—its inability to reconcile the horrors of suffering with the mystery of divine benevolence—is a relevant spiritual practice for preparing Christians to accompany depression sufferers when their suffering and its concomitant theological conundrums persist. With this, Christians might be better equipped to mediate divine presence in the fashion that Palmer, Kantrowitz, and others describe.

Community Action in the Face of Tragic Suffering

Tragic narratives not only contemplate atrocities, but, in so doing, they spur audiences to ethical action, argues Rowan Williams. One might easily assume the opposite—that tragic narratives would engender apathy. When confronted with the senselessness of so much suffering—with their inability to explain it, resolve it, protect themselves and others from it, and reconcile it with their wider understandings of the world—people could find themselves paralyzed by the inevitability of suffering and then resign to it. Williams suggests another collective response to the realities of tragic suffering, however.

According to Williams, collective moral action begins with the shift in perception that tragedies facilitate. These dramas confront communities with "what it is the social order leaves out"—that is, what society elides or covers up in order for the community to get on with its life according to the status quo. For example, the early chapters of this book explored how the drive to justify suffering via claims of inherent purpose reflects and perpetuates a modern Western impulse to downplay the horrors of suffering—in this case, the horrors of depressive suffering. This has long been the theological status quo. A tragic reading of Hagar's suffering and of depressive suffering confronts us with what is "left out" as a result of this modern impulse, in general, and of popular Christian theologies of depression, in particular. They elide those realities of depressive suffering that cannot be explained and that cannot be justified with any coherence before our benevolent God. When communities can perceive what they otherwise tend to erase and "leave out," they are better positioned to consider what they can do about this suffering.

Williams explains, "The act of representing carries implications; the describing of an atrocity changes things by enforcing upon us the urgency of containing its effects."[16] Tragedies, rather than reconciling us to suffering by imposing meaning that downplays their severity or sentencing us to despair, can instill in the community "the urgency of containing its effects." That is, by confronting us with humanity's inability to avoid tragic suffering and by displaying the limits of our efforts to make sense of it, representations of tragic suffering invite us to recognize what we *can* do for one another, particularly for those enduring these atrocities. They spur us to reflect on and actualize what we need to become in order to be a community that can hold and *stay with* others amid this inescapable suffering and fragility.

Williams's link between the contemplative disposition of the tragic imagination and the collective political questions it raises calls to mind Karen Bray's recent project, *Grave Attending*. Bray's exhortation to the theo-ethical practice of "grave attending" in response to moods including depression and anxiety resonates with the contemplative practice of *staying with* suffering in Williams's project. "Acts of grave attention refuse to efface the material mattering of others on the way to our own redemption," writes Bray. "Such a grave attending is an attention to the lamenting cries (those released in word and affect) of those who have been crucified by neoliberalism and its concomitant heteropatriarchal, ableist, and white supremacist ethics. As such, theologically speaking, grave attending is what happens on Holy Saturday, on the day between crucifixion and resurrection."[17] In her description of this theo-ethical practice, Bray names with greater force how the contemplation of suffering can (and should) lead attendants to a recognition of those social structures that facilitate, contribute to, and/or compound the suffering at hand, including depression.

Considerations of depressive suffering as tragic suffering—be it through the application of a cultivated tragic imagination or the practice of grave attending—should urge the church to become a community that can *stay with* the horrors of unresolved, nonsensical

16. Williams, *Tragic Imagination*, 17.

17. Karen Bray, *Grave Attending: A Political Theology for the Unredeemed* (New York: Fordham University, 2020), 27.

suffering while also investigating social factors that contribute to it. In response, the church should do what it can to "contain its effects"—to support possibilities for survival and improved quality of life as depression inexplicably exists and persists.

In my survey of secular interpretations of depression in chapter 1, I gestured toward a variety of existing theories about how oppressive social structures contribute to depressive suffering. While disagreements persist about these theories, any clear-eyed look at the realities of depression will lead one to see that broadscale social injustice contributes to the difficulties of depression in some way. Though depression cannot be reduced to, explained by, or resolved through address of these social realities alone, Christian efforts to "contain the effects" of depression—to mitigate its difficulties—must entail advocacy for social transformation—for revolution, even. In the remainder of this chapter on Christian discipleship, I highlight just two of many needful trajectories for this social transformation in the contemporary United States: Collective advocacy for mental healthcare and collective resistance to mental-health stigma.

Collective Advocacy for Mental Healthcare

This book has made a case for the potential significance of extending theological resources to those struggling to interpret their depression in a Christian frame. I have argued that these theological resources have the potential to curtail some dimensions of the suffering that often accompany depression. Yet, just as in the tragic story of Hagar, supporting the realization of salvation in the context of depression also often entails some very pragmatic, material assistance. Hagar and her son needed water. As Delores Williams points out, they needed a sustainable means for acquiring food, which made Ishmael's skill with a bow a vital salvific affordance (Gen 21:20).[18] Supporting possibilities for survival and quality of life among depression sufferers can likewise take the form of material support.

Often, this material support is provided on an individual basis by the family members or friends of depression sufferers, as I noted

18. Williams, *Sisters in the Wilderness*, 30.

earlier in the chapter. While such offerings are lifesaving for many depression sufferers, it goes without saying that many people do not have the support of individuals who can spare this material support. This is especially the case when it comes to the cost of mental healthcare, which is both costly and difficult to attain. Though there are innumerable stories of friends and family members who have worked on behalf of depression sufferers to access the mental healthcare that loved ones need to survive and aspire to some improved quality of life, these individual contributions are necessary in large part because of the vast inadequacies of the mental healthcare system in the United States. Ensuring depression sufferers the mental healthcare that often enables their survival and quality of life is crucial, and it necessitates the kinds of collective action for which a community such as the church is well positioned to advocate for and enact.

Before pointing to some of the injustices of the U.S. mental healthcare system, I should clarify its important—even salvific—role in the lives of many depression sufferers. William Styron testifies to the importance of hospitalization for his survival. "The hospital also offers mild, oddly gratifying trauma of sudden stabilization—a transfer out of the too familiar surroundings of home, where all is anxiety and discord, into an orderly and benign detention where one's only duty is to try to get well. For me the real healers were seclusion and time."[19] In this sense, he says, as I have noted previously, "The hospital was a way station, a purgatory."[20] Styron speaks figuratively, but his recollection of hospitalization can serve as a heuristic for understanding the soteriological significance of hospitalization for him and so many others who are without alternative means of survival. The hospital supported his survival amid an experience that compromised his ability to sustain his own life. Solomon, too, refers to his medication regimen in a way that strikingly conveys the lifesaving capacity of medical care, writing, "I feel sometimes as though I am swallowing my own funeral twice a day, since without

19. William Styron, *Darkness Visible: A Memoir of Madness* (New York: Vintage Books, 1992), 69.

20. Styron, *Darkness Visible*, 69.

these pills, I'd be long gone."[21] When Solomon was unable to survive on his own—when death was his only conceivable way of moving forward—medicine helped to keep him alive and did so long enough that he could experience additional possibilities for his life with depression.

Some depression sufferers explicitly identify medication and hospitalizations as vehicles of God's saving work in and beyond depression's most incapacitating periods. Pastor Kathryn Greene-McCreight describes medication as a source of survival sent by God: "Those medications that have in fact been helpful . . . have been a strand in the cord that God has woven for me as the lifeline cast out in my free fall. The medications have helped me to rebuild some of 'myself,' so that I can continue to be the kind of mother, priest, and writer that I believe God wants me to be."[22] When Coleman was resistant to taking medication for her depression, a pastor friend suggested that it might be a vehicle of God's grace, saying, "If you really believe that God is in everything, if you really believe that, then you have to know that God is in the medicine too."[23]

These perspectives suggest that medical treatments can mediate God's saving work, enabling depression sufferers to survive a period of depression when they have lost the possibility of sustaining their own survival. This period is frequently met with an eventual expansion of the kinds of possibilities that sufferers experience, but this is not to say that sufferers' dependence on caretakers and medical treatment necessarily ceases nor that many of the qualities of depressive experience fall away completely. Often, emergent possibilities of survival and improved quality of life are continuously sustained by ongoing mental healthcare services.

Despite this, accessible and affordable mental healthcare is scarce in the United States. Even for sufferers with private or employer-provided health insurance, in-network mental healthcare providers can be difficult to access. Those living in rural areas of the United

21. Solomon, *Noonday Demon*, 29.

22. Kathryn Greene-McCreight, *Darkness Is My Only Companion: A Christian Response to Mental Illness* (Grand Rapids, MI: Brazos, 2006), 21.

23. Coleman, *Bipolar Faith*, 280.

States face tremendous challenges in this regard. A 2018 study reported that 65 percent of non-metropolitan counties did not have a psychiatrist, 47 percent had no psychologists, and 81 percent lacked a psychiatric nurse practitioner.[24] Journalist Alisa Roth points to another vulnerable population deprived of quality healthcare: those in the U.S. carceral system. She reports that "the proportion of prisoners with mental illness has continued to go up" in recent years. "In 2010, about 30 percent of people at New York's Rikers Island jail had a mental illness; in 2014, the figure rose to 40 percent, and by 2017, it had gone up to 43 percent."[25] Recent studies find that incarcerated women experience mental illness at a significantly higher rate too: "One study by the U.S. Bureau of Justice Statistics found that 75 percent of women incarcerated in jails and prisons had a mental illness, as compared to just over 60 and 55 percent of men, respectively."[26] Roth details the complex reasons why a population that tends to be less violent than non-mentally ill persons overall is disproportionately prevalent with the U.S. prison system—racism, poverty, and mental-health stigma are all factors. Regardless of the individual or social reasons behind one's entrance into the carceral system, it is clear from Roth's reporting that the mental healthcare one receives there is likely to be woefully inadequate, if not more psychologically damaging.

Even in the best of circumstances—when a sufferer carries insurance that covers mental-health treatment and lives in circumstances where mental healthcare is good and relatively accessible—insurance copays are often high, and treatment coverage is limited by insurance regulations. These are but a few reasons why George Scialabba's reflection on the role of financial insecurity in his experiences of severe depression makes sense: "Chronic depression is very hard on

24. C. Holly A. Andrilla et al., "Geographic Variation in the Supply of Selected Behavioral Health Providers," *American Journal of Preventive Medicine* 54, no. 6 (June 1, 2018): 199–207.

25. Alisa Roth, *Insane: America's Criminal Treatment of Mental Illness* (New York: Basic Books, 2018), 3.

26. Roth, *Insane*, 2–3.

lifetime earnings," he states.[27] Scialabba points to Styron as one who, though having suffered greatly, had the financial means to acquire the treatment he needed when he needed it, a luxury unavailable to many sufferers with greater financial insecurity. In view of this injustice, Scialabba proceeds in his suicide-note-turned-essay to advocate for a massive tax-driven redistribution of wealth that would afford depression sufferers the money they need to sustain life amid the ups and downs of this often-debilitating condition and its treatment costs. His proposal hits home how the financial burdens of mental healthcare can impede access to material means of survival and quality of life among depression sufferers.

Offering another example of the critical need for mental healthcare reform, David Finnegan-Hosey, whose most recent book on depression focuses on the injustices of the U.S. mental healthcare system, exhorts Christian communities to take a stand against the practice of denying insurance coverage to individuals with "pre-existing conditions," of which depression is one.[28] Though, beginning in 2014, the Affordable Care Act (ACA) made it illegal to deny insurance coverage to those with pre-existing conditions, efforts to overturn the ACA continue, and some Christian organizations champion these efforts. A repeal of the ACA—or at least its rules regarding pre-existing conditions—would jeopardize the already-limited-but-vital support that health insurance presently affords many depression sufferers.

This brief look at the U.S. mental-health system evinces why comprehensive healthcare reform that includes affordable and accessible mental healthcare is a social justice issue of material consequence for survival and improved quality of life among those with depression. It also demonstrates the concomitant need for broadscale criminal-justice and economic reform. When a tragic perspective on depressive suffering confronts Christians with the reality that they cannot prevent or avoid or explain depression, the church must ask what it, as a community of disciples, *can do* to mitigate its difficulties. These social reform efforts are but a few that Christians can advance to

27. George Scialabba, *How to Be Depressed* (Philadelphia: University of Pennsylvania, 2020), 3.

28. David Finnegan-Hosey, *Grace Is A Pre-Existing Condition: Faith, Systems, and Mental Healthcare* (New York: Church Publishing, 2020).

substantially and materially support sufferers' survival and quality of life.

Collective Resistance to Mental-Health Stigma

When considering what a community can do to mitigate the difficulties of depressive suffering on a broadscale, resisting mental-health stigma is often one of the first efforts that comes to mind, and rightly so. Recall from chapter 3 that stigma is a social process by which certain individuals are disfavored and devalued because of a characteristic they possess or are affiliated with. In the case of mental-health stigma, those with conditions such as depression are socially devalued simply because of conscious and unconscious assumptions (often, misconceptions) about their condition. This comes at the cost of not only relationships and social opportunities but also psychological well-being. When depression sufferers internalize these social judgements, as often occurs, stigma can magnify their suffering.

Though stigma is elusive in that it is constituted by a set of negative evaluations that a community habitually associates with a group of people, many scholars attending to mental-health stigma note the connection between ideas about depressed people and the prevailing values of American society. They show how stigmatizing ideas about people with mental-health conditions are entangled in broader stereotypes and cultural mores. Thus, addressing mental-health stigma requires more than correcting wrongful ideas about depression. It requires the more radical transformation of multiple, often entangled cultural ideals.

For example, David Karp observes that even before an official diagnosis of depression, many sufferers anticipate the judgement their symptoms will accrue due to their conflict with socially acceptable ideals of personhood. His analysis shows that two key characteristics underwrite the ideal self that renders these early experiences of depression taboo in the eyes of sufferers: First, a person should be happy, and second, a person ought to be wholly self-determining, which includes control of one's affect. Karp argues that the modern economy mediates this happiness imperative and normalizes the willful suppression of any feeling that undermines a cheery disposition. Workers who cannot properly "manage their hearts" are deemed morally insufficient for their inability to actualize the ideals of neoliberalism and globalization.[29]

Scholarship on the gendering and racialization of the social imperative to "put on a happy face" supports and concretizes Karp's claim.[30] Dana Crowley Jack observes how gendered affect norms shape the depression of white women in heterosexual marriages, who regularly suppress negative feelings in order to embody the ideal of the "good wife" who is "friendly and smiling all the time."[31] Western society has long promised white women that actualizing this ideal will bring self-satisfaction and meaningful intimacy. But as Betty Friedan famously conveys in *The Feminine Mystique*, and as cultural critic Sara Ahmed more recently shows, these assurances are predicated on the erasure of many women's realities.[32] When women find themselves unable to reach and sustain this idealized image of the "happy wife," they often judge and blame themselves for their failure; this in turn magnifies the self-loathing and isolation of depression, perpetuating a cycle of self-stigma.[33] In conversation with Crowley Jack, Chanequa Walker-Barnes illustrates how this imperative is mediated in the lives of Black women by the archetype of the "StrongBlackWoman."[34] "Emotional strength [or] regulation is the central defining characteristic of the StrongBlackWoman," she explains.[35] This "controlling image" leads Black women to repress negative emotions to their own detriment, which Walker-Barnes

29. David Karp, *Speaking of Sadness: Depression, Disconnection and the Meanings of Illness*, updated and expanded ed. (New York: Oxford University, 2017), 115.

30. Karp, *Speaking of Sadness*, 116.

31. Dana Crowley Jack, *Silencing the Self: Women and Depression* (New York: HarperCollins, 1993), 56.

32. Crowley Jack, *Silencing the Self*, 84–88; Betty Friedan, *The Feminine Mystique*, 50th anniversary ed. (New York: W.W. Norton, 1963); Chanequa Walker-Barnes also analyzes this in her look at the "cult of true womanhood" and social constructions of the "good woman" in *Too Heavy a Yoke: Black Women and the Burden of Strength* (Eugene, OR: Cascade: 2014), 4, 90–94.

33. Crowley Jack, *Silencing the Self*, 89–127.

34. Walker-Barnes, *Too Heavy a Yoke*, 80–108.

35. Walker-Barnes, *Too Heavy a Yoke*, 18.

demonstrates with a devasting look at mental-health struggles among Black women in the United States today.[36]

The research of these scholars and myriad others demonstrates that at least some of the difficulty of depression is social. And though depression does not appear to be reducible to these social causes, these contributing factors to mental-health stigma are ones that the Christian community can and should address in an effort to curtail at least some of the struggles of depression. Churches can name and critique the happiness imperative, which disproportionately affects individuals along gender and racial lines. Christians can likewise critique the illusion of absolute self-governance, which runs counter to the fundamentals of Christian anthropology and which shames sufferers who cannot will themselves out of depression. Critiquing these prevailing social ideals can contribute to the dismantling of mental-health stigma and may support another salvific step in support of sufferers' survival and quality of life.

This research provides but one example of how social realities such as sexism, racism, and capitalism contribute to the difficulties of depression. White Christians, especially, should note that this is precisely what Black and womanist theologians, including Delores Williams, have been saying in various settings and in relation to a wide range of psychological struggles for a long time: Racism, sexism, and economic injustice are mental-health issues.[37] Increasing rates of suicide among members of the LGBTQ community expose hetero- and cis-normativity as mental-health issues in this regard too. A 2016 study found the 29.4 percent of lesbian, gay, and bisexual

36. Walker-Barnes, *Too Heavy a Yoke*, 52–63.

37. See, for example, Phillis Isabella Sheppard, *Self, Culture, and Other in Womanist Practical Theology* (New York: Palgrave Macmillan, 2011); Cheryl Townsend Gilkes, "The 'Loves' and 'Troubles' of African-American Women's Bodies: The Womanist Challenge to Cultural Humiliation and Community Ambivalence," in *Womanist Theological Ethics*, ed. Katie Geneva Cannon, Emilie M. Townes, and Angela D. Sims (Louisville, KY: Westminster John Knox, 2011), 81–97; Stephanie M. Crumpton, *A Womanist Pastoral Theology against Intimate and Cultural Violence* (New York: Palgrave Macmillan, 2014); Wynnetta Wimberley, *Depression in American Clergy* (New York: Palgrave Macmillan, 2016).

youth in grades 9–12 in the US had attempted suicide compared to 6.4 percent of their heterosexual peers.[38]

With a powerful litany of questions, theologian Elizabeth Antus beckons religious ethicists to attend to the social injustices that contribute to struggles that often occasion suicide, including the sense of oneself as a "burden"—a perception undoubtedly tied up with social stigmas of various kinds and a social landscape that demonizes, marginalizes, and shames some social groups more than others. Christian communities concerned with depression in all its forms would do well to heed her exhortation:

> If it is true that suicide results not only from the capacity for self-inflicted violence but also from a deep sense of being a burden and of not belonging, then religious ethicists should analyze the structural and social conditions that push people to such agony. What makes entire groups of people feel alone, burdensome, and inured to violence against themselves? How exactly do the oppressive realities of wealth inequality, chronic poverty, lack of affordable health care and housing, environmental degradation, sexual violence, white supremacist terror, and the prison industrial complex damage the mental state of socially and psychologically vulnerable groups of people? To what extent does this country peddle the punitive and ultimately carceral narrative that your oppression is your own fault? Further, what is the role of religious scripts here? For example, LGBTQ+ people have noticeably higher suicide rates than that of the general population. How has Christianity's homophobic and transphobic rhetoric of shame enabled that?[39]

An important component of Antus's inquiries is her recognition of the church's own complicity in many of the social and structural conditions that mark some groups of individuals as burdensome and outsiders. Just as supporting depression sufferers entails resistance to widespread social realities such as sexism, racism, capitalism,

---

38. Laura Kann et al., "Sexual Identity, Sex of Sexual Contacts, and Health-Related Behaviors Among Students in Grades 9–12—United States and Selected Sites, 2015," *Surveillance Summaries* 65, no. 9 (August 12, 2016): 1–202.

39. Elizabeth L. Antus in "Covid-19 and Religious Ethics," *Journal of Religious Ethics* 48, no. 3 (September 2020): 380–381.

homophobia, and cis-normativity, it also demands an inward-facing interrogation of these dynamics within Christian communities. If Christian communities are to resist mental-health stigma, then they must address their own complicities in the social structures and beliefs that have denigrated the personhood of so many depressed individuals.[40] Churches cannot sufficiently support the survival and quality of life of depression sufferers until they do.

God, Salvation, and Discipleship

Bringing together a tragic interpretation of the story of Hagar and the testimony of depression sufferers, chapters 7 and 8 have offered three interconnected theological trajectories for further reflection on God, salvation, and discipleship alongside those with depression. The image of the present and concerned God that some depression sufferers have identified as compelling and comforting can also serve as a model for Christians who desire to support depression sufferers without imposition. The notion of salvation as survival and improved quality of life that I have drawn from Delores Williams's reading of Hagar—where salvation consists not in resolving suffering through the assertion of quick theological fixes but rather in supporting possibilities for survival and quality of life through offerings of theological, social, and material resources—also directs Christians to a way of life that strives to advance God's saving work in support of depression sufferers.

The contextual insights into these interconnected loci provide the beginning of what depression sufferers might explore further on their own terms and with the theological companions of their choosing. As it stands, I hope to have demonstrated that a Christian interpretation of depression that withholds the imposition of meaning and divine justifications for suffering is not only possible but can also bear rich possibilities for ongoing theological reflection from within the Christian faith.

40. See Cody J. Sanders, *Christianity, LGBTQ Suicide, and the Souls of Queer Folk* (Lanham, MD: Lexington, 2020).

Conclusion

A Wilderness Within

I first heard the phrase "dust in the blood" while driving down a frozen highway in central Minnesota, a long way from the towering trees of my childhood and the wilderness of my depression. White-knuckled and surveying for black ice, I had turned on the radio show "Fresh Air" for the consoling voices of the familiar interviewer, Terry Gross, and her guest, Kay Redfield Jamison. Jamison was an intellectual acquaintance of sorts. Her memoir, *An Unquiet Mind*, had been an important source for the dissertation on depression I had just submitted.[1] But it was the release of another book, her biography of the acclaimed poet Robert Lowell, that occasioned the interview that day.

Lowell was the kind of creative Jamison had become fascinated with in recent years—one who lived with severe bipolar depression that fueled his genius and also eventually destroyed him. His name was vaguely familiar to me—familiar enough to know that I ought to know more about him than I did. But I had no idea that Lowell had been a professor of poetry at my alma mater and no idea he had taught Anne Sexton, the Boston-based poet whose melancholic writing I had grown to love while living there. I did not know of his four stays at McLean Psychiatric Hospital, whose verdant boundaries stood just a few miles from my old apartment and which may

---

1. Kay Redfield Jamison, *An Unquiet Mind: A Memoir of Moods and Madness* (New York: Vintage Books, 1996).

have been the ones that haunted my dreams during the worst of my depression.

Not long into the interview, Gross commented on the appearance of mania and depression in Lowell's writing. "He described mania as, like, striking matches that brought my blood to a boil. He described depression as dust in the blood, which is a great description."

"Yes, yes," affirmed Jamison. "Yes . . . [a]nd one of the things he writes about time and time again is how tied to his temperament and who he is are these manias and depressions. And that he wishes otherwise, but he knows that that is—you know, the fear of them is part of him. The experience of them is part of him."[2]

At that arresting phrase—"dust in the blood"—I wanted to pull my car over to the side of the road, though I quickly concluded that a sudden shift was unwise under the winter conditions. I could not stop everything to indulge my urge to *just be* with these words. So instead, I drove on, stunned and pondering what it was about them that so demanded my attention.

I have since learned that this is what good poetry does. Though many people assume that the purpose of the genre's figurative language is to obfuscate meaning, to hide its secret messages, Matthew Zapruder argues that poetry's language aims to do the opposite: The poet uses words to draw our attention to the world exactly as it is, just exactly how it feels.[3] For the poet knows that the most exacting way to convey some things, some truths, is to do it poetically—at a slant, with the wink of a rhyme, or through the strange imagery of a metaphor.

In Lowell's words, "dust in the blood," I instantly recognized a truth of what depression was like for me. Having encompassed every dimension of what I experienced, having permeated every inch of my body, depression had been like the blood running through my veins. And though depression no longer consumed my life as it had at its most severe, the experience of living trapped in another terri-

2. "'River On Fire' Explores Genus, Madness and the Poetry of Robert Lowell," *Fresh Air* (February 28, 2017), https://www.npr.org/2017/02/28/517706249/river-on-fire-explores-genius-madness-and-the-poetry-of-robert-lowell.

3. Matthew Zapruder, *Why Poetry* (New York: HarperCollins, 2017).

fying world leaves its mark. My body still held remnants of another landscape latent within. My heart still pulses with dust in the blood.

That Lowell's description also harkened the earthy imagery of the depression memoirs I had read as well as the wilderness of my own depression dreams undoubtedly contributed to the halting effect of this phrase. I wanted to look more closely at this truth he had named. I wanted to stop everything to attend to what these words revealed about his depression and about mine. I made a private vow to myself that day that if I ever wrote the book about depression that I wanted to write, then this is what I would call it. And in keeping with this vow, I have tried, like a poet, to present the truths of depression as best I can.

Theologians are in the business of truth-telling, too, of course. At least we aspire to be. Writing this book has confronted me with how much Christian theologians struggle to actualize this aspiration, however, not only when we speak of the absolute Mystery of God, which is predictably elusive, but likewise when we try to speak the truths of our own lives and of other finite and fragile creatures as well.

This is clear from chapter 1, where I explored the question of what depression is. I showed that expert observers and depression sufferers alike struggle to identify what constitutes this engrossing condition. Overwhelmingly, scholars pursue more precise accounts of depression through the application of their disciplines' respective etiological frameworks, which strive to pinpoint depression's cause, standardize a map of its course, and identify a cure or at least some reliable means of mitigation. And yet in the process, many scholarly accounts of depression oversimplify and depart from the experiential dimensions of depression that sufferers identify as constitutive. So in response and in pursuit of a closer account of what depressive suffering is, I turned to the first-person narratives of depression sufferers and read them with the analytical insights of phenomenology, which "bracket" etiological concerns for the sake of describing experiences as they present themselves to the sufferer. What resulted was a narrative-phenomenological account of depression as a particular form of *unhomelikeness* (*Unheimlichkeit*), one that often resists meaningfulness with a stubbornness unlike other iterations.

In chapter 2, I advanced this exploration of what depression is with a look at popular Christian theologies of depression in the contemporary United States. I presented these prevailing interpretations in two categories: first, depression as a self-imposed moral evil and, second, depression as divine instruction. As in secular accounts of depression, these theological interpretations entail claims about the condition's causes, the purpose that guides its course, and the interventions that should resolve it. The etiological underpinnings of these theologies are evident in their resonances with well-known Christian theodicies, which resulted from the modern Western impulse to explain and justify all things by way of human reason, including matters theological.

Chapters 3 and 4 investigated whether these Christian accounts of depression are adequate not only in content but also in their methodological approach to depressive suffering. Critics of popular theologies of depression and other suffering argue that these theologies of depression erase important dimensions of what depression is like, what God is like, and the ethical implications of theological claims about this condition. Their critiques suggest that replacing these with better ideas would result in more satisfactory theologies of depression. Yet I argued that Karen Kilby's work exposes how both popular Christian theologies of depression and the critiques hedged against them miss a more important and perhaps more difficult truth about this condition: They elide the persistent, unresolvable mystery that Christians confront when interpreting suffering in view of Christianity's benevolent and absolutely mysterious God. And they mandate a reconciliation to depression that is immoral. Heeding these truths requires theologians and other Christians to exercise theological restraint, a disposition to suffering that Kilby outlines with parameters for who is and is not in a position to assign meaning to suffering. I showed that Kilby's argument that meaning can be assigned to suffering only in the first person has a number of strengths for reflection on depression, in particular, and it meets the concerns of content critics in a number of ways.

Building on Kilby's position, I argued that proper theological restraint in the face of depression cannot mean resignation to utter silence about this suffering or about God's relationship to it. To resign in this way would only leave depression sufferers with the existing theological resources for interpreting God and their suffering, which, though generative and sustaining for some Christians, nevertheless fail other depression sufferers. What theologians and other Christians ought to do, then, is to offer up more theological resources for depression sufferers to engage, if they so choose, and to accompany them in that engagement in an ongoing way, if they wish. This must unfold while acknowledging what one does not and cannot know as an outsider to the suffering at hand. To equip both sufferers and those who accompany them for these delicate situations of first-person theologizing, developing theological resources that serve as alternatives to prevailing theologies of depression are especially worthy of the energies and expertise of theologians, I argued. Perhaps especially needed are theological perspectives that depart from the modern theodical mindset—that is, perspectives that situate depressive suffering within a Christian frame without eliding its incoherence before God. Expanding and diversifying the theological resources that populate Christian communities will serve those who theologize depression in the first person and those who accompany them.

To this end, I developed my own constructive offerings across the book's remaining chapters. In chapter 5, I presented the theological foundations for interpreting depression as a wilderness experience, a possibility that begins with many depression sufferers' own descriptions of depression and my analysis of them as an experience of displacement into an unhomelike world. Surveying some of the Bible's sacred stories of dislocation into harsh landscapes and their interpretation throughout the Christian theological tradition, I demonstrated the theological precedent for figurative readings of these wildernesses as analogues for contemporary experience, including psychological distress such as depression. I also showed how such readings open up myriad theological possibilities with regard to what depression is, theologically; how God relates to depressive suffering; and how sufferers and others should relate to it—some of which map onto existing popular theologies of depression.

Chapter 6 offered a close reading of one biblical wilderness tale—the story of Hagar—to develop a theological interpretation of depression that departs from prevailing popular Christian theologies. After highlighting phenomenological resonances between Hagar's second wilderness experience in Genesis 21 and characteristics of persistent depression, I identified her suffering as an instance of tragic suffering—suffering that lacks apparent justification and purpose before God—and proposed that depressive suffering could be seen likewise. Interpreting depressive suffering as tragic suffering through this reading of the story of Hagar results in a Christian account of suffering that does not elide its inexplicability and meaninglessness. In so doing, it suspends any accusation of moral responsibility against sufferers or against God. At the same time, it affords an image of God whose presence and concern are not contingent upon the imposition of meaning onto suffering.

Chapter 7 and 8 sketched three theological trajectories that emerge from the tragic reading of depression forwarded in the previous chapter and further engagement with memoirs of depression. First, I identified the image of divine presence and concern in the Hagar story and noted the significance of similar portraits of God in the stories of some Christian depression sufferers. Second, I drew on Delores Williams's *Sisters in the Wilderness* to reflect on the soteriological image of survival/quality of life that emerges in the story of Hagar. Building on Williams's project, I highlighted the significance of this account of salvation for the context of depression, as it both affirms some of the experiences of life-giving transformation that depression sufferers regularly attest to and offers an image of hope for depression sufferers for whom survival and improved quality of life are seeming impossibilities. Third, I explored the image of discipleship that follows from this interpretation of depression through the story of Hagar. I exhorted those who accompany depression sufferers to imitate the God Who Sees through their own embodiment of presence and extensions of material support to depression sufferers. Actualizing this vision of discipleship while also exercising proper theological restraint in relation to the suffering of others requires the cultivation of what Rowan Williams calls a "tragic imagination." I argued that this ability to *stay with* inexplicable and unresolved suffering that characterizes the tragic imagination should also compel

Christians to collective action, including social advocacy for mental healthcare and resistance to mental-health stigma.

Guiding these chapters was a concern for the "double displacement" to which many Christian depression sufferers attest in their accounts of living with this condition. Having found themselves displaced into a state of seemingly endlessness unhomelikeness, many sufferers struggle to locate their experiences within the theological worldview of their Christian communities. With this, the comfort and support of belonging to a community of faith, with its resources for meaning making and purposefulness, can slip away just like the phenomenological at-home-ness that many sufferers once took for granted. Though we cannot explain and contain depression as much as we might like by preventing or reversing the initial existential displacement of depression, Christians can do much more to address this second displacement, this religious crisis that often results from the theological and practical limitations of Christian communities that need not be so.

This book is one contribution to this effort—a small but long-labored offering of support to depression sufferers who, like me, are trying to live in and through this difficult wilderness before God and with the community of faith that has sustained and animated life. To those of us who accompany depression sufferers in this, let us do our best to become the community that sufferers need for survival and improved quality of life, both through our actions and through the theologies that we surround them with. Like our God, may we have ears to hear, eyes to see, and a generous, loving presence—one that can bear with the harrowing wildernesses that so many of us live within and through. And let us do so in loving memory of those who have died in the desolate landscape of depression, with hope that they rise in another world where all the possibilities that make up the very best of living are in abundance, always.

Acknowledgments

First thanks go to my family, especially my parents and brother. I have not lived a single day without the security of their unconditional love. It is the greatest and most humbling gift of my life, and it has given me the assurance I needed to follow my dreams, which include writing this book. I extend this gratitude to the many friends who I love as family. I know that without their encouragement, I could not have done this. Thank you.

Thanks to Hans Christoffersen at Liturgical Press for believing in this project and for bringing it to fruition with such care. Thanks also to Jan Richardson for permission to use her beautiful artwork for the cover.

Thanks to the countless, beloved mentors and colleagues in theology whose encouragement, companionship, and inspiration have sustained this project over many years. As I embarked on researching depression, my dissertation committee at Boston College—Drs. M. Shawn Copeland, Andrew Prevot, John McDargh, and Brian Robinette—engaged my work with immense generosity. Upon finishing the dissertation, Dr. Copeland advised me to write the book that I wanted to write, whatever that may be, and it liberated me to pursue the questions of my heart—questions that make this book what it is today. How grateful I am for an academic mentor who has always wanted true freedom for me, above all.

Of my many cherished friends from the Boston College community, I am particularly grateful for the continued encouragement of Kate Ward; of Katherine Greiner; and of Kim Bauser McBrien, who lent her biblical expertise to this project as well. Thanks also to Dan

227

Horan, the best of friends, who never wavered in his support; thank you for helping me survive.

Thanks to my friends at the Louisville Institute, who privileged me with two years of mentorship and joyful community as I wrote this book: Edwin Aponte, Jean-Pierre Ruiz, Tomi Oredein, Bryce Rich, Liza Anderson, Jonathan Soyars, Allison Norton, and Joung Chul Lee.

Thanks to another invaluable community that bettered my writing during my years in California—the Bay Area Theology Group, which included Filipe Maia; Travis Stevens; Jen Owens-Jofré; Chris Hadley; Julie Rubio; Paul Schutz, whose continued, generous feedback on drafts have refined my thinking and provided much encouragement; and Joe Drexler-Dreis and Anne Carpenter, who were also my colleagues at Saint Mary's College of California, where they shared their friendship, professional wisdom, and reassurance through some particularly challenging periods of writing. Thanks to our colleague, Anna Corwin, and to my long-time mentor, Susan Abraham, for all this too. Another thanks from my time of writing in California goes to the incredible Mary Rakow, who was the guardian angel of the book's early chapters.

I finished this book while making a home in South Bend, Indiana, at Saint Mary's College. Thanks to my wonderful colleagues here and to my research assistant, Madison Drass, whose passion for her faith and for mental-health issues inspired me and whose feedback bettered the project. Thanks to college librarians Joe Thomas and Catherine Pellegrino; without their generous assistance, my research could not have continued during the COVID-19 pandemic. I owe a special word of thanks to Dr. Dave Smith, who has counseled me through my struggles to finish this book and, more importantly, to become a person more at peace with my work and with myself—all things that long seemed impossible.

Thanks to my colleagues in Catholic theology who, despite the threat of stigma, are taking up the work of theologizing mental-health struggles alongside me. Elizabeth Antus does this work with the compassion, courage, and rigor that the topic warrants; she has inspired and challenged me through her work and generous feedback. Marcus Mescher has likewise provided an inspiring example and generous comments on this book.

Additional thanks go to the many other individuals who—in classrooms, conference halls, research discussions, and parish gatherings—disclosed how depression and other mental-health struggles have touched their lives in an effort to spur me on in this project. I am grateful to do this work with you.

At times, it felt as if I had been writing this book my whole life. How does one even begin to acknowledge all those who have contributed to a project like that? I have resigned to the impossibility of thanking all whose generosity and support warrant my recognition here, with hopes that those unnamed already know my love and gratitude.

I offer my final thanks to God, to whom I have dedicated this book. Despite being a theologian, I tend to shy away from such public gestures of personal piety. But the truth is that writing this has been a slow work of faith—a humble effort to remember and respond with gratitude to the God who first accompanied me, the God Who Sees: I remember. Thank you, thank you, thank you.

Index